"With the eye of a psychoanalyst, the conscience of an activist, and the voice of a poet, Dodi Goldman explores the ways imagination and social reality interpenetrate, giving meaning and richness to human experience. The book is devoted both to Goldman's original and informative reading of Winnicott and to his own creative and passionate clinical work. The result is a volume sure to inspire psychotherapists of all persuasions and levels of experience, and to engage others interested in the study of lives in depth."—**Jay Greenberg, Ph.D.**, Editor, *The Psychoanalytic Quarterly*; Recipient, 2015 Mary S. Sigourney Award

"A Beholder's Share *is an exciting event for anyone with a deep interest in human experience and Winnicott. It provides a rare opportunity to observe close-up how an internationally acclaimed scholar connects with Winnicott through shared sensibility, helping him find his way toward psychoanalytic work. Moving seamlessly between Winnicott and his own highly creative and imaginative work, Goldman's essays are complex, wide-ranging, generous, and deeply knowledgeable. All this—in a writing style that goes-on-communicating with the reader and touches the heart."*—**Michal Rieck**, Training and Supervising Analyst, The Israel Psychoanalytic Society; Co-Founder and Co-Director, Israel Winnicott Center, Tel Aviv, Israel

"When we look at art, it summons something from within us; but we also summon something from within it: that is the beholder's share, and Goldman's inspiration. Goldman's writing does not merely inform, it embroiders; and the pattern comes into being as we read, woven together with our experience of the reading. Goldman is that rare thing: a psychoanalytic writer who also happens to be a fine writer. In the first half of the book, this sensibility is revealed in various unexpected developments with his patients; the second half shows us why Goldman and Winnicott are kindred spirits. Goldman's book is subtle, expressive, and frequently surprising. If that description appeals to you, read it. You won't regret it."—**Donnel B. Stern, Ph.D.**, William Alanson White Institute and NYU Postdoctoral Program in Psychotherapy and Psychoanalysis

"Dodi Goldman's engaging and deeply useful book is Winnicottian in the best sense of that word: original, creative, enveloping the reader in the serious play of clinical psychoanalysis. Freedom and safety are

always in sight, whether Goldman is chasing an idea or listening to a patient. At whatever level you join the conversation, prepare to be interestingly transformed."—**Adrienne Harris**, Faculty and Supervisor, NYU Postdoctoral Program in Psychotherapy and Psychoanalysis; Co-Editor, Relational Perspectives Book Series and Author of *Gender as Soft Assembly* (Routledge, 2009)

A Beholder's Share

A Beholder's Share demonstrates how a sense of reality is evoked in the unpredictable space between imagination and adaptation. The world calls forth something in each of us—a beholder's share—which in turn calls forth something in the world. Though usually viewed as opposites, imagination and reality make uneasy but necessary bedfellows.

Part I of *A Beholder's Share* shows how fantasy generates novelty by creating versions of what is already known, while imagination allows what seems familiar to be seen afresh. Goldman's essays offer unexpected takes on common clinical encounters: clashes of belief, the search for generational dialogue, the awkward discomfort of feeling like a fake, the problem of how and when to end analysis, the strains of working with psychotic anxieties.

Part II, "Winnicott's Living Legacy," illuminates Winnicott's preoccupation with difficulties inherent in contact with reality. These chapters bring to life Winnicott's personal struggle with an area of experience his own two analyses failed to touch, the tangled relationship with Masud Khan, his recognition of dissociation as "a queer kind of truth," and how Romantic poets shaped Winnicott's view of what is felt as real.

Bringing together Dodi Goldman's seminal and new writings, *A Beholder's Share* will appeal to psychoanalysts and psychoanalytic psychotherapists, as well as students and teachers of the arts, literature, and humanities.

Dodi Goldman is a Training and Supervising Analyst and Faculty of the William Alanson White Institute and has a private practice in New York. He is a former book review editor of the journal *Contemporary Psychoanalysis* and Author of *In Search of the Real: The Origins and Originality of D.W. Winnicott.*

PSYCHOANALYSIS IN A NEW KEY BOOK SERIES

DONNEL STERN
Series Editor

When music is played in a new key, the melody does not change, but the notes that make up the composition do: change in the context of continuity, continuity that perseveres through change. Psychoanalysis in a New Key publishes books that share the aims psychoanalysts have always had, but that approach them differently. The books in the series are not expected to advance any particular theoretical agenda, although to this date most have been written by analysts from the Interpersonal and Relational orientations.

The most important contribution of a psychoanalytic book is the communication of something that nudges the reader's grasp of clinical theory and practice in an unexpected direction. Psychoanalysis in a New Key creates a deliberate focus on innovative and unsettling clinical thinking. Because that kind of thinking is encouraged by exploration of the sometimes surprising contributions to psychoanalysis of ideas and findings from other fields, Psychoanalysis in a New Key particularly encourages interdisciplinary studies. Books in the series have married psychoanalysis with dissociation, trauma theory, sociology, and criminology. The series is open to the consideration of studies examining the relationship between psychoanalysis and any other field—for instance, biology, literary and art criticism, philosophy, systems theory, anthropology, and political theory.

But innovation also takes place within the boundaries of psychoanalysis, and Psychoanalysis in a New Key therefore also presents work that reformulates thought and practice without leaving the precincts of the field. Books in the series focus, for example, on the significance of personal values in psychoanalytic practice, on the complex interrelationship between the analyst's clinical work and personal life, on the consequences for the clinical situation when patient and analyst are from different cultures, and on the need for psychoanalysts to accept the degree to which they knowingly satisfy their own wishes during treatment hours, often to the patient's detriment.

For a full list of all the titles in the Psychoanalysis in a New Key series, please visit the Routledge website.

RECENT TITLES IN THIS SERIES:

Vol. 36 *Nonlinear Psychoanalysis: Notes from Forty Years of Chaos and Complexity Theory* Robert M. Galatzer-Levy

Vol. 35 *A Beholder's Share: Essays on Winnicott and the Psychoanalytic Imagination* Dodi Goldman

Vol. 34 *The Interpersonal Perspective in Psychoanalysis, 1960s-1990s: Rethinking transference and countertransference* Edited by Donnel B. Stern and Irwin Hirsch

Vol. 33 *Needed Relationships and Psychoanalytic Healing: A Holistic Relational Perspective on the Therapeutic Process* Steven Stern

Vol. 32 *The Age of Perversion: Desire and Technology in Psychoanalysis and Culture* Danielle Knafo and Rocco Lo Bosco

A Beholder's Share

Essays on Winnicott and the Psychoanalytic Imagination

Dodi Goldman

Routledge
Taylor & Francis Group
LONDON AND NEW YORK

First published 2017
by Routledge
2 Park Square, Milton Park, Abingdon, Oxon OX14 4RN

and by Routledge
711 Third Avenue, New York, NY 10017

Routledge is an imprint of the Taylor & Francis Group, an informa business

British Library Cataloguing in Publication Data
A catalogue record for this book is available from the British Library

Library of Congress Cataloging in Publication Data
A catalog record for this book has been requested

ISBN: 978-1-138-28934-5 (hbk)
ISBN: 978-1-138-28936-9 (pbk)
ISBN: 978-1-315-26718-0 (ebk)

Typeset in Times New Roman
by Swales & Willis Ltd, Exeter, Devon, UK

For Sean, Danielle, Robin, and Olive—
imagining your future

Contents

Acknowledgments

Many ideas in this book come from elsewhere, the voices of others intricately woven in these pages. Even ideas I might hazard to claim as my own percolated in dialogue with partners in thought. I include here the book's primary inspiration: individuals I've worked with psychoanalytically, and from whom I've learned so much, in the past 20 years. For obvious reasons, they shall all remain nameless.

The William Alanson White Institute has been a steady and vital base of support. Colleagues too numerous to name afforded me valuable opportunities to learn, teach, formulate, and rethink ideas.

Some chapters gathered in this volume came to fruition because of the good fortune I had to present early iterations in a variety of settings: the Israel Winnicott Center, the Squiggle Foundation and University College in London, the Psychoanalytic Institute of Northern California, the New York University Postdoctoral Program, the American Institute for Psychoanalysis, and the Institute for Contemporary Psychoanalysis in New York. The road from work-in-progress to I'm-now-ready-to let-this-go was full of twists and turns. Encounters with fellow travelers in these venerable institutions added depth and texture to the journey.

This book might never have come into being had it not been for Donnell Stern's conviction that I "had a book in me." Thanks Don. I can't quite decide if you are more Sherpa or shepherd, but your responsive attention and guidance always got me to where I needed to be.

Writing is a solitary pursuit. Deep gratitude to dear friends, classmates, and colleagues, without whom it might also have been a very lonely one: Seth Aronson, Dana Assaf, Naomi Bravman, Peggy Crastnopol, Andy Druck, Melinda Gellman, Daniel Gensler, Deberah Goldman, Evelyn Hartman, Gil Katz, Sharon Kofman, Emily Kuriloff, Mary Libbey, Suzanne

Little, Richard Loewus, Ernesto Mujica, Rachael Peltz, Robert Prince, Bruce Reis, Joseph Schwartz, Alexandra Shelley, Bonnie Steinberg, Sarah Stemp, and Jim Stoeri. I don't know where I'd be without you.

A few chapters originated as contributions to edited volumes. I'd like to thank Jan Abram, Elizabeth Howell, Sheldon Itzkovitz, and Jill Salberg for inviting and encouraging my participation in their projects. Seeing my own work in a broader context gave me new and welcome perspective.

I am grateful as well to the many dedicated members of study groups I've led and been part of over the years. These groups continue to provide a valuable space to think out loud together about matters dear to our hearts. I cherish your support.

Warm appreciation to Dawnmarie Manduca-Molina and Jessica Ferrara. I know I can always trust you to set me straight.

My heartfelt thanks to Ryan Douglas (www.ryandouglasarts.com), who graciously provided a detail from one of his paintings for the cover of the book. One shouldn't judge a book by its cover, but in this case I hope everyone does.

Most of all, I thank my wife, Harriet. Still waters do run deep. You give me so much. No more need be said. I'm lucky. No, blessed.

Copyright permission

Excerpt in Chapter 1 from THE BLIND ASSASSIN by Margaret Atwood. Copyright 2000 by Penguin Random House LLC, Doubleday edition.

Chapter 2 first published as Goldman, D. (1996). An Exquisite Corpse: the strain of working in and out of potential space. *Contemporary Psychoanalysis*, 32: 339–358. Reprinted by permission of Taylor and Francis LLC.

Chapter 3 first published as Goldman, D. (2007). Faking It. *Contemporary Psychoanalysis*, 43: 17–36. Reprinted by permission of Taylor and Francis LLC.

Excerpt in Chapter 3, SHOOTING AN ELEPHANT AND OTHER ESSAYS by George Orwell (Copyright © George Orwell, 1946). Reprinted by permission of Bill Hamilton as the Literary Executor of the Estate of the Late Sonia Brownell Orwell.

Chapter 4 first published as Goldman, D. (2010). As Generations Speak. *Psychoanalytic Psychology*, *27*(4), 475–491. Copyright © 2010. American Psychological Association. Reproduced with permission.

Chapter 5 first published as Goldman, D. (2010). Parting Ways. In Salberg, J. (ed.). GOOD ENOUGH ENDINGS: BREAKS, INTERRUPTIONS, AND TERMINATIONS FROM CONTEMPORARY

RELATIONAL PERSONAL LIVES. Routledge, pp. 241–256. Reproduced with permission of Taylor and Francis LLC; permission conveyed through Copyright Clearance Center, Inc.

[illegible] CALLING OF THE TIMES [illegible]

[illegible] (2016) [illegible] and the Idea of Dissociation'. In Howell, E. and Itzkowitz, S. (eds.) THE DISSOCIATIVE MIND IN PSYCHOANALYSIS [illegible] Routledge, pp. [illegible]

[illegible]

Introduction

Good essays have apparent objects and buried subjects. Revisiting essays, papers, and talks given over the course of 20 years returns me to old haunts, revealing implied yearnings, enduring interests, and how I've changed my mind. Since more goes on in writing than we can possibly know, the form, pattern, and trajectory of things I have unwittingly been trying to work out are discernible only in retrospect. Even when lost, I may have been headed somewhere all along.

One direction I've been heading is working out the difference between the novelty of fantasy and the originality of imagination. We can either generate novelty by creating versions of what is already known or allow what seems familiar to be seen afresh. I think fantasy does the former and imagination the latter.

With fantasy, there may be novel inversions or juxtapositions, but at the end of the day we find ourselves in the same place over and over again. Under the guise of novelty, fantasy carries the deadening effect of the familiar. An urgent search for novelty often substitutes when imagination fails to bring something vital into being between oneself and the world. Stepping out of familiar repetitions requires the work of imagination, which clears a path so the seemingly familiar can be seen as never before. What is seen anew is original in the sense of connecting us to the origin of what had always been there to be found.

A basic quandary at the heart of this book is how a sense of reality is evoked in the unpredictable space between imagination and adaptation. We neither discover an objective reality nor merely invent subjective ones. Usually viewed as opposites, imagination and reality make uneasy but necessary bedfellows. The world "calls forth" something in us that in turn "calls forth" something in the world. What is "called forth" affects the type of attention we accord, even as the type of attention we pay also governs what we find (McGilchrist, 2009, p. 133). Music arises *between* a musician and an instrument, not from either alone.

The book's title, *A Beholder's Share*, coined by art historian Ernest Gombrich, captures the to-and-fro between inner and outer, imagination and adaptation. Art is not art, Gombrich claimed, without the viewer's collaboration. Not only does the beholder perceptually transform a two-dimensional likeness on a canvas into a three-dimensional depiction of the visual world, but it is through imaginative interpretation that a meaningful "picture" is created out of mere pigments on a canvas. Seeing remarkably meshes with seeing-in-the-mind's-eye—the heart's crayon spangling and fulfilling the world (Wilbur, 1997).

To put this in psychoanalytic terms: we all seek a personal way to keep inner and outer separate but interrelated, to adapt without undue loss of personal vitality. There are difficulties inherent in contact with reality, and pleasures and perils along the way. A sense of reality depends on imagination even as reality puts necessary brakes on imaginative life. We also need to live with our essential aloneness, the part of ourselves that does not, and perhaps cannot, communicate directly with the outside world.

****

I trained as a psychoanalyst as a comparative approach to theory was taking hold. Conferences were frequently designed to have analysts of varying persuasions discuss clinical material from contrasting perspectives. *Psychoanalytic Dialogues* emerged as a journal dedicated to exploring convergences and divergences of orientation. Over the years, I often have been invited to "represent a Winnicottian point of view." Although flattered, I generally experience these requests as mildly objectionable. Why? I certainly understand that I am seen, as one colleague recently put it to me, as a "Winnicott maven." And I enjoy hearing multiple viewpoints in conversation. So what is disagreeable about such a legitimate request? What is off-putting to me about it?

What feels vaguely wrong is the sense that it isn't "me" being invited, but "me" as envoy, emissary, or surrogate. I am expected to "represent" an image of Winnicott held in someone else's mind. And not only is this most certainly uncharitable to Winnicott, it is also a certain violation of myself. While Winnicott holds an important place in my development as a psychoanalyst, many other threads—including non-psychoanalytic ones—are no less entwined in my psychoanalytic sensibility. There is a world of difference, I believe, between "identifying with" something and being identified "as something" (both, of course, are expectable, if not inevitable). To be identified "as something" reminds me of why people are often made uneasy by photographs of themselves. I don't believe it is simply a matter of vanity. Photographs freeze instants in time. But life is never static; it emerges from overlapping moments, movements, and moods. To be "known" without the flow of experience turns us into caricatures of ourselves. To be "shot," photographically speaking, is to be "captured," which means sacrificing a bit of aliveness as we are memorialized as frozen images. It is sometimes said that the goal of psychoanalysis is to be fully known. I'd say almost the opposite: to make something fully known makes it unreal. The analyst must, to a certain extent, help "un-know" the person.

As a child, I relished *Fractured Fairy Tales*, the madcap T.V. segment introduced by the ever-earnest squirrel Rocky and plodding dimwitted moose Bullwinkle. In a typical episode, a classic (dare I say "canonical"?) tale was retold, but with a twist. The "Ugly Duckling," for example, was portrayed as victim of discrimination at the hands of the Chinese Emperor's chief cook. The duck, wanting nothing more than to be served up as main course at a royal feast, kept stealthily sneaking onto the platter. The cook, repelled by the duck's awkward comportment, kept shoving him off. At the end of the tale, after much frustration and travail, the wayward duck's fortunes soar once Walt Disney changes his name to "Donald," transforming him into a Hollywood star.

Fractured Fairy Tales introduced me early on to how topsy-turvy the world can be. Although obviously too young to formulate the matter, I had an inkling that a morality tale meant to be revered could be mocked with impunity; that oft-told stories are but one possible version of the truth, that what one sees is not necessarily what one gets. The subversive pleasure I felt was linked to the dawning awareness that there was more to the world than I was supposed to know. From a child's perspective, these were cartoons allowing imagination to run wild. From an adult's point of view, they were ironic spoofs unmasking appearances. I could be credulous and clear-eyed at the same time!

As an activist student during the "American berserk" of the 1960s, I experienced an exhilaration and dread that the center may not hold.

Trained in a mode of dialectical inquiry, analysis meant Marx, not Freud. Conceptual tools helped make sense of the maelstrom: why are people being beaten on bridges in Selma? Must capitalism be cruel? Is my freedom really threatened by peasants in Southeast Asia? Who can I believe? Why do "little boxes made of ticky tacky . . . all look just the same?" (Reynolds, 1964, p. 28). Animated by egalitarian ideals, a desire for a fresh start, and the fantasy of starting from scratch, I moved to an Israeli kibbutz on the Lebanese border, where I lived for many years.

My experiences in Israel included military service, agricultural work, teaching, and deep engagement in community life. Living with people from worlds remarkably different than my own challenged my capacity for give-and-take. Friends, mentors, writers, and labor leaders introduced me to a new and richly textured cultural vocabulary. Their voices still flow through me, contributing to how I think about people, and therefore to my psychoanalytic sensibility. War and direct terror attacks affected how I experience and think about trauma and resilience. Communal life altered my perception of what is public and what is private, drawing attention to the difference between "individuality" and "individualism." I learned to appreciate what the poet Czeslaw Milosz calls "the captive mind": that whatever is familiar is assumed to be the natural order of things. Every culture creates distinctive rules of engagement taken for granted as constituting reality. In a certain sense, we are all true believers.

I also acquired a new spoken language. Words can obviously, if sometimes awkwardly, be translated from one language into another. But the experience of oneself living within and inhabited by a particular language is not readily transferable. Each language—the whole being greater than the sum of associative webs—is marked by its own distinctive apprehension of the world. To be outside this perceptual lens is to be outside an ineffable reality. "Our moods do not believe in each other," Emerson once remarked. In a certain sense, neither do our languages. To this day, I notice myself listening from within two distinct states, and sometimes the contrast is dramatic. Every so often, I even catch myself speaking one language while actually "being" in the other. The other person looks understandably puzzled and I feel that what I've said has fallen flat. Many things are not only lost in translation; they can never be found.

The United States I returned to in the late 1980s seemed hardly recognizable, a jarring cultural shock to my nervous system. The elements were familiar, but the proportions had changed. It seemed that nearly everything had turned into a commodity, from people shaving corporate logos on their heads to gambling on the early demise of the elderly by buying up their life insurance policies. The electronic din and distractions—the fast train of information far outpacing the slow horse of meaning—felt increasingly inescapable and potentially crippling. A confessional culture had taken hold, fostering the illusion that what people confess to in public is who they "really" are. Clichéd voyeuristic thrills and incessant novelty seeking were obliterating subtlety of feeling. Intellectual life had also changed: nobody was having a conversation anymore; everyone engaged in "discourse." Activists had replaced—some might say displaced—an interest in changing society with an almost obsessive fascination with epistemology. The best minds seemed more inclined to deconstruct problems than to solve them. The proliferation of nuclear weapons was of less concern than the proliferation of quotation marks.

It was difficult to locate myself in the new surroundings. I was totally unaccustomed to America's version of professional careerism. As a recent arrival from a rural landscape, I couldn't shake the impression that commodity culture was something people are not only born into, but buy into. Was this moral revulsion or fear that I would fail to fit in? Would vexation forever alternate with numbness? Could I find a way to imaginatively adapt?

One thing that helped was that the vibrant ever-present currents of American idealism, fairness, open-mindedness, innovation, and generosity were making themselves felt in new and exciting ways. America was becoming more diverse and tolerant than I ever remembered it to be. Older generations were learning from younger ones. There was no shortage of people yearning to transcend commodity culture, to salvage their individuality, to find safe havens in which to discover how interesting and imaginative they could be, and to elaborate who they were trying to become. I was not alone.

These zeitgeist frequencies—the acceleration of commercialization, the babel of signals, the public confessionals, the growing acceptance of the great variety of human experience, the yearning to move beyond the soul numbing effects of commodity culture—are inevitably delivered into the analytic space. One cannot practice without encountering them. What is of interest from a psychoanalytic point of view, however, is not generalizations about contemporary culture so much as the bearing these transformations have on psychic life. There is an osmotic process whereby reality and imagination fuse and cultural artifacts impact what is lived and what is dissociated. What we call the self—an inclusive symbolization of one's own being—is enormously permeable.

I eventually found a professional place at City University of New York and the William Alanson White Institute. These institutions are blessed with active, thoughtful individuals dedicated to psychoanalytic work in both its therapeutic and counter-cultural guises. I was taught to appreciate how what might end up as a psychological problem often begins as a solution to difficulties in living with others; that growth requires human relatedness; that people are challenged to adapt to the cultures in which they are embedded; that the mind's natural capacity for dissociation can also go awry. In the end, the content of what I was taught matters less than the company I found. I discovered predecessors and colleagues. Frankly, I don't know where I would be without them. No writer is only himself; he or she is part of the living tribal fabric, the imagined voices of others whispering what needs to be heard again and again.

While learning to become psychoanalysts, we all conjure images of competent others to evoke our own potential. For me, D.W. Winnicott was one such figure. Rather comically, I first encountered his writing working in the kibbutz dairy. I shared an early morning milking shift with a dear friend pursuing a degree in clinical psychology at the University of Tel Aviv. Handing me an article of Winnicott's, he asked my help translating it into Hebrew. With 20 cows and the thump-thump-thump of milking machines as background, I tried my best, but kept stumbling over the elusive language. The phrase "going-on-being" flummoxed me. My first thought was that there is no word in Hebrew for "being," other than the root of the word "God." My puzzlement was obvious. Impatient, my friend chided: "What's your problem? I thought you know English." "I'm sorry," I replied sheepishly, "but I don't know *this* English."

Many years later, I fortuitously chanced upon Winnicott's private letters stored in boxes in the archives of the old Payne Whitney psychiatric clinic. Winnicott's second wife, Clare Britton, had recently transferred the material from London to New York. According to one person involved in the acquisition, Clare had purportedly said that she "wanted to make sure the Kleinians didn't get their hands on them." I immersed myself in these letters. Much of what I gleaned eventually appeared in a book I published in 1993, *In Search of the Real: The Origins and Originality of D.W. Winnicott.*

What I discovered in the letters, well before I had an even good-enough grasp of Winnicott's theory, was what he would have referred to as "a matching headpiece"—a kindred spirit with whom I share a sensibility. And while I recognize that matching headpieces also carry a liability in terms of growth (we don't, after all, grow by only being exposed to sameness), Winnicott's sensibility—in contrast to the specifics of his theorizing—helped me find my way toward psychoanalytic work. Winnicott certainly had his fair share of failings and foibles. And while certain aspects of his theory are troublesome to me, his sensibility, his *way of seeing the world*, allowed me to imagine myself inhabiting the role of psychoanalyst. I realized that some of his preoccupations were also my own.

I do not think it a coincidence that there is no "school" of Winnicott, no institute organized around his theory, no band of zealous disciples believing in the "truth" of his vision. Indeed, one way to understand his notion of "True Self" is to see it as a process within the self that is in opposition to any built up version of THE truth. Would it not be a contradiction to see a Winnicottian orthodoxy? Winnicott surely had his fair share of narcissism—I like to think of him as a "graceful narcissist"—but it was not of the type that demanded followers and admirers as a precondition for self-stability. While he could certainly be fierce about his convictions, he also genuinely preferred to be found and used than to be thought of as "right."

Winnicott was skeptical of the rigidities induced by allegiances to schools. For years, he pleaded with both Klein and Anna Freud to put an end to the divisive "groupings" that were the outcome of the controversial discussions in the British Society. He hoped they would do so while they were still alive as he saw their valuable contributions reduced to clichés, parroted with inauthentic ventriloquism. Klein, for her part, deeply regretted not having taken Winnicott into analysis. Hannah Segal once claimed that Klein believed that had she done so, she could have spared psychoanalysis the damage she believed Winnicott had done.

What Winnicott offers in place of dogma and clichés are highly original, imaginative metaphors that challenge one to explore further. A Cuban analyst once wrote to Winnicott describing how swords and sticks had become, for his 3-year-old son, symbols of the growing boy's penis. "Yes," Winnicott wrote back, "but what is the boy's penis a symbol for?" One readily sees that Winnicott is more interested in the capacity to play—including playing with ideas—than he is in the content of play. Turning Freud on his head even while remaining a Freudian, Winnicott was always more an innovator than a curator. While this poses some difficulty in terms of coordinating his ideas with existing theory, I like that about him.

Whereas psychoanalysis frequently focuses on the extraordinary means by which ordinary people conceal from themselves what they prefer not to know, Winnicott was equally concerned with how people are trying the best they can to communicate. His sensibility is less a hermeneutic of suspicion and more a belief in the individual's unconscious quest to find an environment that can safely be used for self-expression. Rather than ask what the individual needs to do to adapt to reality, Winnicott was concerned with how the reliability of the environment meeting the growing person's assertion and dependence allows individuality to flourish.

Winnicott is sometimes seen as a Romantic. Actually, he recoiled from sentimentality because he understood the disowned aggression it contained. His theory, if read closely, is not an idealization of motherhood so much as a virtual cartography of the delicate relationship between the environment and the psychosomatic makeup necessary for growth. Winnicott's theory of development is not simply one of how mother's attunement enables baby to thrive. Rather, baby's healthy competence to make use of his own inventiveness helps mother remain good enough.

But Winnicott was a Romantic in the sense of the Romantic poets who placed great stock in the vitality of the imagination. "There is creation in the eye," Wordsworth (1805) wrote:

> A virtue which irradiates and exalts
> Objects through widest intercourse of sense.
> (p. 398)

Winnicott, too, made a virtue of what he called "primary creativity." At the heart of his work is an abiding concern for the urge toward life and the consequences of failures to create and discover a world that can tolerate one's own aliveness. Within psychoanalysis, Winnicott represents an important shift in emphasis from the serial substitutions of thwarted desire to how meaningful and authentic is a person's experience and expression of himself. The central organizing thread of development, he suggests, is not the necessary regulation of the forbidden, but the experience of aliveness and the consequences of disruption to the continuity of being. It was as if Winnicott were perpetually reaching for what was most vital and real to a personal self. For him, psychoanalysis has no normalizing function. He was, for better and for worse, more interested in the unique than in the good.

When Winnicott was only 15 years old, a town planning official for the German city of Essen visited his boarding school. Winnicott volunteered an account of the visit for the school newspaper. Contrasting German and British sensibilities, he begins by noting that "Englishmen, taken as a whole . . . would never stand so officious an official for one fortnight." He chastises the Germans for constructing cities based on misguided notions of unitary perfection and overarching principles rather than allowing them to spontaneously flourish through the rough and tumble of life. The Germans, he mockingly concludes, "have difficulty getting even the youngsters to overstep the miniature railings, let alone accustoming the older gravel-pathed generation to walk in the grass."

Winnicott—like Darwin, one of his heroes—had the cultural habit of mind of a British empiricist, preferring ideas derived from observation of the rough and tumble of life over attempts to build coherent or systematic theories based on a priori thought. He creatively transformed concrete observations of what mother and baby did together into potent metaphors for the working of the mind. Holding, handling, object presenting, and transitional space are all metaphors for psychic processes rooted in concrete phenomena observed in child-parent interactions. These metaphors draw our attention to an inherent *difficulty* involved in contact with reality, distinct from what psychoanalysis commonly describes as *conflict* between reality and pleasure.

****

Robert Frost once remarked that whenever he knew the ending of a poem in advance of writing it, the poem turned out to be a damn poor one. Most of the material in Part I of this volume, "A Beholder's Share," shares that sentiment. Each piece takes as a starting point a common clinical experience. They were written, in part, to help me figure out what it was I was thinking at the time. Through the act of writing, I found myself arriving at surprising detours and unexpected conclusions. Although firmly grounded in a psychoanalytic orientation, the material draws equally upon other sources.

The title essay amplifies Gombrich's observation that imagination infuses our perceptions. By examining in detail a woman's religious experience of God's presence, the essay explores the uses and abuses of imagination and the bearing this has on what psychoanalysis calls "contact with reality." What happens when the unconscious movement between the imaginative and the actual is curtailed? Does imagination merely distort reality or, perhaps, be better thought of as necessary for our sense of what feels real? The notion of idiosyncratic imagination may very well clash with Freud's view of fantasy.

The question of "contact with reality" takes a different twist in the essay "An Exquisite Corpse." I first learned about the exquisite corpse—a parlor game played by Surrealist painters—from a young woman who came to me for help. The paper explores a unique strain of "working in areas where psychotic anxieties predominate" (Little, 1985): the precarious and cyclical way potential space—where perception renders fantasy and imagination relatively safe and fantasy and imagination render perception relatively meaningful—is generated, lost and restored.

The essay "Faking It" considers the common human experience of "feeling like a fake." How might we understand this awkward discomfort? May feelings of fakery sometimes actually signal healthy strivings? A desire to imaginatively join in before we have found a way to adaptively fit in? If psychoanalysis teaches us anything, it is the unpredictability of unconscious desire and the fundamental inability of people to be all of themselves at any given time. Drawing upon literary, personal, and analytic examples, the essay makes a plea for an appreciative view of varieties of "faking it."

Embedded in generational cycles, we all navigate, one way or another, among forebears, peers, and "unknown children" waiting in the wings. "As Generations Speak" suggests that during phases of transition, individuals contend with novel versions of themselves and the influences other generations, both older and younger, exert. As a new place within the generational cycle is imagined and inhabited, the need for generational dialogue is rekindled. Samples of analytic work illustrate how the unconscious search for generational dialogue might be engendered or thwarted.

"Parting Ways" was originally a contribution to an edited volume (Salberg, 2010) on contemporary relational perspectives on termination.

It suggests that it makes a world of difference if one thinks of psychoanalysis as a treatment—a cure for an ailment—or as an experience. These two currents—treatment and experience—are always in tension, but especially so in deciding when to stop. It can be useful to note how, at any given moment, a particular person's use of analysis may be in concord, collude, or collide with an analyst's inclination. Both the person's use and the analyst's inclination can, and often do, shift over time.

Part II, "Winnicott's Living Legacy," includes material inspired by years of teaching Winnicott to psychoanalytic colleagues. "Winnicott's Search for Self and Cure" is based on talks given at University College London and the Israel Winnicott Center. It looks at Winnicott's contribution as a mirror of his own subjectivity. One way of understanding Winnicott's theory is that it speaks to parts of himself that his own two analyses failed to touch and as an indirect attempt at self-cure. This should not surprise us. After all, the psychological terrain we know best is that which we know from the inside out.

Much has been written about Winnicott's tangled relationship with the controversial Pakistani-British analyst Masud Khan. Based on the Madeline Davis Memorial Lecture given at the Squiggle Foundation in London, "The Outrageous Prince: The Uncure of Masud Khan" brings an informed imagination to bear on questions related to Winnicott's work with Khan. Drawing upon Khan's personal notebooks and material found in the Winnicott archives, I offer three distinct, yet overlapping, conjectures: Winnicott helped Khan enormously; Winnicott failed to "cure" him; Masud Khan could not be helped.

"'A Queer Kind of Truth': Winnicott and the Uses of Dissociation" was written as a contribution to an edited volume on the dissociative mind in psychoanalysis (Howell and Itzkowitz, 2016). Portions also appeared in *Donald Winnicott Today* (Abram, 2013), under the title "Vital Sparks and the Form of Things Unknown." It highlights Winnicott's keen awareness of the centrality of dissociation in psychic life. Despite operating within an espoused theory privileging repression as an explanatory construct, *in practice* Winnicott relies heavily upon an intuitive grasp of dissociation—both as a healthy natural capacity and as a defensive response to trauma. For Winnicott, it makes a vast difference how and in what context dissociation is used. Examples from Winnicott's clinical material demonstrate how, as engaged witness to dissociated experience rather than as knowing interpreter of the patient's repressed unconscious, the analyst may open a space for renewed vitality.

For Winnicott, primary creativity is at the root of psychic life. What renders this drive *primary* is that it is not an expression or derivative of, nor is it motivated by, anything else. For Winnicott, it is the threat to one's creative aliveness, not one's sexuality, that is bedrock. One non-psychoanalytic source of this view can be found in the English Romantic poets who deepened Winnicott's appreciation of the delicate area between what is perceived and what is conceived. "Weaving with the World: Winnicott's Reimagining of Reality" offers evidence of the impact Wordsworth and Coleridge had upon Winnicott. It revisits a question raised by the title essay of this volume: how might the imagination be implicated in what we call contact with reality?

In writing about Winnicott's living legacy, my emphasis is on the word "living." I have no interest in hagiography or ensconcing Winnicott in an imaginary pantheon. I do, however, make use of his contribution in my own way.

In a passionate letter to Klein, Winnicott once pleaded she allow people to express themselves in their own language:

> It is only in this way that the language will be kept alive. If you make the stipulation that . . . only your language shall be used . . . then the language becomes a dead language, as it has already become in the Society.
> (Rodman, 1987, p. 34)

Hopefully, by offering one beholder's share, this book makes a contribution to keeping the psychoanalytic imagination alive.

References

Abram, J., Ed. (2013). *Donald Winnicott Today.* London and New York: Routledge.

Howell, E. and Itzkowitz, S., Eds. (2016). *The Dissociative Mind in Psychoanalysis: Understanding and Working with Trauma.* London and New York: Routledge.

Little, M. (1985). "Working in Areas Where Psychotic Anxieties Predominate: A Personal Record." *Free Associations*, 1: 9–42.

McGilchrist, I. (2009). *The Master and His Emissary: The Divided Brain and the Making of the Western World.* New Haven, CT: Yale University Press.

Reynolds, M. (1964). *Little Boxes and Other Handmade Songs*. New York: Oak Publications.

Rodman, F.R., Ed. (1987). *The Spontaneous Gesture: Selected Letters of D.W. Winnicott*. Cambridge, MA: Harvard University Press.

Salberg, J., Ed. (2010). *Good Enough Endings: Breaks, Interruptions, and Terminations from Contemporary Relational Perspectives*. London and New York: Routledge.

Wilbur, R. (1997). "At Moorditch." *The New Yorker*, March 24, 1997, p. 46.

Wordsworth, W. (1805). "The Prelude." In *William Wordsworth: The Major Works, Including the Prelude*, Ed. S. Gill. New York: Oxford University Press, 2008, pp. 375–590.

Part I

A beholder's share

Chapter 1

A beholder's share

A faint blush spreads across Joanna's face as she shares what it feels like to experience contact with God. Joanna speaks to God often. And now and then, she believes, God makes Himself manifest; not by sound or visage, but by palpable presence.

Working together for over a year, we are now touching upon a private sphere our relationship might not yet be ready to encompass. Joanna's devout friends are alarmed: "Isn't that psychoanalyst trying to convince you to give up your belief in God?" more than one of them chided. Given Freud's well-known dismissal of religious belief as remnant of infantile need and vestige of humankind's uneducated folly, their unease made sense to me.

"Maybe you, too, are concerned what I might make of it?"

"Not really," she replies, "I believe what I believe."

"Belief"—a simple word threatening to open an unbridgeable chasm between Joanna and myself. From my point of view, to believe means to temporarily take something to be true while accepting the possibility it may not be. What is called "self-awareness" includes a shift from thinking one knows a fact to accepting one "merely" holds a belief. But for Joanna, to believe is to be in contact with a realm beyond what is commonly thought of as "proof"—the burden associated with an imperious demand for evidence. Working with Joanna highlights how descriptions and explanations readily become entangled. Can experiences even be articulated without foisting beliefs upon them? Are experiences the consequence of beliefs, or vice versa? And how far can credulity be strained before we cease trusting altogether?

Many will no doubt recognize moments in psychoanalytic work where one cannot ignore or sidestep a clash of beliefs. But the word "belief" has wandered quite far from its original connotation. Our current doubt-ridden understanding, whereby assertions are expected to be consistent with evidence and facts clearly distinguished from beliefs, wasn't always the case. Ironically, by returning to the root meaning of "belief," Joanna and I are able to continue a psychoanalytic conversation. But, more of that later.

I think it fair to say that what distinguishes a random idea from a belief is how it feels to the mind; a belief is the disposition to *feel* something is true. There is some sentiment attached to our beliefs absent in relation to fiction or fancy, or even to beliefs held by others we do not share. If it weren't for that felt sentiment, the term "fiction" would have no discernible meaning. I wish we had a better vocabulary to describe this special "belief-feeling." But we don't.

When looked at from a purely internal perspective, beliefs appear to be ideas that carry particular weight. But when we shift our angle of vision to how external realities become part of mental life, it is worth considering this might take place by means of the belief feeling. Beliefs are not simply influential ideas, but the vehicles that render reality, or what is taken as such, influential. Belief bestows a *sense of reality* on that which is psychic (Britton, 1998, p. 11). Even if the beliefs are false, they feel real. Perhaps the central paradox of belief is that while resting on probability, it produces the emotional state accompanying conviction. It is quite common to indiscriminately, if mistakenly, conflate conviction with reality.

A moment-to-moment sense of well-being is built up on the basis of the developmental capacity for belief. Long before words are even at our disposal, we may or may not come to trust that reality really is as we imagine it to be, that we and our loved ones will go on being as we always have, that whatever happens next will likely be benign. All this very much depends on the early belief in the reliability of the environment, without which there is no small measure of mental anguish. Perhaps, as Ronald Britton suggests, believing "is in the realm of knowledge what attachment is in the realm of love" (Britton, 1998, p. 12). No wonder deeply held beliefs cannot be relinquished without mourning or why at its psychotic worst—where basic belief in people is severely compromised—every terror is possible and no respite is probable.

From a psychoanalytic point of view, an object felt as concretely real and inside, as opposed to a more ephemeral image or representation, might readily be explained, if not explained away, using language such as Freud's (1900) "hallucinatory regressive" satisfactions, Klein's (1929) "personification of an internal object," or Glover's (1945) "enclave of primitive mental activity." The trouble with this language, at least for me, is how removed it feels from the texture of Joanna's experience. Attempting to understand a person in the light of predetermined ideas runs the risk of condemning experience to eternal silence.

Even though I am acutely aware that doubt is made bearable by the blinders of certitude, with Joanna I resist going there. It is a given that we all need relief from the strain of holding belief and uncertainty simultaneously in mind. But a steadfastness to Joanna's conviction prompts me to pause not on the content of her belief, but on the sincerity with which she holds it.

On the relatively rare and brief occasions God's presence becomes palpable, Joanna neither hears a voice nor feels distress. What occurs is an amplified sense of distinctness. "At those moments," she says, "I have the odd sensation of being the most 'me'. It's as if all my roles and pretensions fade away and what is finally left is 'me.'" From within her new-found boundedness, seemingly stripped of social identity, she discerns God's presence. Joanna uses a medical analogy to help me understand what it means to *notice* God: "It is like being a really good radiologist," she explains. "A top-notch radiologist detects details often missed by others. The evidence is there, but others don't see it, or if they do they don't apprehend what it is they see." Joanna wishes she could be a more skillful radiologist of her own mind, better able to apprehend God's presence. On rare occasion, however, she is in the requisite state of mind for such discernment.

I was curious about that state of mind: what is it like? When did she first experience it? Was there a difference between sensing God's presence and noticing God's presence *in her mind*? Did she believe accessing it was a skill she could consciously cultivate? How did she enter and exit it?

"Absorption" is one word to capture a necessary, if not sufficient, quality of the state in which Joanna perceives God's presence. A mental capacity common to trance, dissociation, meditative states, and playing, absorption occurs when we are caught up in our own fascinations. There is a notably pleasurable dimension, a delight Joanna takes in letting herself be carried away. Notice I say "letting herself," for what she experiences is quite unlike intrusive thoughts, nightmares, or states of fear. I think it fair to say that absorbed states can only be enjoyed if we are free of the dread of getting permanently lost within them; we can "lose ourselves," so to speak, so long as we believe in the promise of finding our way out and back.

Although unable to anticipate God's appearance, Joanna is not alarmed as it is made manifest. An odd aura heralds the moment. She wonders if the aura is similar to what epileptics describe with the onset of seizures or akin to what it might feel like inside the Aurora Borealis. Joanna's attention grows rapt; yet the contours of herself feel, in her word, "thickened." God's presence is just close enough to tantalize, yet all the while beyond reach and comprehension. Joanna knows people who shake or cry in God's presence. She thinks these people are troubled by conscience, which has now been examined by God, and so they tremble. But that is not her experience. She believes God bears witness not to her conscience, but to her consciousness. Alone in God's still presence, Joanna believes she is most deeply in touch with herself.

At one point, I ask if she finds it odd that God feels so palpably present only when alone. "Not at all," she replies. "One must remove oneself from the din and clamor of others to see what is there to be seen." Struck by Joanna's sensorial metaphor, I say, "You see differently, or you see things differently in those moments." Joanna could take what I say as either statement or question. "In some ways I see more, but in others less," she says. Absorbed in quietude, the attention necessary to manage requirements of living narrows substantially—there is no dinner to be cooked, laundry done, or needs of others to tend to. Indeed, if Joanna's attention were to turn to such external tasks, she would quickly be ripped from the absorbed state of mind. Perhaps this is the very nature of absorption: the mind's object and perhaps mind itself is held in thrall, and what the mind dwells upon occupies more attention than whatever else one's eyes and ears perceive. Yet, even as Joanna's attentional field narrows, it simultaneously amplifies. "I don't hear or see anything," she says, "it's as if God's presence is all there is."

Frankly, this remark is something of a relief for me to hear. By noting she "does not hear or see anything," Joanna indicates awareness of something absent from the senses but present in the mind. And saying that "it's as if God's presence is all there is" allows a space for me to stay in contact with her without needing to accept the literalness of her experience. I can, so to speak, play along with her, for she has introduced the "as-if" double register of play: Joanna acknowledges there is a fanciful not-real but at one and the same time a more-real-than-real quality to God's presence; the eerie "unreality" being no less vital than the seeming "hyper-reality." To my ear, the phrase "as-if" suggests the presence of metaphor in the making, the creative impulse to transfer meaning between dissimilar domains. "Metaphor," the Israeli poet Yehuda Amichai says, "is the great human revolution, at least on a par with the invention of the wheel . . . Metaphor is a weapon in the hand-to-hand struggle with reality" (quoted in Gussow, 2000, p. A14). People differ in the mental muscle involved in making metaphors, not to mention taking seriously what is absent from the senses but present in the mind.

Absent from the senses but present in the mind—perhaps there is no better way to describe the play of imagination. It is worth asking: what happens if we think of Joanna as absorbed in the play of imagination? Could one of the functions of imagining be to discover the contours of one's being by generating a psychic space not exactly limited by our skin and not exactly the same as that which can be verified by our sense organs? And does not the play of imagination always alter what is felt to be real?

To attribute Joanna's experience to the play of imagination is not to question the veracity of her description; it is merely a different belief about what constitutes an explanation. To take this one step further: I do not mean to imply, as common parlance might, that Joanna is "just imagining" something that isn't real. Indeed, I want to make a plea for the play of the imagination as constitutive of our subjective sense of reality.

It is a curious matter that Freud, whose entire body of work can be read as a disquisition on imagination, was reluctant to acknowledge its place in psychic life (Castoriadis, 1992). The term "imagination" holds such little cachet it doesn't appear in the Index to the Standard Edition of Freud's collected works. Freud, of course, had his reasons. The notion of an originary, idiosyncratic, and inventive creation of the individual does not fit comfortably with Freud's version of phantasy as either phylogenetically inscribed in the memory of the species or as arising defensively from an "unconscious combination . . . of things experienced and heard" (Freud, 1897, p. 248). He was committed to the view that the psyche merely combines and juxtaposes elements already furnished from elsewhere. For the most part, Freud's psyche pursues serial substitutions for what has been lost. But it never really creates anything new. Despite acknowledging that "the products of imaginative activity" are not "stereotyped or unalterable," Freud saw the underlying motive "of every single phantasy" as a constant—"a correction of unsatisfying reality" (Freud, 1906, pp. 145–146).

On the rare occasion Freud (1917) made space for imagination in the map of inner life, he imaginatively analogized it to a "reservation" or "nature reserve" that "preserves its original state which everywhere else has to our regret been sacrificed to necessity . . . Everything, including what is useless and even what is noxious can grow and proliferate there as it pleases" (pp. 371–372). Unable to subsist on the scanty satisfactions they can extort from reality, human beings compensate themselves with an imaginary realm filled with private bric-a-brac in which they continue to enjoy the freedom from external compulsion long ago relinquished in the name of necessity. For Freud (1906), imagination, like play, is "the opposite of . . . what is real" (p. 144). Or, at least in Freud's psychoanalytic imagination, that is how it appears.

But picture this: an 11-inch-tall hybrid figurine carved from mammoth ivory. The erect body is human, but the head is that of a lion, or perhaps a lioness. Uncovered in a limestone cliff in southwest Germany, the so-called Lion Man of Hohlenstein-Stadel has been carbon dated to approximately 38,000 BCE, making it the oldest known anthropomorphic animal carving in the world. It is also one of the first indisputable examples of art, and probably of religion, and of the ability of the human mind to imagine things that do not actually exist.

Somewhere between 70,000 and 30,000 years ago, there were probably six distinct species of humans on earth. In one of them, a chance reworking of neural networks enabled a prodigious amount of information to be ingested, stored, and transmitted (Harari, 2015). No one is sure what caused it to happen in the brains of Sapiens rather than in any of our hominin siblings—Neanderthals or Erectus, for example. But as a result, our ancestors began to communicate in an extraordinarily supple language, transforming a limited number of sounds into an infinite number of utterances with distinct meanings. And what they communicated deemed crucial for survival was not only the whereabouts of predators and prey, but also who among their own kind was honest and who a cheat, who was friend and who was foe. The evolving social life of humans was built upon a sustained and intense interest shown to every detail as to who is doing what to whom (Dunbar, 1998).

Yet, as the Lion Man of Hohlenstein-Stadel illustrates, what was truly remarkable was not the ability to transmit information about dangers and pleasures in the external world. Rather, it was the unprecedented capacity to imagine, that is, *to picture to themselves*, things they never saw, touched, or smelled. Humans became disposed to depart from veridicality, to invent imaginary creatures and make-believe situations. The hybrid Lion Man as art and possibly religious expression demonstrates the uncanny capacity to conjure and collectively share meaningful fictions. These figments of our fertile imaginations are not lies. Lying subverts trust. Imagined reality, on the other hand, potentially becomes consensual reality—something most everyone believes in. Rather than undermining trust, shared imaginings allow for cooperation among increasingly large numbers of people, thereby exerting an actual force in the world. This is true whether the belief be in a religion's costly commitment to counterintuitive worlds governed by supernatural agents—what Kierkegaard (1955 [1843]) referred to as "a gigantic passion" to dedicate oneself to the "absurd" (p. 35)—or contemporary Western illusions that humans are "endowed with rights" or that money has real value.

But imagination not only conjures what is not available to our senses. Without imagination, there is no perception—or at least that is what neuroscientists such as Eric Kandel believe. What is "seen" in the "mind's eye" goes dramatically beyond what is present in the image cast on the retina of the real eye. With every look, we complete through imagination what Wordsworth called the "something evermore about to be" (Wordsworth, 1996, p. 240). "Because much of the sensory information that we receive through our eyes can be interpreted in a variety of ways," writes Kandel (2012), ". . . we must guess, given the current situation what is the most likely image in front of us" (p. 202).

Perception, Kandel implies, is a guessing game we are generally really good at. We maintain a peculiar contract with the external world; a curious meshing between seeing and seeing-in-the-mind's-eye. Drawing upon memory and imagination, we forecast what we believe the object of our attention is most likely to be. Believing is seeing: we take crude signals and spontaneously conjure a believable picture in our mind. "Our perception of the world," claims the English neuroscientist Chris Frith (2007), "is a fantasy that coincides with reality" (p. 132).

Art historian Ernst Gombrich (1960) refers to this as "the beholder's share": art is not art without the viewer's collaboration. Not only does the viewer perceptually transform a two-dimensional likeness on a canvas into a three-dimensional depiction of the visual world, but it is through the viewer's imaginative interpretation that a meaningful picture is "created" out of mere pigments on a canvas. "No image tells its own story," says

Gombrich (1996). "We need a jolt to remind us of . . . the contribution we make to any [pictorial] representation from the stock of images stored in our mind" (p. 48). Imagination infuses perception. Were we ever to strip away the beholder's share, says Gombrich (1960), "merely a meaningless armature might well be all that would remain" (p. 211).

The iconic American photographer Ansel Adams testifies to the presence of the beholder's share even in the flash of capturing a fleeting image. "When I am ready to make a photograph," writes Adams, "I think what I see in my mind's eye is something that is not literally there. What I am interested in expressing is something . . . built up from within rather than something extracted from without" (quoted in D'Agata, 2016, p. 351). Adams does not simply *take* pictures; he *makes* them. He claims to "revisualize" what he apprehends so that he can "make it look how it feels." Photography, Adams concludes, "is not the duplication of visual reality . . . All my photographs are photographs of myself" (p. 352).

To suggest imaginative elaboration is involved in perception is not the same as believing that so-called "reality" is *nothing but* a feature of our fancy. It is plausible to claim reality is constructed through belief in what we imagine without subscribing to the preposterous notion that whimsy wills things into manifesting themselves. From a psychoanalytic point of view, reality doesn't go away just because we stop believing in it. It is misguided—or at least so believes psychoanalysis—to claim that just because something is a construction it must therefore be *only* an illusion. Experience, as Henry James (1921) once put it, is like a hot air balloon. Thanks to a rope of remarkable length tethered to the earth, we swing "in the more or less commodious car of the imagination; but it is by the rope we know where we are" (p. xxii).

Still, if Kandel and Gombrich and Frith are right, it is also true that there is an inherent *difficulty* involved in "contact with reality," distinct from what psychoanalysis commonly describes as *conflict* between reality and pleasure. We neither simply discover an objective reality nor merely invent a subjective one. Music is evoked *between* a musician and an instrument. It does not arise from either alone. Similarly, the world "calls forth" something in us that in turn "calls forth" something in the world. What is "called forth" affects the type of attention we accord, even as the type of attention we pay also governs what we find (McGilchrist, 2009, p. 133).

Winnicott (1971) intuited this "betweeness" or reciprocal "calling forth": "The fact is, that what we create is already there, but the creativeness lies in the way we get at perception . . . Every moment I have my little experience of omnipotence before I hand this uncomfortable function over to God" (Winnicott, 1986, pp. 49–52). Winnicott's counterintuitive claim—that imagination is vital for contact with reality to feel real—might readily be dismissed as what he called "absurd illogic." But I think Winnicott was searching for a language to capture how for reality to be personal, meaningful, and eventually shareable, the individual's disposition to feel something is true—belief—must attach to what is imaginatively woven with the world. Or, to restate this from the opposite direction: belief is the feeling that what is "called forth in me" through imaginative elaboration corresponds to reality. The problem is: for better *and* for worse, we are all credulous creatures. As Darwin once famously remarked after attending a seance, "nothing is so difficult to decide as where to draw a line between skepticism and credulity" (quoted in Palfreman, 1979, p. 201).

Imagination is not another term for "fantasy" or name for the unconscious. Unless we subscribe to Freud's phylogenetic theory of primal fantasy, it makes sense that from the riot of things beyond order and form, imagination sculpts distinctive unconscious objects and narratives. Shakespeare (1969), who knew a thing or two about imagination, tells us how it works:

> As imagination bodies forth,
> . . . the poet's pen . . . gives airy nothing
> A local habitation and a name.
>
> (p. 125)

Out of "airy nothing," the idiosyncratic and ungovernable imagination creates form out of formlessness, enabling people to bootstrap themselves from within (Modell, 2003, p. 9). Imaginative elaboration offers affective form—a particular shade of consciousness expressive of character—moving the psyche beyond mere imitation.

Developmental research adds to our appreciation of how imagination's access to the not-here and the not-now is intricately implicated in our sense of reality. Beginning in early childhood, imaginative counterfactuals are employed to reason about causal outcomes; novel possibilities—the stuff of endlessly evolving cultural artifacts—are imaginatively generated within make-believe frameworks. Without imagination, we would be locked into the sensory present, denied future horizons, unable to adopt another person's perspective or even respond to eyewitness accounts (Harris, 2000).

Whether constructing a finely crafted argument or telling a well wrought story, actual minds create possible worlds (Bruner, 1986). As Vladimir Nabokov (1967), both a titan of literary storytelling and curator of butterflies at Harvard, famously remarked: "There is no science without fancy, and no art without facts." Reasoned thought employs imagination to envision possible connections before proof becomes available in some formal way. Used this way, imagination acts as a prosthetic for dealing with impersonal causes.

But we also rely upon imagination to navigate the terrain of personal intentions. Narrative thought generates "good stories, gripping dramas, believable (though not necessarily true) historical accounts" (Bruner, 1986, p. 13). Such tales may reach tragic or comic or absurd denouements but they are never conclusive. Fueled by our drive to endow experience with meaning, narrative imagination is, as George Eliot (1990) claimed, "the nearest thing to life" (p. 110).

But this fundamental human capacity—or, better yet, this capacity that makes us fundamentally human—can go awry or take toxic turns. "The lunatic, the lover, and the poet," Shakespeare (1969) reminds us, "are of imagination all compact" (p. 125). Shakespeare has a point: there are potentially perilous misuses of imagination. Asked about literary influences growing up, the British writer Ian McEwan recalled having few books at hand. His family repeatedly relocated while his father, a working-class Scotsman, made his way up the ranks of the British Army. McEwan's mother, meanwhile, was a creative inspiration to him: she anxiously spun elaborate scenarios detailing misfortunes waiting to befall herself and loved ones. "The writer in me is from my mother," says McEwan. "She was a great worrier, which requires an imagination" (quoted in Zalewski, 2009). Worriers have overwrought imaginations.

Jealousy, ruthless ambition, and glory seeking, too, feed off the fertile imagination. Agitated plots are envisioned with other people serving as mere props in fictional flights of humiliation and triumph. Ralph Waldo Emerson was said to have tempered his own ambition by reminding himself to act *as though* people around him were real. "Who knows?" he concluded, "Maybe they are!" (Edmundson, 2012).

Afflictions of imagination sadly sap the spirit, often precipitating the very disaster most feared. Yet, one reason it is nearly impossible to reason with the toxic worrier, the obsessively jealous, or the ruthless glory seeker is that once an imagined reality acquires the status of a belief within a distinct self-state (Bromberg, 1998), it cannot be dismissed as unrealistic conjecture without invalidating the tenacious belief-feeling of that state, which is quite real.

From a certain angle of vision, many difficulties in living can be seen as debased uses of imagination. Imagination may be too pronounced or too pallid; feelings inordinately amplified or life made stale in its absence. Rather than as a bridge to vitalize reality, imagination may be employed only to escape from it. We might fail to adequately distinguish the actual from the imaginary, genuine anxieties blurring into imaginary fears. The often rather sudden appearance of night terrors in children may signal a developmental upsurge in imaginative capacities before imagination is well enough integrated into the personality as a whole. Imaginative imbalances can even be catastrophic (Currie and Ravenscroft, 2002). Autistic children show a marked deficiency of spontaneous pretense (Happe, 1994, p. 37). What Harold Searles (1988) called "dedifferentiation" in schizophrenia is a failure to recognize imagination as such (p. 103). Megalomanic flights of fancy entail a horrifying disregard for anything limiting, or evidentiary. The urgent search for novelty—a stimulant force coming from outside—often substitutes when the imagination fails to bring something vital into being between oneself and what exists out there.

Without sufficient enough overlap between the conjured and the apprehended, external perceptions lack significance, inner experiences lack substance, social cooperation is fraught, and development cannot proceed. The question Freud posed: "Where do we stand in relation to our unconscious fantasies?" and Lacan provocatively elaborated into: "Where do we stand in relation to our desires?" might profitably be augmented to include: "Where do we stand in regard to our imagination?" (Edmundson, 2012).

Armed with imagination, we nervously step over the edge of allowable thought. In health, we use things in the real world to be imaginative about and our imagination makes the world feel more alive. Children engage in pretense and adults are drawn to fiction—including renderings of misery—because we all seek opportunities to generate vivid imaginings. And somewhere between the sterility of dissociative daydreams and the literalness required for mere survival lies the opportunity to blend vision and judgment in due measure so as to imagine realities shareable with others. Perhaps we need to educate ourselves as to the best ways to traffic in such illusion; in R.P. Blackmur's (1935) felicitous phrase, to imaginatively "add to the stock of available reality" (p. 108). Each of us needs to find a personal way to keep inner and outer separate but interrelated, to awaken the world so it can call forth something in us.

It is telling, in this regard, how Joanna describes her earliest experience of noticing God's presence. Twenty years old at the time, Joanna felt "immediately drawn" when invited to a talk by a respected religious authority. She has no recollection of the lecture itself except being "transfixed" by a question posed to the speaker—"*Where* is God?" The simplicity of his response—"Both inside and out"—struck a deep chord. Later that night, alone in her room, Joanna was overcome by a strange vertigo. The light felt oddly different—more haze than beam. She recalls repeatedly whispering to herself, "Where is God? Both inside and out. Where is God? Both inside and out." The aura appeared. She wondered if she was ill, but the dizziness passed and she began feeling unusually invigorated. "My thoughts became something else then," she says, "not the way thoughts usually are in my head. I felt God's presence and I didn't much care if it was inside or out."

Joanna grew up shuttling between secular, contentiously divorced parents, "more hippies than homemakers"—a description reminding me of Erikson's (1993) trenchant observation: "The clinician can only observe that many are proud to be without religion whose children cannot afford their being without it" (p. 243). Stumbling through a chaotic childhood and turbulent adolescence, Joanna had more than her share of familial arguments. After her parents' divorce, her older brother regularly pummeled her as their overwhelmed and ineffectual mother stood by helplessly. At age 14, Joanna stopped attending school and had a sexual affair with a much older man.

I once asked Joanna if she ever had an imaginary friend growing up. "I actually remember as a child wishing I did," she replied. "It would have helped me feel less lonely." "But you've told me that you are not a lonely person. When did that change?" "I don't know exactly. Maybe some point in high school I decided I really don't need other people and I haven't been lonely since. Today, I even prefer traveling alone because I'm always my own best company."

"Human beings", the anthropologist Scott Atran (2002) notes, "create gods who sustain hope beyond sufficient reason and commitment beyond self interest" (p. ix). Since there is no such single entity as "religion," it makes no sense to generalize as to the function "it" serves for Joanna. That people seek solace through activities called "religious" is undeniable. Anxieties related to making vital decisions without certainty as to outcome, grief, and terror in the face of death and loss, consolation for heartbreak, falling short, and brokenness, longings to belong to a virtuous group, bitter resentments that life is unfair, and that goodness does not necessarily triumph all find expression in religious life. Each of these preoccupations felt salient with Joanna at different moments. But Joanna's personal relationship to God brought something else into play.

Earlier, I suggested that by returning to the original meaning of the word "belief," Joanna and I were able to continue a psychoanalytic conversation. The primary modern connotation of the term "belief"—ideas that are either false or which cannot be proven to be true—constitutes a rather drastic historical shift in meaning. Originally, "to believe" simply meant "to hold dear," virtually "to love." It would have made no sense to say to a person in the Middle Ages, "I believe in the Devil and I believe in God," for that would be a logical impossibility. Both God and Devil were assumed to be real. But either you hold one dear or the other; either you align your life, pledge your loyalty, give your love to God, or else you don't (Smith, 1979). We return to this original meaning when we tell those we hold dear, "I believe in you."

As a child, Joanna remembers aching, but not daring, to utter the words "I love you." She waited expectantly for her mother to say the words first. Mother's silence left Joanna frozen. Today, as an adult, Joanna deeply fears she lacks what she calls "an empathy gene." She knows how to behave in a way called for by the dictates of propriety. When someone is hurting, she knows to say, "I'm sorry to hear that." But inside, she feels nothing. She suspects she is deficient in natural feelings of fellowship, affiliation, concern. Valuing self-reliance, she detests affectionate displays.

Except where God is concerned. As a young child—long before the revelatory experience of God made manifest—Joanna recalls absorbed private bedtime monologues directed to a God her parents did not believe in. Prayer for Joanna resembled Margaret Atwood's answer to the question: "Who do I write for?" "Perhaps," says Atwood (2000), "for the same person children are writing for when they scrawl their names in the snow" (p. 43). Joanna harbored a secret hope that someone would take note.

Take note, that is, without intruding. The alive presence of someone who neither obtrudes with demands, nor needs the child to place demands upon them, fosters a capacity for absorbed solitude as opposed to lonely withdrawal. Joanna's early experience in this regard appears to have been precarious. No wonder she shudders at the thought of praying in public. When forced by circumstances, she buries her face behind the prayer book warding off the impulse to immerse herself. To become absorbed in prayer carries the risk of a flood of feeling compromising her composure. Joanna feels too moved and too connected while praying; she needs privacy for loving feelings to be present.

And the meaning of that love has gradually evolved. "My earliest relationship with God was all about me," Joanna says, "what I want, asking Him to do things for me." Coming into her own as an adult, religious observance took on new meaning. Joanna started asking: "What does God want? What can I do for Him? What can I do even if it is hard or unpleasant for me?" Joanna does not wish to return submissively to infantile dependence, but to heal and expand by discovering a more mature form of holding something dear. But before that is possible, there needs to be a shift in Joanna's center of gravity.

For too long, I was mistakenly alert to the wrong collision of beliefs. Holding divergent views of God—she a true believer, I a committed skeptic—was really a secondary matter, a stand-in for a far more salient clash in play. I was privileging Joanna's having a mind of her own—her wanting, fearing, wishing, desiring—a domain of experience too often unthinkingly referred to as "autonomy," or "agency," or "freedom." But in so doing, I was missing what she sought most deeply: an opportunity to no longer have to be the conscious mover of her own life.

Through sheer force of will, Joanna precociously navigated the world, exploiting her keen intelligence, gumption, and grit to obtain a fair measure of external success. But the tenacious application of will left a hole in her heart and a lopsided sense of herself. As is often the case with achievements born of will, Joanna had little access to the sustaining power of faith—that good things, even when lost, can eventually be refound. While conscious will is necessary to pursue purposeful goals and ensure survival, no one wills themselves into life.

Joanna's achievements feel to her "vaguely unreal." This sense of unreality suggests the exchange between inner and outer is unduly circumscribed. Rather than Joanna putting a piece of herself in the outer world and being enriched by the world's offerings, she employs her will to contend with the external world. Force of will is an impoverished place from which to live because it cannot substitute for the unconscious movement between the imaginative and the actual that allows what is "out there" to creatively link up with the "me in here." Without this creative bridge, there may be a lot of fervent activity but little genuine vitality.

The to-and-fro between imagination and adaptation is moved along by an environment that, in Michael Balint's (1968) phrase, "accepts and consents to sustain and carry . . . like the earth or the water sustains and carries a man entrusting his weight to them" (p. 145). The commodious imagination is tethered without undue loss of vitality within such an environment. If absent, the beholder's share is likely to be stripped away and, as Gombrich puts it, only "meaningless armature" will remain. It is one thing to imaginatively adapt while entrusting one's weight to others, but quite another to ask of the will to do the missing work of the environment.

Joanna's absorption in God's presence may be part of her unconscious search for just such an environment. The Japanese psychoanalyst Takeo Doi (1971) writes about "amae," a Japanese word for which there is no equivalent in the English language. "Amae" is the inborn expectation one will be sweetly and indulgently cherished. Joanna's life suggests a shattering of that inborn expectation. When mother's deafening silence froze the words "I love you" on Joanna's lips, something that should have happened did not happen. When her brother physically assaulted her, something that should not have happened did happen. A cleavage (Ferenczi, 1932) ensued, curbing movement between Joanna's imaginative and adaptational capacities: a part of Joanna safeguards survival by unimaginatively contending with external reality while feeling nothing. Another part dwells in an imaginative daydream where the inborn expectation to be cherished and sustained is met; here, Joanna is, so to speak, "kissed by God." And a third part squirrels away and holds all the hurt.

Whether believed to be a remnant of early mental life, the play of imagination, altered state, or supernatural occurrence, Joanna's relationship with God sponsors an exchange that holds the promise of the yet to be lived life she expects. Or at least so I believe. Perhaps, through her belief, Joanna will eventually overcome doubt as to whether she can be loved so as to cultivate her capacity to love.

"Where is love?" Joanna and I wonder. "Inside or out?"

References

Atran, S. (2002). *In Gods We Trust: The Evolutionary Landscape of Religion*. New York: Oxford University Press.

Atwood, M. (2000). *The Blind Assassin*. New York: Nan A. Talese/Doubleday.

Balint, M. (1968). *The Basic Fault*. London: Tavistock.

Blackmur, R.P. (1935). "Statements and Idyls: A Review of Norman Macleod's, 'Horizons of Death,'" *Poetry*, Vol. 14, May 1935, p. 108.

Britton, R. (1998). *Belief and Imagination*. Hove and New York: Brunner-Routledge.

Bromberg, P. (1998). *Standing in the Spaces: Essays on Clinical Process, Trauma, and Dissociation*. Hillsdale, NJ: The Analytic Press.

Bruner, J. (1986). *Actual Minds, Possible Worlds*. Cambridge, MA: Harvard University Press.

Castoriadis, C. (1992). "Logic, Imagination, Reflection." *American Imago*, 49: 3–33.

Currie, G. and Ravenscroft, I. (2002). *Recreative Minds: Imagination in Philosophy and Psychology*. New York: Oxford University Press.

D'Agata, J. (2016). *The Making of the American Essay*. Minneapolis, MN: Graywolf Press.

Doi, T. (1971). *The Anatomy of Dependence*. New York: Kodansha, USA.

Dunbar, R. (1998). *Grooming, Gossip, and the Evolution of Language*. Cambridge, MA: Harvard University Press.

Edmundson, M. (2012). "Imagination: Power and Perils." *Raritan*, Vol. 32, no. 2.

Eliot, G. (1990). *Selected Essays, Poems, and Other Writings*. London: Penguin Classics.

Erikson, E. (1993). *Childhood and Society*. New York: W.W. Norton & Co.

Ferenczi, S. (1932). *The Clinical Diary of Sandor Ferenczi*. Ed. J. Dupont. Trans. M. Balint and N.Z. Jackson. Cambridge, MA: Harvard University Press, 1988.

Freud, S. (1897). *The Complete Letters of Sigmund Freud to Wilhelm Fliess*. Draft L.

Freud, S. (1900). "The Interpretation of Dreams." *The Standard Edition of the Complete Psychological Works of Sigmund Freud*, Vol. IV, pp. ix–627.

Freud, S. (1906). "Creative Writers and Day-Dreaming." *The Standard Edition of the Complete Psychological Works of Sigmund Freud*, Vol. IX, pp. 141–152.

Freud, S. (1917). "Introductory Lectures on Psycho-Analysis, Lecture XXIII: The Paths to the Formation of Symptoms." *The Standard Edition of the Complete Psychological Works of Sigmund Freud*, Vol. XVI, pp. 357–376.

Frith, C. (2007). *Making Up the Mind: How the Brain Creates Our Mental World*. Malden, MA: Blackwell.

Glover, E. (1945). "An Examination of the Klein System of Child Psychology." *Psychoanalytic Study of the Child*, 1: 3–43.

Gombrich, E.H. (1960). *Art and Illusion: A Study in the Psychology of Pictorial Representation*. New York: Pantheon Books.

Gombrich, E.H. (1996). *The Essential Gombrich*. London: Phaidon Press.

Gussow, M. (2000). "Interview with Yehuda Amichai." *New York Times*, September 23, 2000, p. A14.

Happe, F. (1994). *Autism: An Introduction to Psychological Theory*. London: UCL Press.

Harari, Y.N. (2015). *Sapiens: A Brief History of Humankind*. New York: HarperCollins.

Harris, P. (2000). *The Work of Imagination: Understanding Children's Worlds*. Oxford: Blackwell.

James, H. (1921). *The American*. London: Macmillan & Co.

Kandel, E. (2012). *Age of Insight: The Quest to Understand the Unconscious in Art, Mind, and Brain*. New York: Random House.

Kierkegaard, S. (1955 [1843]). *Fear and Trembling*. New York: Doubleday.

Klein, M. (1929). "Personification in the Play of Children." *The International Journal of Psychoanalysis*, 19: 193–204.

McGilchrist, I. (2009). *The Master and His Emissary: The Divided Brain and the Making of the Western World*. New Haven, CT: Yale University Press.

Modell, A. (2003). *Imagination and the Meaningful Brain*. Cambridge, MA: MIT Press.

Nabokov, V. (1967). "Interview with Nabokov." *Wisconsin Studies of Contemporary Literature*, Vol. 8, no. 2, Spring 1967.

Palfreman, J. (1979). "Between Skepticism and Credulity: A Study of Victorian Scientific Attitudes to Modern Spiritualism." In *The Sociological Review*, Vol. 27, Issue Supplement S1, May 1979, pp. 201–236.

Searles, H. (1988). "Sources of Anxiety in Paranoid Schizophrenia." In *Essential Papers on Psychosis*. Ed. P. Buckley. New York: New York University Press.

Shakespeare, W. (1969). "A Midsummer Night's Dream." In *The Complete Pelican Shakespeare: Comedies and Romances*. London: Penguin Books.

Smith, W.C. (1979). *Faith and Belief*. Princeton, NJ: Princeton University Press.

Winnicott, D.W. (1971). *Playing and Reality*. London and New York: Tavistock/Routledge.

Winnicott, D.W. (1986). *Home Is Where We Start From*. New York: W.W. Norton & Co.

Wordsworth, W. (1996). *The Prelude*. London: Penguin Classics, revised edition.

Zalewski, D. (2009). "The Background Hum, Ian McEwan's Art of Unease." *The New Yorker*, February 23, 2009.

Chapter 2

An exquisite corpse

I was unfamiliar with the Surrealist parlor game "The Exquisite Corpse" until Mary introduced me to it. In the game, a player writes or sketches on a sheet of paper, folds it to conceal their contribution, and then passes it to the next player. Stark individual expressions are thereby collectively assembled into a composition. Surrealism founder Andre Breton claims the game began in fun but gradually morphed into an artistic method. It is fitting that Mary is captivated by a game invented by Surrealists.

The jarring disjunctive verbal and visual productions of the exquisite corpse game produce an unusual psychic strain. The mind is forced to irritably search for intelligibility, without which there is only a terrifying void. Yet, if one labors too self-consciously, the already tenuous semblance of sense vaporizes immediately. The moment Mary introduced me to the game, I *felt* it's import: I was being driven mad.

Working with people who go in and out of psychotic states carries many strains. The most obvious, of course, is handling self-destructiveness both in the intentional form of suicidality as well as the consequential damages that follow from anxious disorganization, confusion, or poor judgment. But there is an additional strain the analyst must bear working in areas where psychotic anxieties predominate: the precarious and cyclical way potential space is generated. The analyst's handling of this strain, the person's experience of how the analyst handles the strain, and the unpredictable and shifting contexts within which the strain is negotiated between the two of them become central features of the analytic encounter.

In anatomy, potential space is a region of the body in which two surface membranes adjoin. Winnicott turned it into a metaphor for the realm of the "in-between." It is, in Winnicott's words:

> not inside by any use of the word . . . Nor is it outside, that is to say, it is not part of the repudiated world, the not-me, that which the individual has decided to recognize (with whatever difficulty and even pain) as truly external, which is outside magical control.
>
> (Winnicott, 1971a, p. 41)

Having observed a little boy who became thoroughly obsessed with a piece of string at a time of separation from a depressed mother, Winnicott (1971a) drew conclusions about how string paradoxically both joins and separates (p. 22). The child's relationship to the string was telling Winnicott something about how potential space:

> both joins and separates the infant (child, or adult) and the mother (object). This is the paradox that I accept and do not attempt to resolve. The baby's separating out the world of objects from the self is achieved only through the absence of a space between the infant and mother, the potential space being filled in the way that I am describing (i.e. with illusion, with playing and with symbols).
>
> (Winnicott, 1971b, p. 108)

Winnicott's paradoxical conclusion is that there is a relationally negotiated developmental achievement of a state of mind in which infant and mother are both one and two at the same time.

Potential space was a natural extension of Winnicott's ideas about transitional phenomena. There is a great deal of overlap between the concepts. Nevertheless, I have chosen to focus on potential, rather than transitional, space because of the relative emphases these ideas evoke. The transitional object originally appears in Winnicott's theory as one concrete example, placed in a specific period of development, of the transition from being merged with the environment to being separate from it. Winnicott's later clinical work, on the other hand, became increasingly linked with the idea of playing and communication in the overlap of potential spaces:

> Psychotherapy is done in the overlap of the two play areas, that of the patient and that of the therapist. If the therapist cannot play, then he is not suitable for the work. If the patient cannot play, then something needs to be done to enable the patient to become able to play, after which psychotherapy may begin.
>
> (Winnicott, 1971c, p. 54)

Potential space is a metaphor for a quality of psychic life in which the individual "begins to be" (Winnicott, 1967, p. 98). "Being," at least for Winnicott, means a person feels alive as a human being as opposed to simply surviving or existing. Potential space colors the texture of an individual's affective contact with both internal and external reality. We are not alive *as human beings* if we reside only in the realm of reality or only in the realm of fantasy because in each case we are reflexively reactive rather than creative. In potential space, on the other hand, we come alive as creators or interpreters of our own experience; reality is interpreted in terms of fantasy, and fantasy in terms of reality. Perception renders fantasy relatively safe; fantasy renders perception relatively meaningful. A sense of personal vitality is generated when each prevents the other from becoming too powerful (Ogden, 1989, p. 258).

From another angle, potential space is a way of thinking about how a secure sense of subjectivity is maintained (Grotstein, 1979). Even the most rudimentary sense of "I-ness"—that one is not only reflexively reactive, but is having one's own experience—requires a degree of differentiation between symbol, symbolized, and interpreting subject (Ogden, 1986). What we generally think of as "thinking" is contingent upon this differentiation. "Thinking," as Bion (1962) notes, "has to be called into existence to cope with thoughts" (p. 306). But, in the absence of potential space, "what should be a thought . . . becomes a bad object, indistinguishable from a thing-in-itself, fit only for evacuation" (p. 307). The desperate need to evacuate the "thing-in-itself" forecloses personal meaning and growth.

Subjectivity, an experience of aliveness, thinking as opposed to evacuating thoughts, and meaningful communication with others all require, therefore, a relational negotiation of potential space. Working with more securely organized individuals, potential space can be more or less taken for granted as silent background. Even when absent, its return is unconsciously anticipated by both participants. With more severely disturbed people, on the other hand, there is a noisy painful struggle to create and maintain it. Its loss is traumatizing, since there is no faith that it will return. The treatment process includes repeated mutually generated cycles of creating, sustaining, losing, and regaining potential space. Since the presence of potential space is essential for shared communicative exchanges, its precariousness places a unique strain on the analyst.

Getting to "know" Mary

Mary's life history, riddled with lacunae, was never easy to ascertain. How can one "have" a personal history if one does not experience oneself as a person? In the absence of an interpreting subject who gives meaning to facts, life becomes a discontinuous, arbitrary, and erratic onslaught of happenings. As Mary once said to me, "There are no events in my life, there are only sequences of possibilities."

No wonder Mary needs time at the beginning of many sessions to reassure herself that she and I are both the same people who had met the day before. And toward the end of a session, she is likely to experience various degrees of catastrophic dread because for her there is no guarantee that tomorrow will be another day.

I could impose a narrative structure upon the so-called "facts" of Mary's life. But such a structure would obscure how they were communicated to me: in bits and pieces without form or perspective or sequence or clear delineation of the boundary between the actual and the dream. Mary's state of mind is frequently one in which she either has no access to memory, or else memory is experienced with raw emotional immediacy as if it is occurring here and now. Only rarely can she talk about the past as something toward which she has both a connection and sufficient distance. Mary compels me to struggle to make coherent sense of what she tells me and she is probably more aware of my efforts than of my success. At best, what I do is hold together the threads of her experience, keep the story of her experience alive and viable by putting it together and telling it back. Frequently, I can't or won't make sense of things and she is hurt by my failings, which she attributes to something deeply evil either within me or within herself. At the same time, she can be quite forgiving and capable of providing excellent supervision as to when I'm understanding her and when I am not.

Mary's treatment is not a simple morality tale of progression from bad to better, past to present. It is a process consisting of exchanges that make things seem both better and worse at the same time, and of experiments, some of which have not yet failed. Together, we have come to know a wide variety of states of mind that we struggle to make sense of. Mary is blessed and cursed with verbal sophistication, piercing intellect, and radar-like perceptiveness. Her and my state of mind and the exchanges between us move and shift kaleidoscopically. In her presence, I experience not a particular countertransference reaction, but an intensification of all possible emotional states: childlike bewilderment, dehumanized alienation, terror, dread, grief, sadness, joy, and delight. Sometimes I feel deep affection for her and sometimes I hate her for destroying the functioning of my mind. At times, I don't mind her using me more to *stand* anxiety than to *understand* it, while other times I do. There are moments she wants nothing more than to use me analytically; that is, to give form and shape and consistency to an emotional experience and *think together about* what it might mean. There are many other moments, however, when there is no space beyond the intense literal concreteness of the sensory present.

Existing in a sea of uncanniness

Mary painfully enters the room, literally measuring every step, eyes cast downward except to quickly look up momentarily to see from which way the next blow will inevitably come. When our eyes meet, her face writhes in excruciating pain. She wears torn, patched, and baggy clothes, doing nothing to enhance her natural beauty. Her body is crunched up, tied in knots, her elbows close to her waist, chin at her chest, her piercing blue eyes darting about from behind the hair covering her face. Sometimes she rolls up into a ball in her chair. Other times she sits on top of the chair or crawls around on the floor. She reminds me of a hunted stalked animal, fearful for its life, petrified to either move or remain still. The sessions are so ridden with anxiety that I have difficulty remembering exactly what transpires. If I try to gather information, I feel I am inflicting pain. Agitated, her legs and body shake, her speech becomes incoherent. She mumbles incoherent half-utterances. Everything I say feels intrusive, awkward, off. I cannot connect with her. We are barely able to sit through a session. She dashes out of the room and I am left exhausted by my own efforts to find coherence in her narrative, shaken by the way my mind has been disrupted.

Gradually, we gain some understanding: she is terrified to be known for fear she'll dissolve, and go crazy. She is convinced that the more she tells me about herself, the more grotesque she'll appear. She is trapped: if she fails to tell me things, I will get exasperated with her; if she dares to tell me things, I will get sick. All she has is her broken speech, her difficulty getting words out, the hope and disbelief that she can be understood and tolerated. She wishes desperately to be seen, but then is devastated by a feeling of being exposed. She demarcates a limited territory that I, too, can neither enter nor exit.

As Mary's initial confusional state shifts, the intensity of her destructive inner life becomes more visible. She tells me with obvious pleasure about an earthquake in Los Angeles. She is fascinated by the evil power of natural disasters: the eruption of the earth, the geologic plates shifting, a city destroyed. Earthquakes, she tells me, are LA's only redeeming feature. "The earth swallowing everything. This is not intentional destructiveness—if ants crawl up my arm I smash them to relieve the itch, not to destroy, that's just a consequence." Mary becomes visibly distressed when I prematurely suggest conflict: that the earthquake and civilized parts have trouble living together. She says, "That means nothing. It's a skeleton. Could be about anyone. It's unreal and not the way I think." Taking stock of my mistake—it was too generic, there was no potential space, and she was far from ready to hold conflict in mind—I say, "I guess I missed the point." It might also be that she had been trying to tell me about her love made hungry and I was relating to her love made destructive. Weeks later, she tells me she feels she lives "on the other side of an earthquake."

After a while, it becomes clearer to me that Mary exists—for she is far from feeling alive—in a sea of uncanniness. Most of her life is spent in a depersonalized state, with only a tenuous link to humankind. She has "metal skin" and no secure sense of ongoingness in time and space. She is a "disembodied geometric figure who pops out of dreams into awakeness." Traveling from one place to another, she loses a sense of certainty that she's the same person in both places. She hasn't looked in a mirror in years because the last time she did, her "face was blank and there was nothing there." Disappearing like that is "more terrifying than dying."

Mary experiences "holes in time," feels herself to be in "a recurring loop." She wonders if "what was before might now just be underneath." Plaintively, she prays time would "stretch to fit the contours of my body." Unable to locate herself within time, pots burn on the stove, her bathtub overflows, flooding her mother's apartment. As a session ends, she asks, "Does time just disappear, sink into holes in the floor?" She complains that time has no boundaries. When I point out that she comes to our sessions on time, she says, "Yes, this is a landmark in time. It's clear and regular, but there is nothing else like that, no other edges to time." To be present with me, she must "retain the capacity to disappear at any moment." As she told me frankly after more than a year together, "I know how to disappear while in the room, but know you'll be there when I get back." Frequently, she experiences intense panic at the end of our sessions. This is not only a matter of separation anxiety and the intense discomfort of being left alone with the turmoil created in her head by our working together. This also has to do with her jolting experience that only fleeting minutes have passed since she entered the room. It took me a while to understand that the sense of herself *entering* and *exiting* sessions, *coming in* from the world and *returning to* face it alone, is distinct from the sense of herself *with* me in the office. If potential space is generated within the session, Mary has no secure sense that what transpired will continue to feel real once outside the room.

To survive, Mary must incessantly and vigilantly scan for possible clues to meanings she can't quite fathom. Although she cannot evoke a constant object, she nevertheless catalogues everything in minute detail. It appears to her that I "move my head as if I am emptying it" of her. A paper clip underneath the couch, visible only from the angle of her chair, suddenly disappears, causing her great distress. She actively investigates every nook and cranny of the room. All her energy is used to guard herself; none is left for living. She has to prepare for all contingencies simultaneously. She is cursed with being unable to be indifferent to anything!

In the absence of potential space, objects "attack her." The books in her room, she says, "encroach upon me, overwhelm me, take over my space, my self," until she can no longer be certain "where I end and the books begin." She has no recourse but to "desperately rip and destroy them, drown them in the bathtub, before they suffocate me." Similarly, words, thoughts, and feelings are dangerous corporeal entities causing catastrophic reactions. They irrevocably shatter by highlighting separateness at the expense of union.

The search for contact and potential space

Like an alien on a strange planet, Mary explores with trepidation and childlike wonder the new physical and human environment she encounters in my office. Secretly at first, and then in an ever more open way, she scrutinizes me in exquisite detail, noticing minute changes in my clothes, my gestures, the inflection of my voice, the cadence of my breathing. Like an infant desperately in search of consistent provision, she confesses it would give her comfort if I would wear the same clothes all the time.

She asks to look in the closet in my room, crawls under the couch, panics when tiny leaves fall off a plant. She cautiously touches the tissue box, turns it over again and again, removes tissues to see what might be at the bottom of the box. I watch as she lets the tissues one by one parachute gracefully to the floor and ours is the momentary pleasure of children discovering the motion and rhythm and mastery of play. Mary begins to use the office as a place to bring little bits and pieces of her world. She shows me a photograph of a wolf dog in a pet shop about whom she weaves a family romance. "My mother is a wolf and my father her shadow," she tells me as she gleefully points to the dog's tongue in the picture. She brings in paintings and tells me how "certain colors and lines impose themselves upon the canvas." She makes odd creations, miniature installations, and we sit on the floor and learn what we can from what they have to say. She asks to leave these things in my closet and I agree.

At one point, Mary grows phobic about leaving the house. Her anguish knows no bounds as she desperately tries to sleep and not move a muscle in her body. But she cannot be still because she is plagued by nightmares of her head split open, smashed, her brain oozing out. Since "even while awake these nightmares can appear," she tries to "think horrible thoughts as a way of occupying her mind." When sufficient potential space is generated between us, we are able to understand that she manages to be "asleep while awake" but that she has not yet found a way to be "awake while asleep."

Hesitantly, cryptically, she reveals that she cuts herself; that her legs are full of disfiguring marks. She is convinced that she has "now destroyed everything" by telling me what she needs for me to know and what I mustn't ever know. Razor blades hidden in bars of soap comfort her. Her delicate cutting is experienced as "good pain," which, in her words, "obliterates the logic of the previous situation." Bringing her temporary relief, it fleetingly allows her to feel real. The more we talk about the cutting, the less she cuts. But every change is accompanied by a horrific new anxiety: a source of potential relief has been taken away from her. The part of her that needs to cut experiences the relinquishing of the act as death. She tells me she might have to cut herself "because the cut marks are fading." If she doesn't cut, it will be a "terrible waste of potential cut marks" and she worries "what will happen to the cut marks I don't make?" The cutting part of her self still needs to be heard. So she tries ripping as a substitute. She rips clothes and important papers. The relief is transient. Enough potential space is temporarily generated for us to talk about how cutting is a way of knowing she exists, not a way to die. Ripping, we understand, is sometimes also an act of trying desperately to sever her connection with her mother. Words, she acknowledges, replace, at times, the ripping by giving form and definition to what she feels. But words also remind her that she is separate. There are moments when I have the fleeting impression we are getting somewhere.

One day, Mary tells me she feels "like a nuclear reactor whose shell is not holding." She chides herself for "trying to find relief rather than having sufficient courage to accept the horror of her barbaric repulsiveness." Weeks pass. Mary says that her "putridness" waits for her when she returns home, "contaminating" all her thoughts. She is "enveloped in evil." To me, it seems, this adhesive addiction to a sense of profound badness is Mary's only way of keeping hope alive: if all the badness is in her, she retains the hope that perhaps by eliminating herself, goodness can be preserved.

One morning, Mary enters the room and reaches out to hand me a sealed envelope. I unthinkingly extend my hand to receive the offering but, mid-air, reflexively pull back. An inscription on the envelope surface catches my eye: "Not to be opened until I die." For a few moments, I feel horrendous strain. I can't find my center and she is fully aware of my hesitation. Desperately, she asks if I want her to destroy "it", to rip "it" to shreds. In the absence of potential space, the envelope and her become equivalent. She has no feelings *about* the envelope; she *is* the envelope. Her and my distress accelerate rapidly, and she appears to communicate that I must take the letter if she is to live. I suggest that her giving me that envelope is a way of letting me know she needs me to be thinking about her all the time. Privately, I consider how she has put me in an untenable predicament, forcing me to chose: I can neither accept nor reject the letter. I have momentarily lost my freedom, squeezed in the vice that she experiences every waking moment. I hate her for doing this to me. I say to her, "I am willing to hold on to whatever keeps you alive but I cannot do so alone." I instinctively move a small table between us and suggest to her that the letter be placed there. At first, she is taken aback; then she agrees. For three sessions, the envelope remains on the table, alluded to, looked at, spoken about, held by us both. She is angry at me for rejecting it; glad that it is still there. Two sessions later, she spontaneously takes it back and in its place produces two bottles, linked by an old telephone cord, a small envelope dangling from it. Uncannily, I recognize the representation of the two of us with the letter between us.

These bottles, and a series of ever-changing variations upon them, have remained a feature of our work together. Through them, Mary creates a special language for the two of us as an attempt to create a non-lethal bridge. I keep them in a closet in my office and we frequently negotiate whose job it is to take them from the closet and how they should be placed within the room. In many sessions, she manipulates them in one way or another. They are a potent concrete symbol of things that cannot yet be said directly or which need be expressed this way first. They are "things of action" that presage "objects of contemplation." Paradoxically, the bottles both bring us together through our private secret shared experience of their reality and keep us separate through the distance created by their being external representations of ourselves. Like a true transitional object, we never question the reality of the projection. When she feels ill, she may lay "her bottle" down or tell me that "it feels sick" or "is dying." When I fail her, or "disappear," or her feeling toward me becomes too aggressively or erotically intense, she may suddenly rip the cord out from between the bottles. Sometimes she moves the bottles closer together, sometimes farther apart. At times, she takes most of the cord and stuffs it inside one of the bottles, leaving the other with only a small piece. She has attached bits and pieces of cloth and pens and buttons and wires in various configurations.

Resourcefully, Mary had found a way to communicate. Through countless acts with and upon the bottles, we have been able to understand, for example, the fine distinction between areas in which we are *unconnected*, or not yet connected, and those moments in which we become *disconnected* because a connection that was felt has suddenly been severed. She has used them to help me understand a variety of states of mind: *panic*, when she is alone and no one is there; *disintegration*, when she is with another person and something that should happen doesn't; and *claustrophobia*, when she is with another person and something is happening that shouldn't. These varieties of anxiety alternate with varieties of confusion: there is the confusion and unique pain associated with trying to *avoid* something that is distinct from the confusion experienced as an absence of a point of reference when she is trying to *confront* something. The bottles, I believe, are both an attempt to graphically represent and at the same time seek an exit from her unending futile wanderings in her own internal object world. They are concrete symbols of Mary's struggle to secure potential space with me.

The cyclical collapse and restoration of potential space

Mary exhausts me as I walk a thin line between neither joining nor denying her projections. To her, I am, at times, "a mad scientist, dissecting her, ripping her guts out, eating her flesh." I also embody "all that is good" and she deeply fears her "evil will destroy" my "goodness." She says to me, "You are a camel with your own water supply while I have no water supply of my own."

Mary confesses one day that she has been "spying" on me. She regularly goes to Barnes & Noble and tries to determine "which books you've read, which ones you dislike, and which ones you started but never finished." Also, she looks me up in a directory and discovers where I live. The strain is so great at that moment that I fail to consider the possibility that she is expressing both a desire for more contact with me and some concern about whether I can help her. Instead, I become preoccupied with how obviously paranoid and delusional she is. There is not sufficient potential space between us that might otherwise enable us to explore feelings of attraction and threat. To relieve the strain, I want to pull her quickly into "reality" and get her to stop "spying" on me. I feel compelled to act swiftly to prevent her from entertaining any ideas about coming to my home. Unaware of my own defensiveness, I tell her in a barely disguised disapproving voice that I think perhaps she's frightened of what she might do now that she knows where I live. As I say this, she is consumed with psychotic anxiety: she fears she is "spilling out into the floor, a huge vacuum cleaner pulling her insides out." She says that when her thoughts "get close to the surface" of her brain, "they feel as if they might be ripped" from her.

In the following session, she does not bring out the bottles. I immediately feel a tremendous gap, a glaring absence, a painful rift. I tell her I realized after she left that she had tuned into my own unacknowledged fear about what she might do now that she knows where I live. I admit to her that I tried to shift this onto her by suggesting that *she* was afraid what she might do when in fact *I* was the one who was afraid. We talk about how exquisitely attuned she is to my anxiety and how sometimes she senses it even before I do. She appears temporarily relieved by my admission.

I, too, feel relief. She mentions having felt "violently excluded and knowing that you must despise and hate me." I tell her that sometimes I do. Enough potential space is generated for us to talk about how getting me to hate her is better than the anticipation of my hating her. Then, at least, she can stop worrying about when it will happen. At this point, she walks over to the closet and brings out the bottles. We were both beginning to appreciate the extent to which she desperately needs to find my hate.

A summer break, four years into our work together, brings into sharp relief the question of Mary's capacity to accept my otherness, my externality, my life beyond her omnipotent control. For two weeks after my return, she is electively mute. All she can say is that "it was very confusing" to her that I had returned. In muffled whispers, she asks, "How can I possibly know that you are real?" She curls up into a fetal position and withdraws into silence. I ask her if she has any ideas about what is happening for her. "I must be looking for something," she replies. "What might that be?" "I can't find it outside, so I try to find it inside." "Perhaps," I say, "you are looking for our regular meetings and can't find them." "I felt trapped," she continues. "I couldn't find our meeting outside or inside." Her life, she says, is "like trying to run a marathon with a single breath." The trick, we discuss, is to keep on breathing while "Is anybody out there?" vies with "Is anybody in here?" She tells me, "You're the Cheshire cat, appearing and disappearing, fading in and out of reality." She is "Humpty Dumpty, shattered in shards." Eventually, I comment, "You need everything to remain the same. Either I am always here or gone forever. You need 100 percent certainty. Any change is unbearable. In response, you withdraw into yourself, totally isolated and cut off, unsure what is real and what is your imagination." This momentarily enlivens her, and she says, "I need you to be a machine but you are Hal, the computer from 2001." I say, "A machine designed to be totally reliable, that then destroys everything because it has a mind all its own." We are beginning to get a sense of how in the absence of potential space, any assertion of my separateness becomes a matter of life or death. "I'm foreign to myself," she continues. "I've gone backward into myself and don't know why. I managed for a while when you were gone and then everything dissolved and now you've returned but I don't know if you have and now I don't know what to do."

As weeks pass, Mary cycles between relative calm and feelings of panic. For Mary, safety acts like a warning signal for impending disaster. Feeling better, therefore, is itself a cause for great anxiety; safety is inextricably linked to subsequent catastrophe. My reliability increases her willingness to risk dependence but also transforms me into a source of potential harm. She is tantalized by the promise of connection and hope I hold out to her, but sees me as hateful and hates me for tantalizing her in this way.

One day—after receiving a high mark in a university class she risked taking—she enters my office a bundle of distress. Torture is everywhere. In the absence of a mediating "I," she is neither the torturer nor the tortured; she is the torture itself! She is stunned and horrified at her high grade and distressed even more when she senses my feeling good about her success. She quickly puts the two bottles out of sight of each other. "Your bottle," she explains, "doesn't want to see my bottle." As she does this, my feeling shifts. It is as if a vacuum cleaner has sucked all life out of the room, de-animating everything. Only once I am able to understand that the part of her that I didn't want to see was the one that feels tremendous despair about her own inability to feel good about any success did Mary allow the bottles to "see" each other once again.

Handling the cycles of potential space

The strain induced by the absence of secure potential space can be handled in a variety of ways. One solution is to emphasize the reality pole by employing counterprojective techniques. Sullivan, for example, would sometimes respond to a person's delusion by saying, "Isn't that crazy?" or "Isn't that a little bit cuckoo?" (Blechner, 1995). He insisted that the disturbed person was capable of communicating in a consensually validated manner, if compelled to do so without excessive threat to self-esteem (Sullivan, 1973). The risk with this approach, however, is that the person can be forced, through premature compliance, into making a false adaptation to reality. Rather than be allowed to make use of the treatment in their own way and in their own time, the person has no choice but to adapt to the analyst's sense of reality.

An opposite approach to reducing the strain is to emphasize the fantasy pole. In its most extreme form, this means "joining the patient's delusion" (Lindner, 1955). By abandoning his or her own version of reality, the analyst hopes to establish contact with the ill person's inner world. The risk, however, is that the healthier parts of the person might experience the analyst's "joining" as either a manipulation or as condescending indulgence (Fromm-Reichman, 1954).

At various times during my work with Mary, I found that the strain would become so intense that I was pulled in each of these directions. Often, although not always, this was a response to the absence of potential space between us. I hoped that by either pulling Mary toward my view of reality or allowing myself to be totally immersed in hers, being together could be made more tolerable. Identification—in the primitive Kleinian sense of similar objects being regarded as the same—became, at those moments, a substitute for potential space.

The bottles Mary introduced into the treatment are emblematic of this process. At certain moments, I am literally afraid to touch the *bottles*, lest I traumatize *her*. At other times, I begin to feel irritated that I am "talking to bottles." I recognize, however, that in the absence of potential space between us at those moments, we are unable to mutually sustain the paradoxical illusion that they are *simultaneously* aspects of herself, representations of the state of our relationship, symbols of her and me, and "just bottles." When we are able, on the other hand, to generate sufficient potential space between us, we can playfully use the bottles as a way of communicating.

Another angle of vision from which to regard handling the strain is in terms of "adaptation to need" or "environmental adaptation" (Sechehaye, 1951; Schwing, 1954; Winnicott, 1955). Sullivan (1973), for example, cautioned clinicians to delimit regressive behavior by actively focusing on the person's "meaningful communications." With uncommunicative people, he would sometimes leave abruptly so as to forestall an irritated countertransference reaction on his part. Fromm-Reichman (1939), on the other hand, would often stay for a long time with regressed people, and in her early years suggested that the best way to handle a feces-smearing person is to wear clothing that one doesn't mind getting soiled. It seems to me that these contrasting approaches have at least as much to do with the sensibilities of the individual practitioner as they do with the objective needs of the ill person. Often, the analyst's personal sensibility is elevated into a clinical theory and a proscriptive technical injunction.

Working with Mary required, especially in the earliest phases, a high degree of adaptation on my part. Nevertheless, as time went on, there were repeated collisions of our conflicting needs. My strict maintenance of the treatment frame was a constant hateful reminder to her that I remained, no matter what, beyond her omnipotent control. For me, on the other hand, the frame constituted a welcome protection against a tendency I had to adapt to Mary's need at too high a personal cost. Similarly, increasing limits I imposed on certain of Mary's demands, such as her wish to store unlimited amounts of personal articles in my closet, or asking me to take mementos of her on my vacation, became painful rejecting moments that felt traumatizing to her. Interpretive work around these rebuffed demands *at the moment they were occurring*, and in the absence of potential space, usually only increased Mary's anxiety.

The point I wish to emphasize is that adaptation in and of itself does not generate potential space. Even in Winnicott's developmental theory, it is the mother's gradual titrated *de-adaptation* that facilitates growth. In fact, what the infant requires is not mechanical and infallible perfection of adaptation, but human and personal relating to gradual failures of adaptation. With Mary, each collision of our conflicting needs led to painful negotiations. These negotiations were painful because from her perspective her survival was at stake, while from my perspective it wasn't always clear when I was being "used as an object," in Winnicott's sense of the term (Winnicott, 1969), and when I was being exploited as a person (Bromberg, 1995, p. 179). I believe that it is the repeated cycles of adaptation, de-adaptation, collision, and negotiation that help generate potential space. Both excessive adaptation and premature refusal to adapt can be employed defensively as protection against the strain.

My efforts to reduce the strain on myself mirror Mary's essential lack of a true relationship to either internal or external reality. She could not generate potential space for herself in a way that would allow inner and outer and her and me to remain separate but interrelated. When she became *too immersed* in her own fantasy world or merged with me, she felt overwhelmed, crazy, and on the verge of annihilation. When she became *too abruptly or exclusively focused on external reality* or her separateness from me, she experienced herself as a deadened isolate or suffocating automaton. In the absence of potential space, there is no way to move comfortably toward someone else's reality without a horrific dread of psychic death.

Put another way, within potential space we do not ask the question: "Whose reality is it?" (Modell, 1989). The person's reality is not experienced by the analyst as something to be "penetrated" or "overcome" or "demystified" or "decoded." The analyst's reality is not experienced by the person as an "intrusion" or "impingement" or "confrontation." If the person is relating to the analyst *only* as a self-object in Kohut's sense, or *only* as representing an external world, it is unlikely he or she will be able to make use of the analyst's construction of reality. If the analyst, on the other hand, is relating to the person *only* as a "distorter" or "resister" of reality, or as *only* mired in their inner world, then it is unlikely that person's construction of reality can be fruitfully elaborated. It is probably the hallmark of a "good" analytic hour if one does not quite know which of the participants has made the interpretation. Working within potential space involves a shared construction of reality that allows for simultaneous union and separateness.

Once the paradoxical nature of potential space is appreciated, it becomes clinically meaningless to dichotomize interventions into "confrontational" versus "empathic" or as emphasizing "security" versus "growth." Potential space can only be generated if, in Winnicott's language, there is some prior "repudiation" of the world, some willingness, no matter how painful, to recognize a truly external "not-me," which, by virtue of its being outside magical control, exists as a potential source of influence. At the same time, in the absence of a creative relationship to the "not me," the individual will be unable to use or allow him or herself to be influenced by what the external world offers.

Even in the best of circumstances, potential space has a quality of illusion that is easily disrupted. It must be kept within its own frame, a frame that accepts multiple levels of reality simultaneously (Kafka, 1964). The Dutch historian Huizinga captured this quality well in his discussion of playing as a form of action contained within a separate reality. He offers the following illustration:

> A father found his four year old son sitting at the front of a row of chairs, playing "trains." When he kissed his son the boy said: "Don't kiss the engine Daddy, or the carriages won't think it's real."
>
> (Huizinga, 2016, p. 8)

Imagine the father at this moment of interaction. Perhaps it is Sunday and, in a playful mood, he sits down on the floor for a train ride. Or maybe he has just returned from work, tired and preoccupied, and wants his son to come to the dinner table at that very moment. Perhaps he is enchanted seeing his son play so creatively. But what if it turns out his son has spent every opportunity during the previous month sitting at the front of those chairs? And now is refusing to go to day care?

The point I wish to illustrate is that the father's reaction is going to be determined by a combination of his parental intent and available repertoire of responses at that moment. Similarly, whether the analyst chooses to "join" the delusion, share the illusion, demand greater contact with reality, or bear the strain of the absence of potential space will be determined by a complex mixture of the state of relatedness between the participants, the therapeutic intent, and the available repertoire of responses at any given moment.

Exquisite corpse and squiggles

The Surrealists' exquisite corpse game was the only game Mary remembers playing with her mother growing up. She finds it bizarre and yet beautiful, and she recognizes that most people probably can't tolerate a creation so splendidly grotesque. Once, I introduced Mary to Winnicott's squiggle game. We played it, and then we played with the difference between "her game" and "my game." Mary was quick to recognize that in the Surrealists' game there is no relationship between the players. Nothing is mutual or created together. Every production is starkly cut off from the next—the folded creases on the paper symbolizing and emphasizing this fact. The startling disjunctions create, nevertheless, a shattered whole, which one struggles to take in as such.

Playing the squiggle game leads Mary to spontaneously declare that she now had a good feeling in the session but that she was frightened that any bad feeling she may have will "eat up this good feeling." As we enjoy the delightful moment together, I wonder if the trajectory of her treatment might be along the lines of "from exquisite corpse to squiggle," from painful isolation to tolerable mutuality. I think of how the disjointed, seemingly meaningless, sounds of an infant can go out into the void yet still one day become a conversation. Then, it occurs to me, the reverse may also contain some truth: a person needs to tolerate the startling disjunctions of stark individualities barely coming together. Soon, I caution myself against any ideas relating to the "trajectory" of her treatment. My desire that Mary move from any one way of relating to any other is a double-edged sword: it contains hope that might help her grow as well as expectation that might prove too much for her to bear. We continue to cyclically generate, lose and restore potential space.

References

Bion, W. (1962). "A Theory of Thinking." *The International Journal of Psychoanalysis*, 43: 306–310.

Bromberg, P. (1995). "Resistance, Object-Usage, and Human Relatedness." *Contemporary Psychoanalysis*, 31(2): 173–191.

Blechner, M. (1995). "Schizophrenia." In *Handbook of Interpersonal Psychoanalysis*. Ed. M. Lionells et al. Hillsdale, NJ: The Analytic Press, pp. 375–396.

Fromm-Reichman, F. (1939). "Transference Problems in Schizophrenics." *Psychoanalytic Quarterly*, 8: 412–426.

Fromm-Reichmann, F. (1954). "Psychotherapy of Schizophrenia." In *Psychoanalysis and Psychotherapy*. Ed. D.M. Bullard. Chicago, IL: University of Chicago Press, 1959, pp. 194–209.

Grotstein, J. (1979). "Who Is the Dreamer Who Dreams the Dream and Who Is the Dreamer Who Understands It." *Contemporary Psychoanalysis*, 15: 110–169.

Huizinga, J. (2016). *Homo Ludens: A Study of the Play-Element in Culture*. Kettering, OH: Angelico Press.

Kafka, J. (1964). "Technical Applications of a Concept of Multiple Reality." *The International Journal of Psychoanalysis*, 45: 575–578.

Lindner, R.M. (1955). *The Fifty Minute Hour*. New York: Holt, Rinehart & Winston.

Modell, A. (1989). "The Psychoanalytic Setting as a Container of Multiple Levels of Reality: A Perspective on the Theory of Psychoanalytic Treatment." *Psychoanalytic Inquiry*, 9: 67–87.

Ogden, T. (1986). *The Matrix of the Mind: Object Relations and the Psychoanalytic Dialogue*. Northvale, NJ: Jason Aronson.

Ogden, T. (1989). "Playing, Dreaming, and Interpreting Experience: Comments on Potential Space." In *The Facilitating Environment: Clinical Applications of Winnicott's Theory*. Ed. G. Fromm and B. Smith. Madison, WI: International Universities Press, pp. 255–278.

Schwing, G. (1954). *A Way to the Soul of the Mentally Ill*. New York: IUP.

Sechehaye, M. (1951). *Symbolic Realization*. New York: IUP.

Sullivan, H.S. (1973). *Clinical Studies in Psychiatry*. New York: Norton.

Winnicott, D.W. (1955). "Metapsychological and Clinical Aspects of Regression within the Psycho-Analytical Set-Up." In *Through Pediatrics to Psycho-Analysis*. New York: Basic Books, 1974, pp. 278–294.

Winnicott, D.W. (1967). "The Location of Cultural Experience." In *Playing and Reality*. New York: Basic Books, 1971, pp. 95–103.

Winnicott, D.W. (1969). "The Use of an Object and Relating Through Identifications." In *Playing and Reality*. New York: Basic Books, 1971, pp. 101–111.

Winnicott, D.W. (1971a). "Playing: A Theoretical Statement." In *Playing and Reality*. New York: Basic Books, 1971, pp. 38–52.

Winnicott, D.W. (1971b). "The Place Where We Live." In *Playing and Reality*. New York: Basic Books, 1971, pp. 104–110.

Winnicott, D.W. (1971c). "Playing: Creative Activity and the Search for the Self." In *Playing and Reality*. New York: Basic Books, 1971, pp. 53–64.

Chapter 3

Faking it

In George Orwell's (1936) classic tale "Shooting an Elephant," an elephant in heat ravages a local bazaar in Burma. A British police officer reluctantly sets out, rifle in hand, to appraise the situation. Meanwhile, local citizens flock to the scene. Shouting excitedly, they watch him "as they would a conjurer about to perform a trick." The ever-growing army of people jostling at his heels unnerves the poor officer. "Here was I," he recalls:

> The white man with his gun, standing in front of the unarmed native crowd—seemingly the leading actor of the piece; but in reality I was only an absurd puppet pushed to and fro by the will of those yellow faces behind. I perceived in this moment that the white man . . . becomes a sort of hollow, posing dummy . . . He shall spend his life in trying to impress the "native," and so in every crisis he has got to do what the "natives" expect of him. He wears a mask, and his face grows to fit it. I had got to shoot the elephant. I had committed myself to doing it when I sent for the rifle. A sahib has got to act like a sahib.
>
> (Orwell, 1936, p. 8)

There is only one problem: by the time the poor officer arrives, the elephant is quietly munching grass in the paddy fields below and looks no more dangerous than a cow. The policeman wishes he could just walk away. But thousands of eyes are upon him. He must act quickly, and appear in command. So he does what he does not want to do: he shoots the elephant. "I often wondered," concludes the officer, "whether any of the others grasped that I had done it solely to avoid looking a fool" (p. 8).

Orwell's rendering of the colonialist's dilemma can also be read as a commentary on a familiar human foible. Who doesn't recognize the all-too-human experience of a me-outside-me making sure I am maintaining a level of dignity? And who can deny that one way of managing the discomfort of threats to dignity is by bracketing part of our disposition and faking whatever we conclude is warranted by the given situation? A sahib, after all, must act like a sahib. Or, as H.L. Mencken once quipped, "Self-esteem is the secure feeling that no one, as yet, is suspicious" (quoted in Stephenson, 2004, p. 1).

Faking it. How pejorative these words seem! Therapeutic third ears perk up at the hint of insincerity. Our current ameliorative ethos mobilizes us as guardians of authenticity. We expect ourselves, as Owen Renik (1988) put it, to shun pretense and "get real." But I would like to make a plea for a more appreciative view of the varieties of faking it. Perhaps believing wholeheartedly in our own authenticity is a form of self-delusion. It is, perhaps, the great illusion of our contemporary culture to believe that what we confess to is who we "really" are. Blessed and cursed with what Roger Shattuck (2000) has termed "intermittence"—the fundamental inability of people to be all of themselves at any given time—it would be a shame simply to dismiss all shamming. As Emerson (1983) liked to say, "I am always insincere, as always knowing there are other moods" (p. 587).

Reader beware: hazarding no clear definition, I intend to play footloose and fancy-free with the term "faking it." I hope what is lost in conceptual clarity will be gained in an appreciation of how blended and overlapping experiences of "fakery" can be.

Knaves and fools

Psychoanalytic theory has its favored dichotomies: objects and instincts, realities and fantasies, sexes and genders. But in the categories of discourse predating psychoanalysis—in that Old World animated by vanity, pride, honor, and self-command—part of the human spirit was captured by another contrasting pair: knaves and fools. Knaves deceive and fools succumb to the deceit of others. Anxiety, from this point of view, is less about forbidden impulses threatening to surface than about the peripheral awareness that we might be engaged in a confidence game. Am I being fooled? Or will you find out that I am fooling you? And if unconscious life is a way of describing our own self-deception, is it not also the biggest knave of all?

A supervisee prodded me to think about the positive value of faking it. Eager to learn, she asked if she could bring tape-recorded sessions to supervision. Only at the first sign of trouble—technical, that is—did it even occur to me to question why she preferred recorded material.

A broken tape left her noticeably more anxious than usual. "I feel like such a fraud without the tape," she explained. "Even when I write process notes, I never fully trust them and I feel like I'm just making it all up. I'm afraid when I report from memory I might confuse myself with the patient."

I was particularly struck by her concern she "might confuse herself with the patient." I heard her words both as a striving for accuracy and, perhaps more poignantly, as anxiety about allowing for dedifferentiation and deeper identifications. After all, can we honestly be of help to others if we do not, from time to time, confuse ourselves with them?

Even though reasonably certain that what she was reporting was accurate, the supervisee was plagued by a niggling feeling that she was "just making it up." Who, I began to wonder, is the one making it up and who is the one reluctant to believe in her own veracity? Afterwards, I begin noticing how frequently people refer to particular experiences in terms of faking it.

Varieties of fakery

An obvious example of faking it is the common experience of the novice feigning self-assurance in a new role. I recall my own first-ever encounter with a patient in a hospital clinic. As a new student with little formal training, I was painfully aware of trying to exude confidence in the absence of competence. The patient, a chronic paranoid, was far savvier about therapy than I was. He had seen dozens of novices just like me and had come fully prepared to put me in my place. Announcing he had 10 questions he needed answered before we begin, he took from his pocket a prepared list and read it aloud:

> Question 1: what is your theoretical orientation?
>
> Question 2: how many patients have you cured and in what diagnostic categories?
>
> Question 3: are you a Freudian, Jungian, Adlerian, Kohutian, or eclectic?
>
> Question 4: what are your spiritual beliefs and how do they affect the way you do therapy?

And so on. Needless to say, I did not do very well. He rose from his chair, shouted at me that he knew I wasn't going to answer his questions, and stormed out of the room.

Having gone into the session feeling like "a hollow posing dummy," I left doubting I could ever "wear the mask until my face came to fit it." But it was also true that before I could ever genuinely inhabit my new role, I would have to learn to fake it. There was no "me" who "is" a therapist to call upon—which is probably why faking it often seems so horribly lonely. As an incipient therapist finding my way into the therapeutic culture's tool kit, I would need to imitate—a word in Latin that is also the root of imago. I would, in other words, have to invoke my memory of competent others—pretend to be them—as part of evoking my own competence.

The discomfort of faking it is by no means restricted to the novice assuming a new role. A middle-aged man, expressing frustration that he "is" an artist, but needs "to work" as a teacher, describes a classroom encounter: "I know it went well but I feel like a total fake, out of sync with the environment—like an image imposed on another image, but the borders don't line up." What an artistic and instructive way of describing the anxiety of faking it: an "image imposed on another image but the borders don't line up." While "he" is in the role, an internal image of himself generates a particular discomfort, an "out of syncness," to which attention must be paid.

Or consider a woman invited to a birthday party at which each guest is asked to write a poem or song in lieu of a present. "I feel so awkward," she says. "Who am I, Dylan Thomas?" Reflecting on her predicament, she spontaneously compares her anticipated humiliation with memories of successful professional presentations: "When I give professional talks," she reports, "if I can feel angry at the person who made me do it—it goes really well. But I really like this person whose birthday it is. I can't figure out how to be angry at her so I won't feel like a fake or a fool." For this woman, anger enables access to inner resources protecting her dignity. But if she could better tolerate, or even enjoy, feeling a bit like a fake, she might not need to rely so heavily on rage as an antidote to potential shame.

The uneasiness of faking it can also be a way of questioning the purity of one's own motives. A man, engaged to be married, asks, "How am I supposed to know if she is really the one? I think I love her, but I have no way of knowing and, if I have these doubts, it must mean that I'm actually faking it. I don't know how to prove to myself that my reasons are pure." Like Dostoyevski's Prince Myshkin in The Idiot, this man tortures himself with "double thoughts." "A half-hearted commitment is a fake commitment," he opines. "I am so tainted, but I still intend to marry her." How easy it is to feel tainted by our uncertain or unverifiable motives.

We know people often mistrust the motives even for their own good deeds, thinking of them as fake good deeds. It is common to desire unself-conscious virtue. "Purity of heart," Kierkegaard (1948) once remarked, "is to will one thing" only. But, given the serial meandering of conflicted desire, is there a good-enough psychoanalytic theory to account for "wholeheartedness"? Or, how might we understand the difference between the person who consciously acts the role of an imposter and the person who feels like an imposter while acting a role?

After 9/11, a journalist writes extensively about the absence of official government guidelines for home survival kits. Should iodide be a standard component? What about Cipro? Are gas masks really useful? He studies government websites, interviews physicians, corresponds with antiterrorism experts. Yet, definitive knowledge eludes him. Meanwhile, his anxious wife repeatedly implores him to prepare a safety kit for the family. As she suffers, he dithers. Exasperated, she obtains supplies derived from a list from his most recent article. The floor of the family den is soon cluttered with scattered piles of supplies. Reflecting on the situation, the journalist says, "I feel like such a hypocrite. Here I am, the one doing all the research, but when it comes to actually doing it it's like analysis paralysis. I'm wondering if all my interest is fake. I don't think so. Then why do I feel like such a fake?"

From a psychoanalytic point of view, one is readily drawn to the passive-aggressiveness, obsessional doubting, and potential transference implications of "analysis paralysis." But might there not be other ways of thinking about what is going on here? While "he" is busy gathering information and gaining expertise, there is also a powerful internal image of himself as the one who knows for sure that he must never think he knows for sure. And sure enough: his own father was "a benevolent dictator who always acted as if he knew for sure." So now, as an adult and a father himself, when this man describes "feeling like a fake," he means not only to communicate a negative affect of discomfort due to some insincerity or false pose. Rather, calling himself a "fake" is also a way of proudly capturing his "true" wish not be like his father.

The quandary of what to include in a home survival kit—like the terrorism that spawned it—brings us face-to-face with fate. People naturally struggle managing the ambiguity of not being able ever fully to disentangle fate from one's own efforts. We do ourselves a disservice believing we are the sole author of our own life. Nobody is. As the saying goes, "there but for the grace of God." Besides, even if I work hard and achieve a measurable outcome, I can always wonder how I had the good fortune to be at the right place at the right time. And if I pride myself upon my ability to seize the day, I can always wonder why I was blessed with the capacity to seize the day. What I accomplish through sheer force of will may not register as belonging to the person who is "me." The discomfort of feeling like a fake sometimes communicates this ambiguity.

A man hosts an affair at his home. He sees his wife and children and extended family. He is moved. People seem happy and content. He tells himself he is very fortunate, but he cannot quiet the gnawing sensation it is all a mirage and that he is a fake and a fraud. He knows he is spoiling his own experience, but refuses to believe he has earned his good fortune. It is "all luck." He is "nothing but a fraud." If he were, momentarily, to "sit back and simply take it in," he would be in danger. "It is safer," he says, "to keep myself on edge," and he knows berating himself as a fraud helps keep him on edge. But why? One way we might understand his experience is that, paradoxically, by relating to what he has as "all luck," he protects himself from fully experiencing what is, indeed, beyond his control. His world is full of gods that must never be ignored but cannot be propitiated. Feeling the fake spurs him to action; it is a way of reminding himself there is always more he can do. Unable to bear being at the mercy of fate—which psychoanalysis has reframed as "passive dependence"—he creates a world where all is contingent on him, but his purposeful action never fully brings relief. Sometimes, we even try to fake out fate.

Mirror image

It appears to be a feature of consciousness that while the image of oneself makes possible the knowledge of oneself, it also fosters a degree of self-alienation. Developmentally, the advent of representational thinking allows the self to be experienced as an object among objects. "I" shades into "I am," which shades into "I am Me." Symbolization, or the capacity to generate psychic distance from raw experience, has rewards but comes with a price tag.

It is no coincidence psychoanalytic theory has placed great stock in the importance of the mirror. A witheringly self-critical woman complains of "being invisible." She literally cannot look at herself in the mirror: she is terrified she might see nothing there. Pleadingly, she asks how I can possibly know for sure that it is really her in the room with me. Not surprisingly, she seldom looks me directly in the eye. For quite a while, I feel broaching the subject would constitute a breach. When I finally risk turning our mutual gaze on her avoidance of looking, she responds that she "cannot pretend" and she "avoids looking to make it easier to make up who you are." As long as she can keep me "not real," she does not have to contend with my being "too real."

The startling thing about this woman, however, is that from an external point of view, she has obtained a measure of personal and occupational success. It would be easy, under normal circumstances, to miss completely the extent of her internal distress. Here we have a high level of compliant adaptation. Through active mimicry—of the type for which psychoanalysis has invented the term introjects—she has grown up to be just like those around her. But, although she has attained a show of being real, her internal experience is one of going through motions imitating the kind of person she wishes she could be. At best, she feels like a horrible phony anxiously passing; at worst, like a person with nothing at the center.

Lacan (1977), theorizing about the moment a child first identifies with his own visual gestalt in the mirror, suggests it generates a foundational dissonance. While the child's inner experience is one of disarray, the image in the mirror is of himself collected into a unified whole. The mirror, constituting the basis of the ego, offers a false promise of wholeness. The discrepancy generates shock and with it the assumption of the armor of an alienating identity. Exiled from the reality of the lived self, the child identifies himself with the fictitious or imaginary self, of which the reflected image is the first outline.

While Lacan had what we might think of as an inside-out view of the mirror, Sullivan (1953) took an outside-in approach to mirroring. For Sullivan, the infant's self-system reflects the forbidding gestures and tender awards of significant others outside. Part of this process involves the child's "growing abilities to conceal and to deceive" both through what Sullivan called "verbalisms"—a type of rationalization—and through "as if performances" or "dramatizations." "A great deal of trial and error learning," Sullivan wrote:

> . . . can be observed in the child's playing at acting-like and sounding-like the seniors concerned . . . Probably the progression literally is that one tries first to act like and one tries then to act as if one were . . .
>
> (Sullivan, 1953, p. 209, original emphasis)

Whether we are partial to Lacan's inside-out or to Sullivan's outside-in formulation, they both point toward dissonance or alienation—a "me" that is also "not really me." For Lacan, the split is existential; for Sullivan, a means of warding off anxiety.

That we may not be what we appear to be leaves us susceptible to questioning whether we are misperceived or fooling others. Objective self-awareness—that inherently flawed capacity to see ourselves as others might—carries with it the dread that the "me out there" might be mistaken for "all of who I am." Or, worse yet, that the "me out there" will be exposed as totally unrelated to the "I in here." What makes the mirror alluring is precisely what makes it deadly: the illusion it provides that the image is the self. The discomfort of feeling like a fake is valuable as a way of reminding, at least ourselves, not to be fooled.

That most people do not like photographs of themselves is worth pondering in this context. Usually, the aversion is chalked up to vanity, as if people don't like the photos because they think or wish they looked better. But I suspect there is more to it. Perhaps, psychically, we return to the early somatic traces of becoming objectively self-aware, with the attendant shame and recognition of the limits of our self-awareness. As the Sicilian author Luigi Pirandello put it:

> You can only know yourself when you strike an attitude: a statue: not alive. When one is alive, one lives and does not see himself. To know one's self is to die . . . however much you may try, you can never know yourself as others see you.
>
> (Pirandello, 1933, p. 247)

Photographs freeze instants in time, which is why even the best of photographs often seem vaguely wrong. Life is never static; it emerges from fluid overlapping moments, motions, and moods. To be "shot," photographically speaking, means sacrificing a bit of aliveness as we are memorialized as frozen image.

The vague wrongness of static portraiture became a major preoccupation of Leonardo da Vinci. According to his biographer, Martin Kemp (2004), Leonardo was perpetually frustrated that his drawn objects could not move. Were he alive today, says Kemp (2005), Leonardo would probably prefer the medium of computer-generated images that capture dynamic fluctuation over time.

Echoing Kemp, art historian James Elkins (1996) notes that few oil portraits have the weirdness of snapshots because painters can blend moments. Indeed, a photograph, he says:

> Pushes a small part of the person forward and presents it as the whole . . . and that will tend to hurt the subject's sense of herself. "I am not that exaggerated thing," she might say, "or that gangly model, that stiff mannequin . . . that adolescent poser—and I am certainly not the punch-drunk person in that last photo."
>
> (Elkins, 1996, p. 28)

We are, Elkins implies, hypersensitive to partial versions of who we are. Each photo, he concludes, is "a little travesty, a peculiar caricature" (p. 28). Whether or not we accept Elkins's explanation, it cannot be denied that consciousness of self is all too easily transformed into the painful affect of self-consciousness. As Goethe famously put it: "Know thyself? If I knew myself, I'd run away!" (quoted in Conover, 2002).

Perhaps no one was more familiar with the excruciating form of self-consciousness than the painfully shy German Romantic writer Henreich von Kleist. In his beautifully rendered tale "On the Puppet Theater" (Kleist, 1811), a narrator describes "a young man over whose physical form a marvelous grace seemed to shine" (p. 214). One day, observing himself in a mirror, the graceful young man happens to raise his foot to a stool and thus strikes the exact pose of the famous Spinario statue of a youth removing a thorn from his foot. Smiling proudly at his discovery, he calls it to the attention of the narrator. But the narrator, knave that he is, challenges the boy's vanity. "I indeed had noticed it too," recalls the narrator:

> But . . . I laughed and said he was seeing phantoms. He blushed and raised his foot a second time to prove it to me, but the attempt, as might easily have been foreseen, did not succeed. Confused, he raised his foot a third and a fourth time: he must have raised it ten times more: in vain! He was unable to produce the same movement again. And the movement that he did make had so comical an effect that I could hardly suppress my laughter.
>
> (p. 215)

No real harm done, we might too easily conclude. So what if the young man feels a fool? Kleist captures the disfiguring power of shame: "From that very moment," writes Kleist:

> An inconceivable transformation began. He would stand whole days before the mirror; one charm after the other fell from him. An invisible and incomprehensible force, like an iron net . . . spread over the free play of his gestures, and when one year passed not a trace could be detected of that sweetness which had once so delighted the sight of all who surrounded him.
>
> (p. 215)

Von Kleist portrays self-consciousness as a form of shame emerging from an encounter with an Other (Bose, 1992). Excessive self-consciousness is like the cartoon figure Wile E. Coyote racing off the face of a sheer cliff in hot pursuit of the speedy desert bird. He plummets to the canyon floor below only when he is aware that he can fall. "On the Puppet Theater" suggests the havoc consciousness can cause in the natural grace of a human being and reminds me psychoanalysis has no real theory of poise.

Learning as trauma

From a pedagogic point of view, one root of the psychoanalytic situation can be traced back to the Socratic notion that all learning is recollection. In his classic didactic encounter with Meno's slave boy, Socrates (Plato, 1981) asserts that virtue cannot be taught. Insisting his detailed inquiry is nothing but an act of midwifery, Socrates concludes that one grows not by learning from the other, but by bringing out of the "I" that which it already contains. Freud, too, eschewing all suggestion and influence, believed a person would discover what was always there to be found.

A striking challenge to the idea of learning as recollection is offered by the Greek social theorist Cornelius Castoriadis. Castoriadis (1997) proposes that learning depends on the ability to become something other than what one already is. Eminently pliable—man, Dostoevsky famously remarked, is the animal that can adapt himself to anything—we accomplish self-alteration by negotiating meaning with the world. Offering a gloss on the Freudian adage "Where Id was, there ego shall become," Castoriadis notes that in learning the subject is shaped by, and yet resists, the forces of social circumstance. Learning to become is, in his view, an inherently "violent" activity where the social environment exacts a traumatic price from the psyche (p. 129).

To suggest learning is "inherently violent" is itself jarring. How easy it is to idealize learning as an all-good enrichment or actualization of self. But Castoriadis (1991) provokes us to remember that, to some extent, we have all been coerced into becoming social individuals. As Fay Weldon once remarked, "The greatest advantage of not having children must be that you can go on believing you are a nice person. Once you have children, you understand how wars start" (quoted in Parker, 1995, p. 5). Like Freud, Castoriadis believes we control ourselves, as best we can, for the purpose of forming relationships with others. Learning is accompanied by a certain violence to the self occasioned not by the content of what one learns, but by the very structure of the demand to learn.

Indeed, some analysts, such as Laplanche, see our earliest attachments as saturated with enigmatic projections born of the asymmetry between child and adult. Who we become—including our unconscious life and sexuality—emerges from our initial receptivity and permeability to unthinkable experiences beyond awareness. The question for Castoriadis and Laplanche, therefore, is not whether self-alteration wounds or not, but whether it wounds excessively.

Emmanuel Levinas (1985), the French-Jewish philosopher, also sees learning as inherently traumatic. Placing "otherness" at the heart of learning, he wonders how we might counteract the potential for violence that always exists in our relations. In his words, "The face is exposed, menaced, as if inviting us to an act of violence. At the same time, the face is what forbids us to kill" (p. 86). To be clear: what Levinas means by "the face" or "otherness" is not simply a sociological "other" who is marginalized or that we are all, despite differences, more human than otherwise. For Levinas "the Other is what I myself am not" (Levinas, 1987, p. 83). The Other is not "like me," nor am I "like the Other." Moreover, the psychical bridges we build—whether we put ourselves in the other's shoes through projection, or we put the other into ourselves through identification—merely underscore the chasm separating self from other.

Winnicott held a surprisingly similar view. As he wrote in a personal letter:

> The individual only communicates with a self-created world and the people in the environment only communicate with the individual in so far as they can create him or her. Nevertheless in health there is the illusion of contact and it is this which provides the high spots of human life . . .
>
> (Rodman, 1987, p. 43)

For Winnicott, what offers some relief from both isolation and the threat posed by our permeability to other people is the capacity to traffic in illusion. Engaged in a precarious venture, we discover ourselves by reaching out to others to find what we need. But we need to find it in our own way and in our own time. If contact with otherness is too abrupt, or violent, or off—that is, if we collide with the world instead of finding ourselves—distortions in development ensue, psychosis being the most extreme. Faking it, from this point of view, might signal efforts to traffic in the illusion that keeps us sane. We are, so to speak, testing the waters to determine whether it is safe enough to be ourselves as we risk permanent alteration through learning and participating in what the world has to offer. The problem is how to find the world without losing oneself.

Faking and pretending

A 5-year-old boy is waist-deep in a pool. He knows he cannot swim and hesitates as he approaches water too deep for him to stand. But he repeatedly proclaims to his anxious parents at poolside that he really can swim. Indeed, he swaggers about the pool as if he believes he can. Is this little boy faking it? Yes, and no. He "knows" that he cannot swim. But he also believes the way to swim is to believe he can swim. He must, in other words, fake himself out.

Put differently: what the boy's parents communicate as not true, he experiences as an assault on a reality in the making. Setting for himself an imaginative horizon, he moves toward an image of who he will become. Perhaps one way to grow is gradually to become who you pretend to be.

Returning to the safety of his parents, the little boy dons goggles designed like the face of a shark. He lies down in shallow water, a rubber fin protruding atop his head. Soon he spots his prey: a 7-year-old girl splashing about innocently nearby. Stealthily approaching from the side, he simulates shark sounds. The little girl, caught off guard, is momentarily startled. But once she makes sense of her predicament, she bops the little boy on his fin. "Just because you have a shark mask," she admonishes him, "doesn't mean you are really a shark!" Standing tall, the boy-shark realizes, perhaps for the first time, that the girl is bigger than he is. Slinking away to safer water, he displays his teeth, growls, and barks emphatically for her to hear, "I *am* a shark!"

Of course, from the point of view of the little girl, he is nothing but a little boy masquerading as a shark. But, from his point of view, he both is and is not a shark. He is engaged in a type of play for which we employ the word pretend. As Fonagy and Target (1996) have noted, in pretend mode, "ideas are felt to be representational but their correspondence to reality is not examined (p. 219). Make-believe and reality coexist. So long as the little boy simultaneously holds on to the double accounting of being and not being a shark, he is able to play. As long as the girl suspends her disbelief to play the prey to his predator, nobody will get hurt!

To pretend, we sometimes need partners willing to fake it. The Dutch historian of play, Johan Huizinga, offers the following illustration:

> A father found his four year old son sitting at the front of a row of chairs, playing "trains." When he kissed his son the boy said: "Don't kiss the engine Daddy, or the carriages won't think it's real."
>
> (Huizinga, 2016, p. 8)

Huizinga's example reminds me of a 2-year-old girl named Linda who proclaimed for all to hear that she was Cinderella pretending to be a butterfly pretending to be Linda. What was all this pretending about? Perhaps Linda was testing the contours and durability of her self, checking to see if it would be there for her to come back to! Pretending, in other words, is one way of reminding ourselves that we are real.

What makes the double accounting of pretend play so powerful is the magic of its reversibility. Huizinga's boy can be or not be a train engine. Linda can be or not be a butterfly. Feelings of insufficiency are overcome through superficial imitation requiring no realistic self-assessment (Reich, 1973). And that is precisely what allows the children to play unselfconsciously without feeling fake. How different is the gradual sustained transformation of actually becoming something! Becoming often begins as pretense or fear, which is why a new self is so easily mistaken for resistance or a problem. While becoming, one is liable to be self-conscious of deficiencies that cannot be magically undone. Only in retrospect, and often after much suffering, might one recognize having emerged richer for the experience. And to make matters worse, while becoming, every seeming success carries with it the dread that one will be expected to reproduce what is being currently demonstrated. It is potentially petrifying that others might develop a belief in one's ability. Given no guarantee that this currently highlighted unfamiliar "me" is replicable and enduring, one easily feels like a fake engaged in false advertising (Margaret Crastnopol, personal communication).

While pretend play might be seen as a variation of faking it, there are, nevertheless, also crucial differences between the two. When pretending, we are our own authors, directors, and actors, accessing with pleasure the multiplicity of our inner imaginary worlds. Faking it, in contrast, often entails an unpleasant self-consciousness. It involves playing a role culturally scripted that does not feel like one's own. Pretending allows us momentarily to enjoy leaving the world as we know it; faking it means being disturbed by a world thrust upon us.

Wild turkeys

Hundreds of years ago, Litchfield County was overrun by harems of wild turkeys. Native Americans refused to hunt them. Considering the birds dumb and cowardly, they feared that by ingesting them they would incorporate those unwanted traits. Such literal thinking captures how difficult it can be to disentangle the two attitudes taken toward an object, first detected by Freud—what we would like to have and what we would like to be.

An overweight, sloppily dressed woman, Lauren, is in analysis only briefly and bad feelings already permeate the room. My efforts to understand prove consistently futile as she laughs contemptuously at nearly every remark I utter. "I wish you would stop trying to take me so seriously," she says mockingly. "Don't you understand that it is all an act on my part and that when you pay attention to me it all starts to feel too real? I hate that. None of it is really real." As she laughs nervously, I feel a momentary desire to be rid of her entirely.

The conversation goes from bad to worse, until I comment that perhaps our only hope is to understand what all this unpleasantness is about. Quite spontaneously, Lauren started talking about her sister: "My parents hated my older sister, Norma. She was fat and messy and disorganized and my parents screamed at her all the time. But I remember as a kid Norma was everything to me. I loved Norma. I wanted her all to myself. My mother still says to me, 'Why do you want to be like Norma?' But, I didn't want to be like Norma. I wanted to be Norma." With these words, I suddenly saw Lauren in an entirely new light: the fat, messy, disorganized Lauren, sitting across from me and telling me she didn't know what was real and what was an act was an imitation of the sister she wanted "all to herself." Lauren wanted to be what she could not have.

Lauren's primitive imitation reveals itself as a disturbance in identification. No one has theorized this matter more astutely than Italian analyst Eugenio Gaddini (1969). For Gaddini, while imitation is an essential element of the structure of identification, it can also be employed as a way of defending against the anxiety provoked by identificatory processes. Lauren's attempt to bypass the anxiety of identification through the magical acquisition of a vicarious identity did not provide the basis for an unselfconscious sense that "this is who I am." Instead, it left her with an anxious feeling of unreality—an "ersatz me," a "fake me" for which there is no real counterpart.

Disturbance in identification reveals itself as disturbance in relationship. Masud Khan (1979a, 1979b) describes a type of relating he refers to as a "technique of intimacy." Khan's technique of intimacy employs pseudo-confessional disclosure to deceive and control the other into becoming an accomplice in a scripted scenario. A deep terror of emotional surrender precludes the development of a real relationship. The involvement is quick, intense, and with little hope for a future. The intimacy, in short, is fake.

I was reminded of Khan's idea when Mark, a person I had never met, left a message on my answering machine: "Hey, Dodi, hope you are doing OK. I would like you and me to have a chat when you're free. I'm a little hard to reach, but maybe we can get together soon. I got your name from Bill, who thought it would be cool for us to talk." Mark eventually came to see me. For years, he had been a facilitator with "Landmark Education," a spin-off of what was formerly called EST. His intimate life consisted, for the most part, of intense weekend encounters with strangers who disappear from his life as quickly as they appear.

Khan's "technique of intimacy" is a creative elaboration of what Fairbairn (1952) earlier described as the "de-emotionalization of the object relationship." To manage the stifling consequences of the absence of real emotional giving, it becomes necessary to resort to artificial methods of being with people. Two of the most successful strategies Fairbairn outlines are "playing of roles" without one's own personality being involved and "showing" or "displaying" when no actual emotional "giving" occurs. As I spent more time with Mark—I purposely do not say "got to know him better"—I was increasingly impressed with Fairbairn's idea, particularly the implication that the fakery is not only a problem, it is also a solution. Mark's mother related to him as her sole possession and lone creation. His father was totally ablated. Mark's only refuge was to retreat into a suffocating loneliness that can be relieved momentarily through fake intimacy. Faking it allowed Mark to breathe.

Skin shame, deep shame

It is a shame that once shame entered the purview of psychoanalytic theorizing, it was understood primarily as a curb to curiosities and a damper to desires to display. I agree with those who make the claim that shame is part of what constitutes our humanity. In Sartre's words, "Through shame we confer on the Other an indubitable presence" (Sartre, 1964, p. 251). For Sartre, shame derives not from this or that particular fault, but simply as a consequence of having "'fallen' into the world in the midst of things" needing "the mediation of the Other . . . to be what I am" (p. 264).

The Czech playwright-politician Vaclav Havel, accepting an honorary degree from the Hebrew University, said, "This is far from the first honorary degree I have received, but I accept it with the same sensation I always do: deep shame." Describing his accomplishments as attempts to "vindicate my permanently questionable right to exist," Havel concluded, "I thank you for the honor, and after what I've said here, I'm ashamed to repeat that I accept it with a sense of shame" (*The New York Review of Books*, September 27, 1990). Havel's statement might too readily be heard as a pose, a posture, or a piece of pathology. I prefer to see it as an expression of his humanity.

Havel suggests we consider creative endeavors as originating in a need to vindicate—Klein would say to repair—the burden our existence inevitably places on others. Shame, in another language, might also be the mother of invention. Stephen Spender once asked the poet Auden if he might ever hope to be any good as a poet. "Of course," Auden replied. "Because you are so infinitely capable of being humiliated. Art is born of humiliation" (*The New Yorker*, February 28, 1994, p. 76). I don't know whether, as Auden suggests, all art is born of humiliation, but I do accept that bearing and transforming humiliation is part of what makes us human.

A tribe in New Guinea draws an emotional distinction between "skin shame" and "deep shame" (Hultberg, 1988). Urinating in public or being caught unaware generates "skin shame." "Deep shame," in contrast, occurs when one insults the spirits of one's ancestors. The distinction alerts us to shame's paradoxical double function. Shame certainly acts as a powerful inducement to social compliance. But, on a deeper level, shame also guards an inner sanctum by silently crying out, "It is nobody's business!" Each of us safeguards privacy with a unique threshold that may be high or low, rigid or flexible. But crucial to our humanity is that we be allowed to retain—as Winnicott (1963) put it—the right not to communicate. That is why one of the elementary situations in the passage to adulthood, one of the prime conflicts adolescents have with parents, is some version of the claim to a private lock and key. "We enter adulthood," says Milan Kundera, "through the rebellion of shame" (*The New York Review of Books*, September 21, 1995). Shame, I am suggesting, not only serves the interest of conformity, but also preserves inwardness, personal distinctiveness, and integrity. Perhaps we need to differentiate between those things that produce shame because they are an affront to general opinion and those that are shameful because they betray a vital value, offending the lattice of our deepest convictions.

But here's the rub: convictions might be just another name for character. And if Freud was correct that character is constituted by identification—the ego likening itself to what it once loved—then character becomes, to borrow from Judith Butler, a copy of a copy for which there is no original. The potential for infinite regress leaves us—as many postmodernists have asserted—without a core or place within to locate authentic convictions. Contrast this idea with Bion's (1981) notion of a "Truth Instinct," Winnicott's (1952) "center of gravity," Lacan's (1977) "full speech," and Loewald's (1960) focus on a patient's "emerging core." What these four ideas share in common is a distinction between moments when the person is vitally and generatively animated, and those characterized by empty lifeless accommodation. For each of those authors, the integrity of the personality is more than an accumulation of introjects. In contrast to a theory of life as consisting of performative acts—imitations without originals—they believe analysts can challenge a person's complicated armor to communicate with the viscera it protects. Each asks how we might find our way with as little pretense and denial as we can muster, what poet Jane Miller refers to as "extend[ing] ourselves far enough back from . . . superficial multiplicities to register a sense of the whole" (Miller, 1992, p. 16).

The feelings of shame that accompany "faking it" might be a signal of a struggle to identify without losing identity, to be anchored to the tribal fabric that says "I am because you are," while simultaneously remaining tethered to a reliable inner gyroscope "I am because I am." "Faking it" means that shame—as both promoter of conformity and guardian of private integrity—is bearable enough to be representable in one's own mind. It is only when shame cannot be adequately contained in mind that it perniciously devolves into truncating humiliation or defiant shamelessness. Complexity is replaced by caricature: real imposters never know the shame of feeling like a fake.

Irony as antidote

In what is probably a profitable and creative reading of Freud, Lacan suggests a distinction between an ego ideal and an ideal ego. The ego ideal structures the ego within a symbolic system. The ideal ego is the repository of grandiose fantasies. The former spurs aspirations; the later promotes pretense.

Jonathan Lear (2003) argues that the capacity for irony facilitates psychic organization by bringing aspirations and pretenses into communication with each other. Words are given to aspirations and pretenses exposed for what they are. Appreciating the irony of the gap between how one is and how one would like to be is part of the project of becoming more human. Lear's emphasis on the gap between aspiration and pretense—the place where "faking it" may reside—is probably also one of the roots of spiritual impulse: figuring out how to live while knowing one falls short.

It is perhaps out of appreciation of irony that Jane Miller (1992, p. 7) refers to identity as a "posture of status." Adaptation requires compromise not only with the environment, but also with potential selves. There is no performance without inhibition elsewhere. Every identity contains the grief of foreclosure. Is it not a common characteristic of adolescents on the brink of consolidating identity that they bristle at false solutions, wish fervently to live a number of lives besides their own, conflate compromise with settling? Engaged in trying to find a self to be true to, adolescents cannot abide the way adults go through life faking it.

Faking it, in other words, can signal a healthy striving for compromise—a sign that a person seeks a livable solution that takes into account the intractability of limits, a sturdy enough bridge between ego ideals and ideal egos, personas and possible selves. The awkward discomfort of feeling like a fake communicates the strain of wanting to join in before we have found a way to fit in.

The psychoanalytic situation, as originally envisioned by Freud, was organized around the ironic premise that speaking as truthfully as possible would bring self-deception into relief. But it is also the case that becoming conscious of one's self-deception can arouse the paralyzing affect of self-consciousness. For this reason, it is not enough to speak of psychoanalytic treatment only as making the unconscious conscious. Better perhaps to think of establishing a relationship through which one expands ironic self-awareness and diminishes anxious self-preoccupation.

Not only might the patient benefit from a healthy dose of playful irony. The analyst, too, may need to accept the irony of his earnest efforts to alter someone's psyche through conversation. He aspires to help, but knows how little he has to offer. The analyst plays at being and not being the mask he wears. One moment, he sees himself in his patient's eyes and recognizes how essentially alike they are. Another, he sees himself through his patient's eyes—he sees the patient seeing him. The analyst improvises as he acts the parts in the unpredictable play of transference and the unguarded exposure of who he "really" is. The analyst is and is not only himself. He is and is not only an analyst. How ironic: despite whatever experience, knowledge, and care the analyst musters, his expertise is also in faking it.

References

Bion, W.R. (1981). "Notes on Desire for Knowledge." *The International Journal of Psychoanalysis*, 63: 73–80.

Bose, J. (1992). "Stage Fright in Psychotherapy." *Contemporary Psychoanalysis*, 28(3): 503–511.

Castoriadis, C. (1991). "Power, Politics, Autonomy." In *Philosophy, Politics, Autonomy: Essays in Political Philosophy*. Ed. and trans. D.A. Curtis. Oxford: Oxford University Press, pp. 143–174.

Castoriadis, C. (1997). "Psychoanalysis and Politics." In *World in Fragments: Writings on Politics, Society, Psychoanalysis, and the Imagination*. Ed. and trans. D.A. Curtis. Stanford, CA: Stanford University Press, pp. 125–136.

Conover, M. (2002). *The Quotehouse: Johann Wolfgang von Goethe*. http://homemetcarrier.com/conover/Authors/Goethe.html.

Elkins, J. (1996). *The Object Stares Back: On the Nature of Seeing*. San Diego, CA: Harcourt Brace & Co.

Emerson, R.W. (1983). *Emerson: Essays and Lectures*. New York: Library of America.

Fairbairn, W.R.D. (1952). "Schizoid Factors in the Personality." In *Psychoanalytic Studies on the Personality*. London: Tavistock.

Fonagy, P. and Target, M. (1996). "Playing with Reality: I. Theory of Mind and the Normal Development of Psychic Reality." *The International Journal of Psychoanalysis*, 77: 217–233.

Gaddini, E. (1969). "On Imitation." In E. Gaddini (1992). *A Psychoanalytic Theory of Infantile Experience: Conceptual and Clinical Reflections*. Ed. A. Limentani. London: Tavistock/Routledge.

Hultberg, P. (1988). "Shame: A Hidden Emotion." *Journal of Analytical Psychology*, 33(2): 109–126.

Huizinga, J. (2016). *Homo Ludens: A Study of the Play-Element in Culture*. Kettering, OH: Angelico Press.

Kemp, M. (2004). *Leonardo*. London: Oxford University Press.

Kemp, M. (2005). *Interview with Dick Gordon*. www.theconnection.org/shows/2005/01/20050114_b_main.asp. Aired January 14, 2005.

Khan, M.R. (1979a). "The Role of Polymorph-Perverse Body Experiences and Object-Relations in Ego-Integration." In *Alienation in Perversions*. Madison, CT: IUP.

Khan, M.R. (1979b). "Intimacy, Complicity, and Mutuality in Perversions." In. *Alienation in Perversions*. Madison, CT: IUP.

Kierkegaard, S. (1948). *Purity of Heart*. New York: Harper & Row.

Kleist, H. (1811). "On the Puppet Theater." In *An Abyss Deep Enough: The Letters of Heinrich von Kleist with a Selection of Essays and Anecdotes*. Ed. and trans. P. Miller, 1982. New York: Dutton.

Lacan, J. (1977). *Ecrits: A Selection*. Trans. A. Sheridon. New York: Norton.

Lear, J. (2003). *Therapeutic Action: An Earnest Please for Irony*. New York: Other Press.

Levinas, E. (1985). *Ethics and Infinity*. Trans. R.A. Cohen. Pittsburgh, PA: Duquesne University Press.

Levinas, E. (1987). *Time and the Other and Additional Essays*. Trans. R.A. Cohen. Pittsburgh, PA: Duquesne University Press.

Loewald, H. (1960). "On the Therapeutic Action of Psychoanalysis." *The International Journal of Psychoanalysis*, 41: 16–33.

Miller, J. (1992). *Working Time: Essays on Poetry, Culture, and Travel*. Ann Arbor, MI: University of Michigan Press.

Orwell, G. (1936). "Shooting an Elephant." In *The Orwell Reader: Fiction, Essays, and Reportage*. New York: Harcourt, Brace, & Co., 1984, pp. 3–8.

Parker, R. (1995). *Mother Love, Mother Hate*. New York: Basic Books.

Pirandello, L. (1933). *One, None, and a Hundred Thousand*. Trans. S. Putnam. New York: Dutton.

Plato (1981). *Meno*. Trans. G.M.A. Grube. Indianapolis, IN: Hackett.

Reich, A. (1973). *Psychoanalytic Contributions*. New York: IUP.

Renik, O. (1998). "Getting Real in Analysis." *The Psychoanalytic Quarterly*, 67: 566–593.

Rodman, F.R. (1987). *The Spontaneous Gesture: Selected Letters of D.W. Winnicott*. Cambridge, MA: Harvard University Press.

Sartre, J.-P. (1964). *Being and Nothingness*. Trans. H.E. Barnes. New York: Citadel Press.

Shattuck, R. (2000). *Proust's Way: A Field Guide to "In Search of Lost Time."* New York: W.W. Norton.

Stephenson, F. (2004). *Self Esteem: What Is It?* Research in Review, Florida State University. www.research.fsu.edu/researchr/summer2004.

Sullivan, H.S. (1953). *The Interpersonal Theory of Psychiatry*. New York: W.W. Norton.

Winnicott, D.W. (1952). "Anxiety Associated with Insecurity." In *Collected Papers: Through Pediatrics to Psychoanalysis*. New York: Basic Books, 1958, pp. 97–100.

Winnicott, D.W. (1963). "Communicating and Not Communicating Leading to a Study of Certain Opposites." In *The Maturational Processes and the Facilitating Environment*. London: Hogarth Press.

Chapter 4

As generations speak

"Do you know what Facebook is?" Megyn asks the first time we meet. With gaze sheepishly averted and shoulders angling toward her ears, Megyn seems to wordlessly say, "I don't mean to insult you, but someone your age probably cannot understand what I'm talking about." I notice my surprise and tinge of hurt feeling. "Yes I do," I say, mustering a measured matter-of-fact tone. But I am also aware of a formless inner upset quickly transformed into an unmistakable impulse to avenge my wounded vanity by shouting back, "How old do you think I am*?* How out of touch?"

"Do you know what cyberstalking is?" the next question rolls off Megyn's lips. A visceral change swiftly comes over me: forget the insult of being "too old to possibly understand", this 21-year-old may be in trouble! "Yes, I do," I respond. "Well," she continues, "I've decided to remove my profile from Facebook because I've been cyberstalking myself."

"Cyberstalking yourself?" the puzzlement clearly evident in my voice. Perhaps her earlier averted gaze was warranted after all. I don't have a clue what she is talking about.

"Yeah," she replies, "I realized I was checking my home page repeatedly just to figure out how other people see me. That's crazy. I mean, why should I need to be thinking so much about how other people see me? Why can't I just be who I am? Don't you think it is a rather strange kind of mirror?"

The word "mirror" catches my attention. Yet, I resist the obvious chain of explanatory associations. Attempting to understand a person in light of predetermined ideas runs the risk of condemning genuine suffering to eternal silence. Her mirror, the strange one about which she is speaking, may not necessarily be only a derivative of mother's face or, as Lacan suggests, a source of shock that comes from encountering one's internal disarray in the form of an imaginary unified whole. Facebook is a place where she is seen by her peers—a place where the word "friend" is often a synonym for "coincidence"—and she has already communicated an awareness she and I are from different generations. Perhaps that mattered more than I cared to believe. Does the gaze of peers carry the same portent as the gaze of parents? Early identifications are not necessarily primary identifications.

Later that week, 85-year-old Marie, with sons about my age, shuffles into my office with a walker. Having had her hip replaced two months prior, she is deeply frustrated that her usually active life is suddenly so circumscribed. Unaccustomed to disability, Marie bemoans "feeling for the first time" in her life "rather old." Her thoughts turn back in time to teenage years when she fled with her parents from Nazi-occupied France. A flood of memories surface: particular pieces of art left on the walls of her parents' home; walking arm-in-arm with a younger sister as they approach the border with Spain. However, as Marie conjures up these memories, I notice a subtle shift in her manner of speaking. What had begun as poignant recollection devolves into the retelling of an oft-recounted tale. Whereas the earlier memories felt "fresh," she is now on autopilot, treading a well-worn path. I interrupt and point out the change: "A moment earlier," I say, "you seemed to be remembering something very much alive in you. But, just now, it felt more like you are repeating a very familiar story."

"Yes," she replies, "I know what you mean."

"Any idea what happened?"

"All I know is earlier I think I was talking to myself, but then, I suddenly became aware of speaking to you."

"And when you became aware of speaking to me?"

"Well, I guess I realized there is no way you could ever really understand."

"You mean I couldn't imagine myself in that place?"

"Oh no," she replies, "I know you can imagine yourself in that place. There is just no way you could imagine yourself at that TIME."

Both these women—one young enough to be my daughter and one old enough to be my mother—each communicates an awareness of generational differences forming a salient backdrop to our conversation. What was sayable, what was unsayable, and what did not need to be said, were determined in part by the present perception of generational identities forged in time.

Generations, like cultures, create shared rules of engagement. These include distinctive ways of playing with boundaries: what is public and what private, how much "space"—physical or psychological—one person need give to the next, when interest expressed is sympathy and when intrusiveness, what is considered a beautiful body or cause for disgust, which acts are trumpeted as bold and which condemned as reckless, what is dismissed as aggressive and what valued as forthright, what is fair game to be mocked and what is to be revered. To remain outside such common agreements—to be a member of a different generation—is to partake of a different felt reality.

From a psychoanalytic point of view, what has most often been considered meaningful about generational differences is how they reiterate Oedipal struggle. The "portentous domestic encounter" (Gay, 1985, p. 95) became an explanatory lens through which to understand suffering and civilized life. A phylogenetically inscribed parricidal motive—the universal feature of mental life Freud (1905, p. 226n) once referred to as the "shibboleth" of psychoanalysis—is recapitulated as personal destiny and generational conflict. The psychoanalytic account of development suggests that to fit in we must first accept where we don't. Growth demands an acceptance of difference—sexual and generational.

Freud had compelling reasons for privileging the Oedipal moment. One may, of course, profitably question its developmental timing, whether it is more variable than simple affection toward a cross-sex parent and rivalry toward the opposite one, what it means to "win" and "lose" the struggle, and if later difficulties in living are best accounted for by earlier experiences of triangulation. But, it is hard to deny that somewhere between the ages of 3 and 6, children undergo a transformative experience toward a more richly textured social life that includes intense and oscillating feelings of love, hate, exclusion, possessiveness, potency, humiliation, and seductiveness (Greenberg, 1991).

The child wakes up to the realization he is one mind among many and, to complicate matters, he, himself, is of more than one mind! The Oedipal moment, in other words, announces the arrival of awareness of "the oddity of possessing a mind of one's own" (Bollas, 1992), the presence of perspective, and the discovery of the multiplicity of points of view.

Participation in increasingly larger groups of people radically challenges the original family structure. A child goes out and discovers, usually to his bafflement, that each peer has a different family with its own laws, habits, justice, and perception of reality. Families of origin are discovered to be too weak to extend their power away from home. A multiplicity of perspectives and affiliations dissolves the primacy of dyadic and triadic structures even as relief from complexity is simultaneously sought by returning to these very structures.

Erik Erikson (1980) was the first to elevate generational relations into a serviceable psychoanalytic construct. One of his central insights—that "whatever individuation has been experienced by the individual must . . . join generationally in the mutual activation offered by the adult world" (p. 215)—draws our attention to the psychological implications of generational dialogue.

Embedded in generational cycles, we all navigate one way or another among "well-known forebears," "familiar peers," and the "unknown children" waiting in the wings.[1] Generational dialogue refers to both developmental shifts in relatedness between generations as well as how the otherness of predecessors and successors are negotiated internally.[2]

The Israeli author David Grossman (2014) poignantly portrays the desperate psychic press for generational dialogue in his novella *Falling Out of Time*, written after his own son was killed in battle. A ghostlike "walking man" leads villagers, pied-piper style, on a long and harrowing journey in search of their deceased children. The dead are not erased, Grossman suggests, but are elsewhere. Hauntingly calling out to his own lost child, the "walking man" intones: "It is you/who decides/how to appear in me/and when" (p. 84).

Generational dialogue is not about how parents and children (of any age) consciously speak to one another. Nor is it solely about how an isolated individual manages anxieties. Rather, generational dialogue is the process by which *shifts in generational relations* are mutually negotiated, both consciously and unconsciously. Since each new generation's place needs to be claimed and not simply conferred, clashes are inevitable. Earlier generations do not seamlessly relinquish their position, nor do successive generations benefit psychically by inheriting without struggle. Generational dialogue includes the hopes and dreads of development and the perception of how other generations weather the change themselves.

While not all development involves such dialogue, transitions throughout the life span often heighten the unconscious salience of generational dialogue. As a new place within the life cycle is inhabited, the individual contends with a novel version of the self and the influence other generations, both older and younger, exert. These pressures readily raise doubts about the self and require a "sorting out" process: what to dispose of, what to keep, what to give in love, and what to give in hate, who to be like, and who to be different from. Repeatedly, the individual is challenged to remain separate but interrelated without collapsing into merger or isolation.

Generational dialogue can also easily "shut down." Anxieties associated with change may generate emotional investment in temporarily foreclosing active *mutual* dialogue. Nonrecognition between generations may even be engineered so as to shore up a precarious sense of autonomy—a process quite common in adolescence. Nevertheless, as Winnicott (1963) once noted about the game of hide-and-seek, while it may be a joy to be hidden, it is also disaster not to be found.

Generational identity

As a descriptive concept, "identity"—personal or generational—has never held much cache from a psychoanalytic point of view. The notion of identity, Kohut (1971) wrote:

> Is not indigenous to psychoanalytic psychology; it belongs to a different theoretical framework which is more in harmony with the observation of social behavior and the description of the (pre)conscious experience of oneself in the interaction with others than with the observations of depth psychology.
>
> (p. xiv)

There is merit to this position. "Identity" should not be conflated with "self-experience"—a more inclusive idea grounded in the imaginative elaboration of bodily rhythms and processes in interaction with others.

Nevertheless, if we accept as workable premises that the psyche does not start off as a unitary whole (Winnicott, 1945), there is no such thing as a single integrated self, and a multiplicity of self-other configurations only gradually come to be experienced with a degree of cohesiveness (Mitchell, 1993; Davies, 1996; Stern, 1997; Bromberg, 1998), then it makes sense that the various building blocks of identity—the ways large and small I am both me and we—are crucial in forging an inwardly believable and morally acceptable functional linking of potentially odd combinations and irreconcilable realities. Identities enact the age-old conflict between wandering and wanting a home, not unlike Moby Dick's narrator, Ishmael (Melville, 2002), who first declares, "I try all things;

I achieve what I can" (p. 378), but then later asks, "Where lies the final harbor, whence we unmoor no more?" (p. 535).

Each of us carries a generational identity. But what, exactly, constitutes a generation? In common parlance, a generation refers to the 25-year-or-so interval between parents and children. But many theorists of current popular culture identify new forms of generational consciousness emerging about every 10 years. If this is so, then in contemporary culture no generation parents the one that immediately follows. There is always some intermediate cluster that carries a different generational stamp.

Only in their teens or early twenties do people become aware of their distinct generational consciousness. As childhood, adolescence, and young adulthood are viewed as a continuous whole, we begin to objectify our place in time (Bollas, 1992).

Here is one way Oedipal formulations potentially fall short: a recognition of generational difference is quite different than carrying a stable consciousness of a distinctive generational identity—at least in the double sense of the term "identity." While navigating Oedipal destiny, I may come to accept a persistent sameness *within myself*—I am a boy and not a girl—but that does not necessarily mean I also recognize a persistent sharing of collective memory *with others of similar age*—that I belong to a generational cohort. Being *spatially* smaller than my parents and excluded from their doings is quite different than *temporally* sharing memories *over time* with a group of people forging a generational consciousness.

Gradually, we discover memory is not simply a recollection of the past, but evidence the future, too, will have a past. Appreciating the *future-oriented* aspect of memory—seeing the experiences one lives through as part of a story later to be told—includes recognizing being *situated in time between generations*. It is no coincidence, therefore, generational consciousness comes to full fruition not only in relation to *previous* generations, but once a *future* cohort is already within sight. Each generation reaches a potentially disorienting point *as the anxiety of influence meets the anxiety of succession*.

Generational identity is fashioned out of a culture of chosen objects. As Salman Rushdie (1991) notes, the "imaginary homelands" we call "identity" are "a shaky edifice we build out of scraps, dogmas, childhood injuries, newspaper articles, chance remarks, old films, small victories, people hated, people loved" (p. 12). Bollas (1992) coins the term "generational objects" to signify how certain of these objects store memories collectively shared. By unconsciously selecting particular objects from the available cultural tool kit—heroes, events, causes, mannerisms, styles—each generation, in the words of Wallace Stevens, "turns to its own figurations and declares, 'This image, this love, I compose myself/Of these'" (Stevens, 1990, p. 245).

But, whereas marginal inspirations are easily forgotten, the fixed shape given to unconsciously chosen generational objects keeps them from vanishing from recollection. Artistic inventions in particular—music, film, fashion—are often the nursery in which larva-like imaginings mature to emerge as cultural memory. A curious mix of the fashioned, the accidental, and the imposed, generational objects carry with them the mark of events and happenings—wars, economic changes, social tensions—well beyond conscious control.

No generation legitimately claims absolute originality for what it creates (Ogden, 2006). Along with the wish to be free of forbears, we all must contend with an awareness of indebtedness to them. Since creativity has an unpredictable relationship to memory, the reinventions and innovations of a younger generation might be hostile to its predecessors or serve as homage to them. Gratitude may be expressed by thriving or envy by spoiling. Indeed, people often have feelings about the past of their progenitors, which is why it is not uncommon to look back at one's parents' youth with a mixture of pity and envy. Every generation also has its own way of amplifying, validating, and privileging certain orientations at the expense of others, which is why it is common for some individuals to feel out of sync with their own generation.

Generations collide because people are more than the sum of the loves they have lost. They need also to differentiate themselves from the loves they have. "To put it simply," writes Joseph Brodsky (1986), "one is changed by what one loves, sometimes to the point of losing one's identity" (p. 365). The anxiety of influence, Brodsky implies, exposes our vulnerability to losing ourselves out of love.To not lose ourselves, there must be space to both become like our lost loves and to collide with and distinguish ourselves from them. Even in loving relations, convenient hatreds can be exploited to foster differentiation (Gabbard, 1993).

At various points in the life cycle, searching for a way to love without losing ourselves rekindles the need for generational dialogue. People need time and space to create new versions of themselves without precipitously abandoning the "me" that feels most familiar. These developmental junctures require navigating both vertically and horizontally: holding in mind both differences and similarities between generations, tolerating collisions between them, finding a place among peers, and imaginatively elaborating who one is gradually becoming.

When the press of this challenge stalls development, the individual risks the doldrums. The word "doldrums" refers to a region near the equator where various trade winds neutralize each other such that sailing vessels remain temporarily motionless. In human development, the conflicting winds of self-sameness, change, and generational loyalties can create a type of doldrums—a crisis that precludes movement. Often confused with depression, the doldrums carry the pain of wanting to inhabit a newly emerging position in the life cycle without finding a workable way to do so. A confused paralysis accompanies the desperate desire to remain true to oneself while seeking a secure enough new version of oneself to be true to. Generational dialogue—the sorting out of similarities, differences, antipathies, and loyalties between generations—often helps lift the doldrums so development can proceed.

In another language: vitality involves generational dialogue around the active adjustment to emerging desires and feelings throughout the life cycle. It includes discovering one's personal way of mastering experience is, at the same time, a successful variant of a group's way of mastering experience and that one is recognized within a generational dialogue. "A child who has just found himself able to walk," writes Erikson (1968):

> Seems not only driven to repeat and perfect the act of walking by the promise of libidinal pleasure in the sense of Freud's locomotor erotism . . .; he also becomes aware of the new status and stature of "one who can walk," with whatever connotation this happens to have in the coordinates of his culture's life plan—be it "one who will swiftly run after fleeing prey," "one who will go far," "one who will be upright," or "one who might go too far."
>
> (p. 49)

Creative accommodation to novelty—retaining a sense of who I am with you even as I change—is the psychic equivalent of the passage from sucking to chewing, from baby talk to words to full-fledged speech. It accompanies the appearance of pubic hair, the first erection, menstruation, leaving home, having children, losing our parents, growing old.

Psychical growth requires some willingness, no matter how painful, to find a place within for the "not-me"—bodily changes as well as shifts in relationship to other generations—which, by virtue of being beyond control, easily makes me momentarily unrecognizable to myself. In this active accommodation to novelty, the individual does not simply identify with, or "take in" static object images, but encounters the process of relationship with those images, including the enigmatic way the past has been transmitted.

The past is transmitted enigmatically because long before we learn to speak, we are spoken about, each of us bearing what Lacan (1980, p. 135) refers to as a lineal "curse." Every life is constituted through the obscured inheritance of the generations preceding it. Our births have been longed for or dreaded. We are given names stuffed with hope, fear, and expectations. Each of us is entangled in a history belonging to someone else. We have a relationship with the lives our parents lived before we ever came upon the scene. Haydee Faimberg (2005) refers to this as the "telescoping of generations." We are inscribed, Faimberg argues, with "alienated identifications"—alienated because they are rooted in conflicts of generations not our own. Or, as Lacan suggests, all identities are to some extent mistaken. It is precisely because of how readily prone we are to feel like strangers to ourselves—particularly during developmental transitions—that generational dialogue is so vital. The breakdown or absence of generational dialogue can hamper a person's capacity to accommodate to his own emerging self leaving him mystified, muddled, or alienated from a part of himself.

Unconscious destruction is inevitably a part of generational dialogue. Indeed, it is precisely when one generation's aesthetic and authority are being vitiated that we become aware of the emergence of a new generation. Loewald (1979, p. 396) refers to this as "passionate appropriation." "If we do not shrink from blunt language," writes Loewald, "in our role as children of our parents . . . we do kill something vital in them—not all in one blow and not in all respects, but contributing to their dying" (p. 395). But destructiveness in and of itself, Loewald emphasizes, is not the intent. Nor does the impulse arise as a fearful response to the threat of castration. Rather, a new generation's destructiveness toward predecessors—Ogden (2006) calls it "loving murder" (p. 655)—is a natural byproduct, or collateral damage, accompanying the "urge for emancipation" (Loewald, 1979) we call growth.

One clear implication of Loewald's formulation is that the Oedipal complex is not to be understood simply as an intrapsychic event occurring in early childhood, but rather a set of living generational object relations experienced throughout a lifetime. True, a younger generation must learn to tolerate feelings of rivalry, exclusion, and difference. But older generations must choose whether to give way generatively or meet the new age with hostility and destructiveness of their own. A younger generation might be inhibited from claiming authority for itself just as an older generation might resent being reminded of moving closer to death or resist sadly though proudly taking its place as cherished ancestors. As older generations are altered by younger ones, they may or may not find joy in their offspring being just like them or, to the contrary, quite unlike them. The dialogue between generations is as indispensable for the renewal of the older generation's life as it is for the next generation. Difficulties arise not from parricidal fantasies per se or from bitterness at having to pass the torch, but when the quality of the living tie between generations does not permit safe collisions and periodic re-envisioning over time.

We are all more mediated than otherwise

From a psychoanalytic point of view, the inscription of events upon memory never takes the form of a simple engram. A variety of internal meditational processes are involved in the registration of external reality. Freud suggested memory traces are constituted by particular "facilitations" and that memory traces are dispersed among multiple mnemic systems.

Another angle of vision from which to think about the registration of reality is that the families and cultures within which we live constitute mediational pathways. We are born into a class or caste, in war or peacetime, during a period of prosperity or decay, of rapid change or social stagnation. Indeed, perhaps the most important matters of our lives actually happen in our absence as none of us choose where, when, or to whom to be born. As Seneca, the first-century Stoic, observed, there are two choices in life: one can be led by fate, or dragged by fate. We have no choice but to make a place for the aspect of our lives that preceded us.

Cultural mediational pathways—carriers of our often unrecognized fate—might even be usefully thought of as extensions of the human nervous system. Margaret Mead (1970) presciently observed some 40 years ago how human relationships are radically altered by technological change.

Early forms of cultural organization were characterized by the profound continuity symbolized by a grandfather holding a grandchild in his arms and knowing the future of the newborn would be identical to his own past. Predecessors, in other words, imagined the future through recall. In the newly emerging cultural form, however, there is a dramatic shift from significant continuities to significant discontinuities. "As long as any adult," writes Mead, "thinks that he, like the parents and teachers of old can . . . invoke his own youth to understand the youth before him, then he is lost" (pp. 80–81). Mead was documenting a change in the structure of generational dialogue. Rather than a culture in which children learn from elders, Mead envisioned a culture in which adults must learn from their children. Memory could no longer serve as a reliable guide.

Of course, any effort to describe generational differences contains an element of folly; diversity within a generation is always and significantly larger than perceived gaps between generations. Still, the incubating environment of any generation clearly matters. For example, the dizzying pace of social change means the four current generational clusters in America—Depression era, Baby Boomers, Generation Xers, and Millennials—have somewhat different relationships to the artifacts of cultural mediation. It has been well documented that whereas Baby Boomers as a group tend to use the Net primarily to transact, Millennials use it far more frequently to interact. For Depression era individuals, with little reflective sense of creating their own reality, the opposite of real is phony. Baby Boomers, too, are often preoccupied with what is artificial and what is authentic. Many Millennials, in contrast, more readily than their predecessors, assume the objects, places, and mannerisms constituting culture are merely representational. They are all created and designed and could just as well have been otherwise; identity, custom, and lifestyle are something to have, not something you are. In their mediated world, the opposite of real isn't phony, it's optional.

From a psychoanalytic point of view, however, what is of interest is not these gross generalizations about generational differences, but rather how mediational artifacts impact what is lived and what is dissociated, and whether unconscious life is somehow altered by the great electronic din. What we call the self—an inclusive symbolization of one's own being—is enormously sensitive to the flow of history, including transformations in the means of mediation. The question is: what bearing might these transformations have on the structure of psychic life and quality of generational dialogue?

The thrust of mediating representations today is to flatter by creating the illusion everything is addressed to me personally and the world an open book allowing me to fashion myself in accordance with my heart's desire. "Reality" is packaged so as to be worthy of a claim on my attention. Interchangeable spectacles, wildly out of scale with one another, clamor in recursive loops of nervous effervescence making it difficult to get an emotional read on their significance. Everything is simultaneously vital and disposable. Evolving mediational pathways challenge people to accommodate their continuous partial attention to the accelerated babel of signals.

These zeitgeist frequencies are inevitably delivered into the analytic space, particularly by the generation most recently crossing over from the riotous country of adolescence. Here's an example: a precocious, seemingly self-assured, and savvy 22-year-old asks if I would like to hear a dream he does not remember. Baffled, I ask how we might do that. "I recorded it last night on my cell phone," he replies, looking at me a bit askance as if this should have been self-evident. I then have my first ever experience of being with a person listening to their own groggy voice as they wake from a dream they no longer recall. While listening to his dream on the cell phone, a ring alerts him to an incoming call. And he answers. Soon, he is caught up in a lively conversation with a friend about plans to meet later in the day. When he finishes, he starts talking about a different matter. I interrupt him and say, "I notice we lost track of your dream." "Oh," he replies, "are you still interested in that!" And then, adding the inevitable shoulder shrug, "Whatever!"

Whatever. No word or gesture could possibly better capture and distill this young man's generational experience of negotiating the field of options incessantly competing for his attention. On the one hand, a virtual feast of possibilities, an experience of culture as offering whatever he wants, a flattered self addressed by the media as if whatever is being offered is really about him. And yet, this same environment creates an aura of thinness, a hollow shallowness, to things. Haunting the moment of "I can experience whatever I want" is the moment of shrug that declares, "But what difference does it really make?"

As a psychoanalyst, I privilege steady and undissipated attentiveness situated in the delicate area between "looking for" and "waiting for." The chaotic indiscriminateness of the young man's shifting focus makes him appear to belong less to himself than to every object that happens to catch his notice. I want to be a scuba diver in the sea of his words and he wants to zip along the surface like a guy on a Jet Ski. I want to find what feels real and he sees everything as an interesting simulation. His rapid mobility among options precludes poignancy. What accelerates, among other things, is the pace of moving from being curious to being jaded, from caring to numbness.

In a later session, the young man tells me how disturbed he feels with slowness, and uncomfortable with silence. For all the immediacy of the images he chases, they too often become electronic phantoms. "I get bored if it's not all going at once, if there are gaps," he says. "I skip from lily pad to lily pad; if I stop for a moment, I'll sink. I can't afford to rely on anyone; the risk is all mine. Everybody in my generation has to tread lightly but quickly."

Tread lightly but quickly. Psychoanalysis suggests we all employ an array of manic defenses to blunt the grief of helplessness. Put differently: we use reality to gain reassurance against death inside. I think we see this in the hustle and bustle of commercial activities, the pleasures of entertainment, the liveliness of our creative endeavors. But, perhaps with the discordant rhythm of contemporary life, the external objects we rely on to enliven are themselves prematurely deadened. In that case, the needed reassurance through external reality becomes increasingly elusive. The torrent of clutter makes it harder to locate aliveness within or without.

While there are, no doubt, transferential implications to this young man's pronouncement he "can't rely on anyone," another way to hear his statement about risk and "his generation" is that he is also alerting me to his awareness of a generational experience different from my own. He emerged into generational consciousness well after the Washington Consensus began dismantling public support networks, Margaret Thatcher triumphantly declared, "There is no such thing as society," and Bill Gates exuberantly promoted the social fantasy of "friction-free capitalism." Welfare liberalism, at its best, was succeeding in a broader recruitment of elites but was failing to promote a systematic rise in the general level of competence. While unheard of fast fortunes were being made by an ever slimmer and younger segment of the population, for the broader masses it was becoming increasingly difficult to reach even the first rung up the ladder of achievement. Is it any wonder this young man's generation needs to devise its own codes as to what to expect of themselves and how much to trust others? Despite whatever personal support they may receive from their particular set of parents—divorced, blended, or otherwise—they often feel "out there all by themselves." Many of them wonder which will come first—nuclear or environmental annihilation. Few of them believe social security will be there for them when they get older. For his generation, the nation-state has become too small for the big problems of life and too big for the small problems.

Nevertheless, understanding historical context does not alter my critical state of mind: I want to change him. I want him to cultivate the faculty of voluntarily reigning in his wandering attention, to transition from youthful distraction to mature contemplation, to put an end to the hurry, bustle, and agitation that are the symptoms of a frivolous mind.

I find myself, at this moment, sympathetic to Chasseguet-Smirgel's (1984) contention that postmodern culture, with its eradication of differences—between generations, sexes, and aesthetic values—is essentially perverse. I am drawn to Kristeva's (1997) view that the forms of deep narration necessary for symbolizing experience are absent in media-driven culture, leaving people psychically impoverished. The young man appears to me to be suffering from the malady Wordsworth (1800) called the "degrading thirst after outrageous stimulation."

The moment I am describing—of shrugged shoulder, "whatever," and my irritation—is a moment of collision unable to be processed within a generational dialogue. The disruption is evident both in his manner and in how readily I reduce him to "nothing but" a vacuous, distracted, shallow simulation of a person. He is not a full human being; he is only a prototype of his peers. I am not a full human being; I am just one more demand on his rapidly shifting attention. We are failing to make contact, in part because of what each of us dissociates at that moment.

For buried in my negative judgment is also the first glimpse of how I want to change him because of my own dread and envy. While I want him to better bear psychic pain, I cannot help but notice his relative freedom from the bodily pains that come with age. His mercurial mind pays no heed to joints or muscles or bladders, arteries or eyes. His vigorous body romps in a world, changing so fast it will surely pass me by, leave me to die. And I realize: I am annoyed with him—prefer to think of him as "degraded," "impoverished," "perverse"—because he is, among other things, communicating his disillusionment, not only with his own childhood, but with my generation's promise as well. His presence revives memories of my own youth left unfulfilled and forces me to become more aware of what I prefer to dissociate: the abandoned imagination of my adolescence.

And what is more: I envy the young man's amplified shapeshifting because it is better suited to the restlessness and flux of our time than anything I can possibly muster. He is comfortable with simultaneity while my mind is primed for the sequential. He has developed, far better than I, what Robert J. Lifton (1993) calls a "protean self." As Homer tells us in the *Odyssey*, Proteus first:

> takes on a whiskered lion's shape
> a serpent then a leopard; a great boar
> then sousing water; then a tall green tree.
> (quoted in Lifton, 1993, p. 5)

Lifton sees proteanism as an expression of human resilience in an age of fragmentation. The young man, Lifton reminds me, has adjusted to accelerated distractions where I have not. The future, in other words, is more his than mine.

But I am not the only one who, at this particular moment of encounter, empties his mind of disturbing truths. For the moment of "whatever" also hides the very pain that brings this young man to treatment: the precipitous loss of his father and seeming incapacity to engage life productively. The precocious maturity he developed early in life has become an empty pose. Imitating the adult he does not really feel himself to be leaves a chronic undercurrent of hollow unreality. While he appears to be at ease everywhere, he is, in fact, going nowhere. Well suited for accelerated distractions, he is ill-equipped to expand his potential to actively accommodate emerging desires and feelings in the context of new relationships. He desperately needs to find an inner presence upon which he can rely but finds in me only the familiar absence. It is not that he is shallow; it is that our generational dialogue at this moment is shallow!

A space to speak

Ethnographers of contemporary culture marshal strong evidence that in parts of the Western world, horizontal networks are outstripping vertical orientations. Younger generations grow up in a universe defined largely by their contemporaries such that the cocoon of custom binding earlier generations to their ancestors has seemingly vanished. Carlo Strenger (2004) argues these changes are so profound that psychoanalysis cannot treat these young people using outdated practices and notions of Oedipal conflict. Their psychic makeup, he claims, is just too different. Rather than modeling themselves after or reacting to early parental introjects, these "self-designed" individuals navigate a course of hyper-reflective choice. "The ambivalent mix of love and hate, respect and disdain that characterized earlier generations in their rebellion against parents," writes Strenger, "has given way to a faint sense of irrelevance" (p. xii). In the language of psychoanalysis, Strenger describes a generational culture founded on the ablation of the paternal.

One need not necessarily believe the psyche to be constituted by a determining triangular struggle, however, to accept that as we grow we must learn to tolerate difference—sexual, generational, and otherwise. To be involved only with one's peers is to be condemned to a shallow, narrow world of sibling sameness and rivalry that constricts growth. At best, this provides the warmth of a band of brothers; at worst, the terror of warring death gangs. Growth requires a depth of colliding with and relating to, not ablating, parental images.

And even if fathers or their surrogates appear irrelevant in terms of the transmission of conscious cultural identifications, they nevertheless remain vital sources of unconscious implicit knowledge about how people relate to one another. Well beyond awareness, paternal figures offer implicit maps by which we unreflectively navigate our way with, over, through, around, and without other people. While conscious connection to father may seem relatively dormant, at some transitional stage of life a renewed generational dialogue might be actively sought. Here is an example:

"I've just sold a webisode," Sam, a 29-year-old new media entrepreneur tells me.

"What is a 'webisode'?" I ask.

There is a moment of despairing silence. Sam's eyes turn toward his feet and an old familiar fidgetiness takes possession of his lanky frame. Sam was first referred to me at age 17 because of brooding withdrawal at home and angry outbursts at school. Matters were particularly tense between Sam and his father. "It is like they are suddenly from different universes," his mother told me over the phone in a version of "Fathers are from Venus and sons are from Mars." "It wasn't always like this. They used to be so close." I saw Sam for about a year and thought I had helped him in overcoming a developmental hump. He went away to college and I hadn't seen him for more than a decade. Naturally, I am curious when he resurfaces, telling me his girlfriend encouraged him to speak with someone about his persistent moodiness. A picture of the intervening years emerges: Sam had immersed himself in a cultural life quite different from his father's. He drank heavily, whereas his father did not drink at all. He consumed a great deal of popular culture; his father, intellectually highbrow, rarely watched television. He spent his days and nights immersing himself in simulated interactive Multi-User Domain games, constructing elaborate virtual identities, and living a "life on the screen" (Turkle, 1997) that felt far realer to him than what he called "RL" or "real life." In college, Sam increasingly lubricated his ill ease and oft-shifting sense of self with ironic and mocking gestures. His father despaired over how his son "was wasting his life in childish and useless pursuits." Mother, meanwhile, painfully felt her family torn asunder as the men in her life drifted further and further apart. For years, father and son rarely spoke, and when they did the conversations quickly devolved into awkward silences. Eventually, Sam graduated, and pursued a line of work far from home that would be anathema to his father. He moved from one media job to the next, frequently complaining his peer colleagues never seemed "quite serious enough." Recently, he accepted a creative opportunity, which brought him back to his hometown, making it more difficult to avoid his father. At the same time, he was beginning to wonder if he "really fit in with his peers."

"Something just happened when I asked you what a webisode is," I remark.

"Not really," Sam replies.

"To me it seemed you were momentarily taken over by a mood."

"Sometimes I feel like there's no point," he says, beginning at least to acknowledge the sudden shift in his own state of mind. "No point in explaining myself."

Gradually, we gain some understanding: the moment I displayed my lack of knowledge about the activity in which he was engaged, Sam experienced familiar feelings of hopelessness. A gap between us—a piece of cultural knowledge not shared by us both—readily became an unbridgeable gulf of despair over never being able to find a connection to his father. My ignorance confirmed once again his conscious warranted belief there is little guidance to be gained from his father as to how to navigate his cultural world.

What was striking about this encounter, however, was what came next. As we came to understand his despair over how his cultural world was incomprehensible to his father, Sam acknowledged how he had begun recently to wonder about how similar the two of them really are. His girlfriend had drawn his attention to this: "There is something in the way you do things," she had observed, "not what you do, but how you do it—that reminds me sometimes of your father. How persistent, reliable, and honest you are. How you seem to think you must do everything on your own. That's just like your father!" Sam was moved, but taken aback by her comment. It flattered yet confused him, and he was struggling what to make of it. Here was a woman of his generation and cultural sensibility who he could even imagine marrying, sharing a perception discrepant with his sense of reality that nevertheless felt uncannily true.

And as the shock of recognition settled in, Sam recalled feeling safe and loved as a child by his father. He knew no matter the distance between them, his father cared deeply. Indeed, Sam formulated for the first time an awareness of an obscure feeling of meaning "too much" to his father; it was as if Sam needed to relieve his father of some unspoken burden. As we explored these feelings, Sam raised a piece of family history he had never before considered relevant and about which I had been totally ignorant. "I always knew my father was very distant from his own father," Sam remarked, "but it never occurred to me until now that had anything to do with me. Maybe it is a family curse—fathers begetting sons who inflict pain on each other." And as Sam more fully appreciated his involvement in a history belonging to someone else, he was poignantly moved by how earnestly his father, too, yearned for something different between them. Discovering the loneliness ran both ways reduced Sam's shame. The shift in perspective allowed him to move closer toward his father as a person. Sam began enjoying his father's company, valuing what he had to offer, as he sorted out what to make or not make his own.

As I think about the trajectory of Sam's life, I imagine he could afford to recognize he was like his father because, paradoxically, he was coming more into his own. Sam was entertaining the idea of creating a family. But to fully imagine himself a husband or father, he could not rely solely on images of his peers; he needed also to reconnect somehow with the lost father of his childhood. Sam, on the cusp of a developmental threshold with a new sense of timescale entering consciousness, was discovering his own authority by revisiting a dormant paternal relationship and accessing the otherness of the forgotten father in himself.

The rekindled generational dialogue facilitated an active "sorting out" of who Sam was in relation to his father, helping him emerge from the doldrums.

Sam was better able to articulate for himself what to keep and what to dispose of, how to love and how to be loved by, his father. The renewed dialogue, I suspect, was as vital to the father as it was to the son.

To state my point in terms of transference: Sam was involved, culturally, in a generational life quite mystifying to his father. He consciously, and to an extent accurately, believed no guidance could be gained from his father. But he was also carrying within implicit knowledge gained from father about what it means to be a man, a husband, a father, a productive worker, as well as a longing for generational dialogue. Sam's moment of moodiness was not simply a repetition within the transference of an Oedipal relationship. I was not, in the transference, only a person whose imagined success stands as constant reproach. He was not only projecting on to me an image of a dismissive or rejecting father with whom he must compete. Rather, Sam's moodiness might profitably be seen as an attempt on his part to involve me as a generative being. It expressed an unconscious plea to restore the generational dialogue. What Sam needed in this dialogue was not his father's approval so much as the opportunity to collide with him in a way that included his father being able to hold in mind an accurate perception of Sam's own experience of himself (Laing, 1962). He needed recognition, not approbation—room for the process of becoming able to accept both difference and similarity. What initially appeared as radical generational discontinuity between father and son can be understood in retrospect as a masking of a failure of intimacy.

Transference, in this case, was not about guilt and rivalry between an excluded child and dreaded father. It communicated a deep yearning for a loving, but lost father whose influence he could comfortably accept without losing himself. Sam's experience suggests, from a psychoanalytic point of view, that the myth of Telemachus' longing for his father Odysseus' return[3] is perhaps no less relevant to human development than Oedipus' tale of triumph and guilt. Transference carries the hope of being heard as generations speak.

Notes

1 The terms "well-known forebears," "familiar peers," and "unknown children" are taken from Margaret Mead's typology of cultures.

2 There are certain historical conditions—migrations, decimations, pioneering, or revolutionary ventures—that may preclude or radically curtail elements of the

generational dialogue. It is beyond the scope of this paper, however, to consider the deep psychological impact of these circumstances.

3 "My mother certainly says I am Odysseus' son, but for myself I cannot tell. It's a wise child that knows its own father" (Telemachus to Athena as the Taphian stranger, Homer, *Odyssey* 1.215, quoted in http://homepage.mac.com/cparada/GML/Telemachus.html).

References

Bollas, C. (1992). *Being a Character: Psychoanalysis & Self Experience*. New York: Hill & Wang.

Brodsky, J. (1986). *Less Than One: Selected Essays*. New York: Farrar, Strauss & Giroux.

Bromberg, P. (1998). *Standing in the Spaces: Essays on Clinical Process, Trauma & Dissociation*. Hillsdale, NJ: The Analytic Press.

Chasseguet-Smirgel, J. (1984). *Creativity and Perversion*. New York: Norton.

Davies, J. (1996). "Linking the 'Pre-Analytic' with the Postclassical: Integration, Dissociation, and the Multiplicity of Unconscious Process." *Contemporary Psychoanalysis*, 32: 553–576.

Erikson, E. (1968). *Identity: Youth and Crisis*. New York: Norton.

Erikson, E. (1980). "On the Generational Cycle: An Address." *The International Journal of Psychoanalysis*, 61: 212–223.

Faimberg, H. (2005). *The Telescoping of Generations: Listening to the Narcissistic Links between Generations*. The New Library of Psychoanalysis. London and New York: Routledge.

Freud, S. (1905). "Three Essays on the Theory of Sexuality." *The Standard Edition of the Complete Psychological Works of Sigmund Freud*, Vol. VII, p. 125.

Gabbard, G.O. (1993). "On Hate in Love Relationships: The Narcissism of Minor Differences Revisited." *The Psychoanalytic Quarterly*, 62: 229–238.

Gay, P. (1985). *Freud for Historians*. New York: Oxford University Press.

Greenberg, J. (1991). *Oedipus and Beyond: A Clinical Theory*. Cambridge, MA: Harvard University Press.

Grossman, D. (2014). *Falling Out of Time*. New York: Vintage Books.

Kohut, H. (1971). *The Analysis of the Self: A Systematic Approach to the Psychoanalytic Treatment of Narcissistic Personality Disorders*. New York: IUP.

Kristeva, J. (1997). *New Maladies of the Soul*. New York: Columbia University Press.

Lacan, (1980). *Television: A Challenge to the Psychoanalytic Establishment*. New York: W.W. Norton.

Laing, R.D. (1962). *The Self and Others*. Chicago, IL: Quadrangle.

Lifton, R.J (1993). *The Protean Self: Human Resilience in an Age of Fragmentation*. New York: Basic Books.

Loewald, H. (1979). "The Waning of the Oedipus Complex." In *Papers on Psychoanalysis*. New Haven, CT: Yale University Press, 1980, pp. 384–404.

Mead, M. (1970). *Culture and Commitment: A Study of the Generation Gap*. New York: American Museum of Natural History, Natural History Press.

Melville, H. (2002). *Moby Dick or, The Whale*. New York: Penguin Classics, revised edition.

Mitchell, S.A. (1993). *Hope and Dread in Psychoanalysis*. New York: Basic Books.

Ogden, T. (2006) "Reading Loewald: Oedipus Reconceived." *The International Journal of Psychoanalysis*, 87: 651–666.

Rushdie, S. (1991). *Imaginary Homelands*. New York: Viking Press.

Stern, D.B. (1997). *Unformulated Experience: From Dissociations to Imagination in Psychoanalysis*. Hillsdale, NJ: The Analytic Press.

Stevens, W. (1990). "Poem with Rhythms." In *The Collected Poems of Wallace Stevens*. New York and London: Vintage Books.

Strenger, C. (2004). *The Designed Self: Psychoanalysis and Contemporary Identities*. Hillsdale, NJ: The Analytic Press.

Turkle, S. (1997). *Life on the Screen: Identity in the Age of the Internet*. New York: Touchstone.

Winnicott, D.W. (1945). "Primitive Emotional Development." In *Through Paediatrics to Psycho-Analysis*. New York: Basic Books, 1975, pp. 145–156.

Winnicott, D.W. (1963). "Communicating and Not Communicating Leading to a Study of Certain Opposites." In *The Maturational Processes and the Facilitating Environment*. London: The Hogarth Press, pp. 179–192.

Wordsworth, W. (1800). "Preface to Lyrical Ballads 1800." *Famous Prefaces. The Harvard Classics. 1909–14*. December 14, 2004. www.bartleby.com/39/36.html#txt1.

Chapter 5

Parting ways

It obviously makes a difference if one thinks of psychoanalysis as a treatment—a cure for an ailment—or as an experience. Accounts of psychoanalysis as treatment demand plausibility and coherence, not to mention intelligibly formulated criteria, for professional efficacy. From the point of view of treatment, psychoanalysis is an elaborate exercise expected to adhere to the satisfying narrative structure of beginning, middle, and, preferably, happy end. But to the extent the purview of psychoanalysis is experience—the place where the singularity of a person's idiosyncratic desire meets the contingencies of life—it is virtually impossible to create a consensual vocabulary for knowing when enough is enough.

Of all aspects of the psychoanalytic process, it is perhaps the ending that most vividly brings into relief the tension between professional accountability and the unpredictability of desire. The language of accountability insists on words such as "analyzability," "boundaries," and, yes, "termination." But the language of unconscious desire—and the freedom to live with its accidental consequences—is captured by Emerson (1904):

> The results of life are uncalculated and uncalculable . . . The persons who compose our company converse, and come and go, and design and execute many things, and somewhat come of it all, but an unlooked-for result. The individual is always mistaken. He designed many things, and drew in other persons as coadjutors, quarreled with some or all, blundered much, and something is done; all are a little advanced, but the individual is always mistaken. It turns out somewhat new and very unlike what he promised himself.
>
> (Vol. 3, pp. 69–70)

The experience of psychoanalysis, as Emerson suggests, is quite unlike what we promise ourselves. More often than not, it creates an unlooked-for result.

When inclined toward psychoanalysis as treatment, the analyst holds in mind a linear trajectory evidenced by alteration of symptoms, enhanced capacities, and developmental achievement. From the outset, the therapist is at the beginning of treatment while the person seeking professional help is somewhere in the middle, because his own efforts at self-cure have thus far failed. Criteria for ending—in the language of whatever theory they might be cast—serve as benchmarks in an instrumental relationship designed for a purpose external to the relationship itself. No matter how long the treatment takes, the unalterable "not-me" aspect of time—what Kipling calls "the unforgiving minute"—is always, in some way, of the essence. Although the constricting repetitions—the unconscious limiting of potential life stories—that bring people to analysis carry the appearance of time having stopped, the person also knows very well otherwise. For the analyst to not monitor movement in time, to seductively ablate awareness of time passing, does a disservice.

While inclined toward psychoanalysis as experience, on the other hand, the analyst participates in the kaleidoscope of unconscious life without necessarily concerning himself with purpose, direction, or time. Or, to state this in more nuanced terms: the sense of time in play is less a linear trajectory moving toward something as it is the recognition that ends are recursively consonant with origins. Furthermore, endings, like beginnings, can be delinked from chronological implications and instead be understood as "states of mind" in which one feels one is either leaving a familiar situation or facing a new one. From this point of view, analysis is a potentially infinite series of beginnings and endings (Schlesinger, 2005). Are there not many moments in the course of an analysis when, on the brink of entering uncharted territory, the person suddenly experiences the analyst as an unsafe stranger? For the analyst concerned with safeguarding analysis as experience, the question is not: what is the model best suited to explain and facilitate a "successful termination?" But rather: how are the multiple beginnings and endings experienced by the two participants? Undue emphasis on prescribed theories of mourning, growth, loss, or developmental achievements runs the risk of silencing some aspect of the person's internal world. As Malcolm Bowie (1993) suggests, "Perhaps the best hope for the psychoanalyst lies not in 'theory' at all, but in the old fashioned arts of speaking opportunely and knowing when to stop" (p. 46).

A particular analyst's inclination—his sensibility regarding these currents—will inevitably tilt how the ending of a treatment is negotiated. The point being: it is inadequate to think of the timing of ending analysis as simply a matter of the person's pace—what Freud once referred to as the "length" of an analysand's "stride." Instead, the analyst's own preference will also have significant bearing on the how and the when of ending. It can be useful to note, at any given moment, how a particular person's use of analysis may concord, collude, or collide with an analyst's inclination. And to be clear, both the person's use and the analyst's inclination can, and often do, shift over time. Whether formulated or not, the two participants continuously feel each other out both transferentially and in actuality: is it safe to stay? Is it time to go? What's the rush? When will it end? Idiosyncratic rhythms of engagement—seeking contact and safeguarding solitude—certainly play their part in the dance over time. A person communicating, whether in words or not, "When will this treatment start working?" may prompt the analyst to communicate, "Can't you let the experience be?" Similarly, a person's apparent obliviousness to change might prompt the same analyst to communicate, "We don't have all the time in the world!" Concordant and complementary identifications (Racker, 1968) and dissociated self-states (Bromberg, 1998) play out in unpredictable ways. There are, as Paul Simon put it, 50 ways to leave (or not leave) your lover.

This is not to say people necessarily know what they really want. Central to Freud's original project was drawing attention to how people are, in Emerson's sense, "always mistaken." Freud was, therefore, equally suspicious of analysand's stopping—be it chains of associations or commitments to battle their neuroses—as he was about their continuing treatment indefinitely. Stopping and not stopping can each readily be viewed as "resistance." Ludwig Wittgenstein seemed particularly struck by this aspect of psychoanalysis when he remarked that Freud's:

> Procedure of free association and so on is queer, because Freud never shows how we know where to stop—where is the right solution. Sometimes he says that the right solution, or the right analysis, is the one which satisfies the patient. Sometimes he says that the doctor

> knows what the right solution or analysis of the dream is, whereas the patient doesn't: the doctor can say that the patient is wrong. The reason why he calls one sort of analysis the right one does not seem to be a matter of evidence.
>
> (Wittgenstein and Rhees, 1968, pp. 376–377)

Perhaps what Wittgenstein found "queer" about psychoanalysis was the paradox that Freud's method of free association—which by its very nature has no end point—was employed as a treatment designed to come to a satisfactory conclusion. Essential to Freud's vision of unconscious life are what Malcolm Bowie (1993) refers to as "unstoppable transformational processes" (p. 127) that "prevents meaning from reaching fullness, completion, closure, consummation" (p. 98). Freud ironically presumed that speaking as truthfully as possible with no end in sight would necessarily bring self-deception into plain view. But how does one ever find the "right solution" as to where to stop if some measure of self-deception is vital to psychic survival? And how—given the unstoppability of the signifying process described by Bowie—can either participant possibly "know" with conviction when an analysis should come to an end?

From the point of view of psychoanalysis as a treatment, the main obstacle to finding the "right solution" to knowing when to stop has generally been understood to be the person's stubborn self-protective obstructionism or "resistances." More specifically, the reason held responsible for analyses failing to successfully self-terminate is that people have an unrealistic grasp of the satisfactions to be expected from love and life. Describing termination as the "Achilles heel" of psychoanalysis, Martin Bergmann (1997) notes:

> For many analysands, transference love is the best love relationship that life has offered. Understandably, they are reluctant to give it up . . . In real life, only death and hostility bring a libidinal relationship to an end. The kind of termination psychoanalysis demands is without precedent.
>
> (p. 163)

As long as the analytic bond was thought of primarily as a "libidinal relationship," the ending of treatment could only be envisioned in terms of the individual "overcoming" unrealistic childish wishes. Ferenczi would even suggest the battle waged against these wishes was usually won, if at all, by sheer attrition. "The proper ending of an analysis," writes Ferenczi (1955):

> Is when neither the physician nor the patient put an end to it, but when it dies of exhaustion . . . a truly cured patient frees himself from analysis slowly but surely; so long as he wishes to come to analysis he should continue to do so . . . The patient finally becomes convinced that he is continuing analysis only because he is treating it as a new but still a fantasy source of gratification, which in terms of reality yields him nothing.
>
> (p. 85)

It is worth considering, however, what happens when we view ending an analysis from a lens other than one of misplaced libidinal gratification. What if the question of ending is not seen as a matter of the patient's inadequacy in relinquishing forbidden desire or accepting reality? After all, Freud's hermeneutic of suspicion—the state of mind aiming to expose that which we conceal from ourselves—is only part of what constitutes the psychoanalytic enterprise. No less potent than the desire to conceal is the human urge to communicate. People don't only want to hide; they also seek other people to know, to be known by, and to know themselves.

One interesting trend in psychoanalytic theorizing is the increasing emphasis on how the analyst becomes, as Emerson put it, a "coadjutor, quarreled with . . . blundered much," as part of the individual's project to be recognized (Emerson, 1904, p. 70). And in the midst of the conversing, the quarreling, and the blundering—as the patient clamors to be heard—there is no escaping that the analyst is also always in some way mistaken.

Put differently, just as the language of "libidinal gratification" is inadequate to describe why people come together, "termination" is an inappropriate term to describe what happens when a relationship ends. Obviously, people part—in anger or sorrow, disgust, or relief; people stop doing things together—working, living in the same city, or sleeping in the same bed. People may never see each other again or even consciously think about each other. But one can never know or control how the departed, forgotten, exiled, abandoned, or lost other might return unbidden as one's own mood or to haunt one's dreams. As the Israeli author David Grossman (2014) writes in his novella *Falling Out of Time*, "It is you/who decides/how to appear in me/and when" (p. 84). Echoes of objects reverberate in ways not readily predictable. And these echoes—their role in pain, suffering, witnessing, and self-transformation—bear significantly upon how endings are experienced.

Freud (1926) asks: "When does separation from an object produce anxiety, when does it produce mourning, and when does it produce, it may be, only pain?" (p. 169). As is often the case, the question Freud asks is more interesting—in the sense of opening possibilities—than the answer he provides. What is striking about the choices Freud offers—anxiety, mourning, and pain—is that despite his general emphasis on fantasized relations, actual separation from an object is viewed as a loss with significant consequences. Even mourning, which, from Freud's point of view, "occurs under the influence of reality testing" and categorically demands of the bereaved a "detachment of libido," involves a greater degree of continuity of relationship than Freud acknowledges. Attachments, it turns out, are far less interchangeable than Freud's theory of libido might suggest.

More telling than the range of emotional choices Freud highlights is his intriguing proposal that some forms of separation might involve "only pain." "Pain" is an affective state Freud sidelined after his first speculative musings in the "Project for a Scientific Psychology" (Pontalis, 1977). In that early work, the primary distinction Freud draws is not between pleasure and unpleasure (which are on a single tension continuum), but between pleasure/unpleasure, on the one hand, and pain, on the other. The experience of pain is independent of the experience of unsatisfied desire. Pain—which involves a traumatic break in the stimulus barrier—is of an entirely different order than frustration or thwarted desire.

It is the newborn's experience of helplessness when separated from mother that generates the earliest experiences of pain. Helplessness—and the traumatic pain accompanying it—Freud suggests is the primordial condition of the human species. As an affective state, pain is not the result of a fantasized danger; it is a reaction appropriate to an actual loss. The primitive psyche cannot think about, transform, or elaborate pain. By introducing the distinction between anxiety, mourning, and "only pain" as possible consequences of separation, Freud was revisiting an earlier notion that certain traumatizing experiences cannot be psychically elaborated.

Bion (1970), picking up this aspect of Freud's thinking, provides his own compelling version. "Patients," he writes:

> experience pain but not suffering . . . The intensity of the patient's pain contributes to his fear of suffering pain . . . Pain is inflicted or accepted but is not suffered except in the view of the analyst or other observer.
> (p. 19)

Mental pain, Bion suggests, emerges when the person lacks a capacity to suffer. Suffering, which is associated with the capacity for containment and psychic elaboration of painful emotions, is suitable for description in words. Pain—a "nameless dread"—resists elaboration and is thereby devoid of meaning. But if psychoanalysis teaches us anything, it is that pain can be transformed by applying words to wounds. But for words to carry a transformative potential, it is not enough they simply be spoken; they need also to be heard.

For Winnicott, too, there is a meaningful difference between pain and suffering. Suffering, for Winnicott as for Bion, is a developmental achievement associated with a relatively healthy relationship to the difficulties inherent in life. "Probably the greatest suffering in the human world," writes Winnicott (1988):

> is the suffering of normal or healthy or mature persons. This is not generally recognized. It is a false guide to observe manifest perplexity, misery, and pain in a mental hospital. Nevertheless it is usual for degree of suffering to be assessed in this superficial way.
> (p. 80)

Christian upbringing probably drew both Bion and Winnicott to the word "suffering" to capture the profundity of love, loss, lack, and life (psychoanalytic theory offers a rich vocabulary to explain transformations of excitement, but is rendered silent when it comes to describing what makes an experience poignant). It may also be that Bion and Winnicott were quite consciously wanting to highlight an intriguing overlap between religious and psychoanalytic experiences. As Masud Khan (1981) observed:

> It is my inference from what I know of the history of religions, especially the three monotheistic ones, that it is precisely this need in the human individual for his or her psychic pain to be witnessed silently

> and unobtrusively by the other that led to the creation of the omnipresence of God in human lives. Over the past two centuries and more, with the increasing disappearance of God as the witnessing other from man's privacy with himself, the experience of psychic pain has changed from tolerated and accepted suffering to its pathological substitutes, and the need has rapidly increased for psycho-therapeutic interventions to alleviate these pathological masochistic states.
>
> (p. 414)

Putting aside Khan's assertion that the "disappearance of God" gives rise to increased masochism and need for psychotherapy, it is precisely what he refers to as "this need in the individual" to have psychic pain transformed by an Other that links—despite meaningful differences—Winnicott's "holding" with Bion's "containment." Winnicott's mother safeguards the infant's spontaneous rhythms—his experience of aliveness—in part by insulating him from premature awareness of the painful "not-me" aspects of the passage of time (Ogden, 2004; Goldman, 2013). For Bion, mother does the unconscious psychological work of dreaming the infant's unbearable pain and making it available in a form that can be made use of in dreaming his own experience. For each of them, the mother is reliably available not only as an object of desire, but as an animating presence. We are, both Winnicott and Bion suggest, vitally enmeshed in relatedness with an Other prior to the time we can mentally represent them in our minds. The vestiges of this early sensorimotor environmental setup (distinct from what is traditionally thought of as "libidinally cathected" or "object-related") becomes the rudiment of our later well-being.

Christopher Bollas (1987) coins the term "transformational object" to capture an aspect of embedded relatedness implied by Winnicott and Bion. Bollas describes the transformational object as:

> experientially identified by the infant with processes that alter self experience. It is an identification . . . where the first object is "known" not so much by putting it into an object representation, but as a recurrent experience of being—a more existential as opposed to representational knowing. As the mother helps to integrate the infant's being . . . the rhythms of this process . . . inform the nature of the "object" relation rather than the qualities of the object as object.
>
> (p. 14)

Bollas's transformational object—like Winnicott's environmental mother—originates before there is a mental representation. It is, we might say, a pre-object relationship emerging not from desire but from a perceptual identification of the object with its function as transformer of the rhythms of self-experience.

This form of early relating, Bollas suggests, "lives on in certain forms of object seeking in adult life" (p. 14). People search for transformational objects not to possess them so much as "to surrender to them as a medium that alters the self" (p. 14). The patient's use of the analyst as a transformational object, Bollas (1992) believes, is aimed less at gaining understanding than to free "the instinct to elaborate oneself" (p. 70). But, if this is to happen—and it is a big "if"—the analyst has to be available in a way that allows the individual to discover his or her own inventiveness. It is a catastrophe, Bollas implies, to be trapped in someone else's preconceptions—including the analyst's theory of successful endings.

To state all this in terms of the question at hand: if, as Freud suggests, pain is a primordial condition of the human species beyond the pleasure/unpleasure principle; and if, as Winnicott and Bion suggest, relationships are essential to transform pain into suffering and suffering is a way of describing what makes living meaningful; and, as Khan and the evidence of major religions suggest, having one's pain transformed by an unobtrusive Other is a fundamental human need; and, as Bollas claims, there is a lifelong search for transformational objects; why, it must be asked, should an analytic relationship ever be expected to come to an end? Not: what obstacle in the patient is obstructing termination? But rather: how does each analytic couple wish to negotiate this basic human situation over time?

And to take this one step further: why must psychoanalysis only be about pain and suffering? There is, after all, an inherent pleasure, of the kind that accompanies exercising one's faculties and competencies—stretching one's psychic muscles so to speak—that is often a part of the analytic experience. Why might we tend to disparage an individual for simply finding pleasure in psychoanalysis? And what do we do when it becomes an addictive pleasure?

Addiction, it has been said, is what happens when we can never get enough of what we don't really want. And if psychoanalysis teaches us anything, it is that we often don't know what we really want. Bergmann (1997), discussing an early paper on termination by Ferenczi and Rank, notes that:

> in keeping with Freud's idea that during psychoanalysis the infantile neurosis is transformed into a transference neurosis, they advocated the analyst set termination date the moment this transference occurs. They believed that only then could a repetition of clinging to the early object be avoided.
>
> (p. 164)

Clinging—the dread of a patient never leaving because of an "addiction" to psychoanalysis—was sympathetically and usefully explored by the Hungarian analyst Imre Hermann. The natural instinctive urge to cling to mother, says Hermann, eventually becomes a source of shame. "We come to the conclusion," writes Hermann (1976):

> that . . . the human child is torn from his mother's body prematurely perhaps, among other things, as the consequence of an egotistical act on the part of the primal father. The urge to cling, therefore, continues to exist, reflecting a yearning for the primal state in which mother and child constitute an undivided dual unit. The fulfillment of that yearning is thwarted by a trauma, in actual fact by a series of traumata, repeated over and over again.
>
> (p. 7)

Hermann—an unacknowledged ancestor of attachment theory—describes a psychic conflict between the urge to cling to, and the reactive tendency to be free of, mother. These conflicting tendencies support two contrary phantasies: the phantasy of the lost unity and the phantasy of total independence. The instinct to cling inevitably remains unsatisfied because any real object will merely be an insufficient substitute for the sought after primal object. Human attachments, Hermann implies, are immersed in a sphere of nostalgia, inconsolability, and reactive detachment (Van Haute and Geyskens, 2007).

At first glance, Hermann appears to offer an instinctual twist on the traumatic pain of helplessness described by Freud. But there is a distinction that makes all the difference: for Freud, helplessness is understood in terms of the basic experiences of hunger and thirst. Attachment—the remedy for helplessness—is akin to an emergency measure to manage the tension of needs (Klein will add to this a fear of the death instinct). But for Hermann, clinging is an innate tendency adaptationally designed to manage a universal insecurity he calls "Haltlosigkeit"—a lack of hold or being without foothold (Van Haute and Geyskens, 2007). The primal catastrophe, according to Hermann, is not a question of hunger or innate destructiveness, but the traumatic separation from mother to whom we cling so as to feel grounded. Hermann introduces us to the idea that clinging might be thought of as a grasping for groundedness. Is it not common, while entertaining the idea of ending important relationships, to experience sensations of "losing support," "feeling unmoored," "dropped," or "being on shaky ground?"

Hermann's view of "the yearning to cling" as "thwarted by trauma" implies that the negotiation of this adaptational tendency is a fundamentally relational event. We are, in other words, all vulnerable to the shame of having the need for supportive grounding dismissed. Perhaps that is why mutual shame is a common emotional current running between analyst and patient when ending is contemplated. The patient may be wondering if the analyst can still love him despite the ways he hasn't changed. And the analyst might feel a need to cling to the patient so as to avoid the recognition of his own limitations. Referring to this as "the blood and guts" of therapy, Peggy Crastnopol writes:

> The clinging of the patient seems to be about the need for reassurance that "staying the same" in some ways, even on termination, is acceptable to the analyst. The patient keeps wanting to discover whether the analyst can value him *notwithstanding* his or her remaining imperfection. On the analyst's side, clinging to the patient often comes from a residual "sticky devotedness" to the patient and their shared process. To this we'd have to add the analyst's wish to convince himself that he really can cure the hardest things about the patient, and to avert feelings of failure at what still remains of the patient's neurosis.
>
> (Peggy Crastnopol, personal correspondence, March 12, 2009, emphasis in original)

Another angle of vision from which to consider this matter of clinging and ending—the way we are poised between inconsolability and detachment—is a potentially terrifying element at the core of Winnicott's vision. "I think we must take it for granted," Winnicott wrote privately to Money-Kyrle:

> that emotionally there is no contribution from the individual to the environment or from the environment to the individual. The individual

> only communicates with a self-created world and the people in the environment only communicate with the individual in so far as they can create him or her. Nevertheless, in health, there is the illusion of contact and it is this which provides the high spots of human life.
>
> (quoted in Rodman, 1987, p. 43)

Contact, the sustaining nutrient of relationship constituting the "high spots of human life," is, Winnicott suggests, a certain kind of illusion (Hermann might say neurosis is a pathology of contact). Or, to turn the matter around: it is the capacity for illusion—the "blood and vital juices of our minds," as Wordsworth (1974, I: 103) once said—that allows an experience of contact. Indeed, it is not a far stretch to suggest that what we call psychopathologies—the irksome maladies that bring people to psychoanalysis as a treatment—have as their common denominator an insufficiency or misuse of healthy illusion. "Panic seized her. Blood seemed to pour from her shoes," writes Virginia Woolf (1941). "This is death, death, death . . . when illusion fails" (p. 125). Illusion—the root of all symbolism that allows a thing to be itself and something else at the same time—Marion Milner (1969), reminds us:

> is needed for restoring broken links, bridges, to the outer world, as well as forming the first bridges. As necessary for healthy living as night dreams seem to be—and as playing is.
>
> (p. 416)

Milner's plea is not for illusion as a substitute for reality, but rather as a formative and restorative bridge to reality. Whether cast in the language of "ego mastery," "renunciation of omnipotence," "having the reality principle supplant (and protect) the pleasure principle," "achieving the depressive position," or "developing a mature capacity for mourning," psychoanalysis suggests the individual needs to tolerate a not-me reality beyond magical control. Some form of loss, in other words, is believed to structure the psyche's relationship to external reality. But the question that animated Milner was: how does the acceptance of loss become something other than an empty lifeless accommodation? How does a person navigate between the "thingness" of the world and his own subjectivity so that brute reality may be gradually brought to life with meaning?

The problem of knowing when to end is not simply about learning to accept reality—Freud's bleak pursuit of an illusion free existence based on truth. The truth must "dazzle gradually," Emily Dickinson reminds us, or else it only "blinds" (Wikisource). Psychoanalysis, it might be said, takes place in the space where reality—or at least the effort to speak as truthfully as possible about reality—meets up with the vital illusory "juices" of our minds such that one is not blind to, nor blinded by, the truth.

"It is the disillusionment accompanying termination," suggests Bruce Reis, "it's (tolerably) failed treatment goals, and/or the inability to ever provide 'enough,' which helps to create subjective meaning . . . Because psychoanalysis takes place in between timelessness and temporality, and in between reality and unreality, the dissolution of a treatment could also be thought of as the gift of reality that accompanies loss, a further structuring of the inside occurring as a result of what happens (in illusion) on the outside" (Reis, personal communication, March 14, 2009).

For Reis, tolerable disillusionment—including disillusionment with psychoanalysis itself—helps create the "gift" of finding meaning in reality. Or, to state this in its active form: it is misleading to think it helpful for the analyst to insist on the externality of external things. The patient does not come to simply accept reality, but to make use of disillusionment.

The capacity to "make use of disillusionment" in ending, however, does not reside solely within the patient. It is also a shared moment allowing for simultaneous union and separateness held in mind by both parties without either needing to dissociate the experience (Bromberg, 1998). It is an expression of what is containable within the context of the relationship at any given time. Just as the hallmark of a "good" analytic hour is not quite knowing for sure which of the participants made the interpretation, it is probably a feature of a "good-enough" ending to not know whose decision it "really" was.

Making use of disillusionment includes retaining felt connection despite one's "essential aloneness" (Winnicott, 1988). "At the start," Winnicott notes:

> is an essential aloneness. At the same time this aloneness can only take place under maximum conditions of dependence. Throughout the life of the individual there continues a fundamental unalterable and inherent aloneness, along with which goes unawareness of the conditions that are essential to the state of aloneness.
>
> (p. 132)

Whatever else stopping psychoanalysis means—no matter how well or how badly it ends—it is liable to reintroduce us to our essential aloneness made bearable, Winnicott suggests, only through "conditions" about which we are not aware. While Winnicott (1958) tells us about how the "capacity to be alone" comes about—having its roots in an early experience of being alone in the presence of an other—he tells us little about what that capacity actually entails, except to intriguingly suggest:

> When alone in the sense that I am using the term, and only when alone, the infant is able to do the equivalent of what in an adult would be called relaxing. The infant is able to become unintegrated, to flounder, to be in a state in which there is no orientation, to be able to exist for a time without being either a reactor to an external impingement or an active person with a direction of interest or movement.
>
> (p. 34)

It is worth pondering what bearing this capacity to be alone, in Winnicott's sense, might have on endings. Winnicott draws our attention not to an end state so much as to a freedom to drift about—"to flounder, to be in a state in which there is no orientation"—without needing any prematurely built-up coherent version of a self (Winnicott is the first analyst to propose that, in addition to a desiring subject, there is a nonsensical subject). What makes the pulses of drifting and gelling—transitioning from state to state without needing to immediately make sense—life-enhancing as opposed to alarming is the tether of connection to an Other of which we need not, indeed cannot, be aware. Coherence—including coherent explanations of endings—might suggest too vigilant a need for self-holding, a precipitate foreclosure of the non-purposive resting state essential for creative reaching out to take place. "Free association that reveals a coherent theme," Winnicott (1971) writes elsewhere, "is already affected by anxiety, and the cohesion of ideas is a defence organization" (pp. 55–56).

Winnicott's emphasis on the freedom to drift about without needing to prematurely integrate has implications for what might constitute a good enough ending. To put it bluntly: it is misguided to presume the goal of psychoanalysis is for a person to be fully known. To make something fully known is to make it unreal. Disney World, fast food restaurant chains, and the static world of television sitcoms are examples of the comforting predictability of fully known worlds (Boswell, 2008).

Only when the unrecognizable beyond immediate comprehension is allowed for can meaningful experience emerge. From this point of view, the work of analysis is less about "knowing a patient" and more about "unknowing a character."

In another language: one way to think about what might make stopping possible is in terms of the individual no longer needing to vigilantly make familiar sense. It is a mistaken notion worth dispelling that psychoanalysis helps a person "make sense of their life." At best, it contributes to the lesser, but still quite valuable, feat of appreciating the ways people need and try to make sense of their lives.

Psychoanalysis can, among other things, bring to awareness clamoring internal perspectives—as Emerson (1983) once put it, how "our moods do not believe in each other" (p. 406). In a speculative leap, Bollas (1992) suggests that to find relief from the "ordinary unbearableness" of this complexity, people take flight—they "regress"—into the collusive consolation of couples, families, and groups. It is as if joining the "madness" of others is preferable to being left alone with one's own "madness." "We call this regression 'marriage' or 'partnership,'" writes Bollas:

> In which the person becomes part of a mutually interdependent couple that evokes and sustains the bodies of the mother and the father, the warmth of the pre-Oedipal vision of life, before the solitary recognition of subjectivity grips the child.
>
> (p. 242)

Bollas's view of coupling as a relief from the oddity of one's own mind is consistent with the observation that securely married and socially connected individuals often find it easier to end psychoanalysis than those more isolated and "alone." Could it be that some seemingly unattached people are individuals who actually found other people's madness more disturbing than their own? And that for them the psychoanalytic setup affords the necessary opportunity to be with another and bear their own minds? Might a form of "regression"—in Bollas's sense—also account for why some endings—including certain psychoanalyses or marriages—stubbornly stall?

While negotiating endings, each analytic dyad takes measure of their madness. Sanity—whatever else it entails—includes some acceptance of the enigma of the rhythm of relationship, the natural course of living experiences together. To be sane, one also needs to take some comfort in completion—an arc with a beginning, a middle, and an end—no matter how incomplete. Like all languages, psychoanalysis seeks freedom of expression but also benefits from punctuation. Is this particular moment—when one person pauses—a comma, a period, or an exclamation point? How do analyst and patient alike feel when treatment benchmarks that seemed fitting at the outset later lose their luster? Or when the experience of psychoanalysis outlives its usefulness? Not only: how is the treatment progressing? But also: how are the analyst and patient currently treating each other? Are analyst and patient collaborating, colluding, or colliding?

While analysts anticipate people are likely to end treatment consistent with the way they generally experience relationships—perhaps a definition of a "good treatment" is one that ends differently than would have been expected—it is not easy to gauge how "well" or how "badly" a psychoanalysis really ends. There are even highly unusual cases where the beginning does not simply foreshadow the end but actually is the end.

This was vividly brought home to me by a young man, engaged to be married, who came for a consultation. He was experiencing "odd, disorienting, sensations" that his fiancée kept reassuring him were "nothing but wedding jitters." He knew he had wedding jitters, but was convinced that something else was also going on. "I'm nervous about the wedding," he says. "It's a big step and I'm scared, but this isn't that!" "Well, if these aren't the jitters," I ask him, "what do they feel like?" "A blunt pain," he replies, "it is just a blunt pain." This blunt pain—he had no other word to say how he was feeling—troubled his days, disturbed his nights, and, tellingly, "interrupted his dreams." He confides how much he loves his fiancée, how he knows he'll need to adjust to her "quirks," yet how hopeful he is about their future together. "That's why this pain makes no sense at all."

"I see how hard you are trying to make sense of it," I say. "With the wedding coming up, I imagine it might even feel somewhat urgent."

"Odd that you say that," he replies. "It does feel urgent because of the wedding, but at the same time I have the eerie feeling this has been with me my whole life."

At this point in our conversation, the young man surprises himself: "I can't believe I'm thinking about this right now. But I'm remembering a specific moment—I must have been in second grade—I was in school, at my desk, and suddenly, out of the blue, I had this acute realization that nobody—not the teacher, or my mother, or my father, or my sister—can ever really know what's inside my head. And I can never really know what is inside theirs!"

At the time, he found the realization both "exhilarating" and "terrifying." And he remembers how it preoccupied him for quite a while and put him into a mood similar to the one he has been in lately.

"You figured out you are all alone with a mind of your own," I comment.

"I did," he replies, "and I will remain alone even though I love my fiancée to death and she loves me too."

We talk about this a bit more, and as the session approaches its end I am acutely aware that I do not know if I will see this likable young man ever again. From the point of view of psychoanalysis as treatment—the "work" felt as if it had just begun. But, from the point of view of psychoanalysis as an experience, this man seems—there is no way to know for sure—to have found what he hadn't even known he was looking for. He had taken a risk, used our time together, and, as in all forms of playing, could be rid of something after getting what he wanted from it.

"I guess I don't need to see you again," he remarks.

As he utters these words, I surprise myself by replying, "'Guess' feels to me like just the right word."

He smiles. And so we part ways. What happens next is anybody's guess.

References

Bergmann, M. (1997). "Termination: The Achilles Heel of Psychoanalytic Technique." *Psychoanalytic Psychology*, 14: 163–174.

Bion, W. (1970). *Attention and Interpretation*. London: Maresfield Library.

Bollas, C. (1987). *The Shadow of the Object: Psychoanalysis of the Unthought Known*. New York: Columbia University Press.

Bollas, C. (1992). *Being a Character: Psychoanalysis & Self Experience*. New York: Hill & Wang.

Boswell, R. (2008). *The Half-Known World: On Writing Fiction*. Saint Paul, MN: Graywolf Press.

Bowie, M. (1993). *Psychoanalysis and the Future of Theory*. Oxford and Cambridge, MA: Blackwell.

Bromberg, P. (1998). *Standing in the Spaces: Essays on Clinical Process, Trauma & Dissociation*. Hillsdale, NJ: The Analytic Press.

Dickinson, E. https://en.wikisource.org/wiki/Tell_all_the_Truth_but_tell_it_slant_%E2%80%94.

Emerson, R.W. (1904). *The Compete Works of Ralph Emerson*. Boston, MA, and New York: Houghton, Mifflin & Co.

Emerson, R.W. (1983). "Circles." Essay X in *Emerson: Essays and Lectures*. New York: Library of America.

Ferenczi, S. (1955). "The Problem of Termination of the Analysis." In *Final Contributions to the Problems and Methods of Psycho-Analysis*. Ed. M. Balint. London: Hogarth Press, pp. 77–86.

Freud, S. (1926). "Inhibitions, Symptoms, and Anxiety." *The Standard Edition of the Complete Psychological Works of Sigmund Freud*, Vol. XX.

Goldman, D. (2013). "Vital Sparks and the Form of Things Unknown." In *Donald Winnicott Today*. Ed. J. Abram. London: Routledge.

Grossman, D. (2014). *Falling Out of Time*. New York: Vintage Books.

Hermann, I. (1976). "Clinging—Going-In-Search—A Contrasting Pair of Instincts and Their Relation to Masochism and Sadism." *The Psychoanalytic Quarterly*, 45: 5–36.

Khan, M.R. (1981). "From Masochism to Psychic Pain." *Contemporary Psychoanalysis*, 17: 413–421.

Milner, M. (1969). *The Hands of the Living God*. London: Hogarth Press.

Ogden, T. (2004). "On Holding and Containing, Being and Dreaming." *The International Journal of Psychoanalysis*, 85: 1349–1364.

Pontalis, J.-B. (1977). *Frontiers in Psychoanalysis: Between the Dream and Psychic Pain*. New York: IUP.

Racker, H. (1968). *Transference and Countertransference*. New York: IUP.

Rodman, R.F. (1987). *The Spontaneous Gesture: Selected Letters of D.W. Winnicott*. Cambridge, MA, and London: Harvard University Press.

Schlesinger, H.J. (2005). *Endings & Beginnings: On Terminating Psychotherapy and Psychoanalysis*. Hillsdale, NJ: The Analytic Press.

Van Haute, P. and Geyskens, T. (2007). *From Death Instinct to Attachment Theory*. New York: Other Press.

Winnicott, D.W. (1958). "The Capacity to Be Alone." In *The Maturational Processes and the Facilitating Environment*. London: Hogarth Press, pp. 29–36.

Winnicott, D.W. (1971). *Playing and Reality*. London and New York: Routledge.

Winnicott, D.W. (1988). *Human Nature*. New York: Schocken Books.

Wittgenstein, L. and Rhees, R. (1968). "Conversations on Freud." *Psychoanalytic Review*, 55: 376–386.

Woolf, V. (1941). *Between the Acts*. Harmondsworth, UK: Penguin.

Wordsworth, W. (1974). The Prose Works of William Wordsworth. Ed. W.J.B Owen and J. Worthington Smyser, 3 vols. London: Oxford University Press.

Part II

Winnicott's living legacy

Chapter 6

Winnicott's search for self and cure

In the early history of psychoanalysis, it was common to claim that dissidents were motivated by a resistance to the truth of Freud's discoveries. Jung, Adler, Rank, Ferenczi, and Horney were, each in turn, thought to be neurotically denying either the formative drive of childhood sexuality or the centrality of the Oedipus complex. Alternative ideas were devalued by ad hominem references to unanalyzed conflict.

It is probably no accident that D.W. Winnicott was one of the first to suggest deeper and better reasons for challenging Freud's theory. In an idiosyncratic review of Jung's autobiography, Winnicott (1964a) advises we might all profit not by taking sides with either Freud or Jung, but by allowing "the two to meet and to go together and to separate" (p. 482). Approaching Jung with admirable empathy, he concludes that Jung parted with Freud because Freud's theory had little to offer him in terms of his own illness. Having built up a complex defense organization in recovering from childhood schizophrenia, Jung could not have been helped by Freud because Freud's model of a repressed unconscious was insufficient to account for Jung's dissociatively split mind. So Jung sought his own self-cure, and the theory he eventually articulated was an expression of his search for both self and cure.

Winnicott's insight is not only a new view of what drove Jung's dissidence. It is—like many observations we have of others—a way of saying something about himself. Nietzsche had it right when he noted that every philosophy is a confession on the part of its author and an involuntary unconscious memoir. Winnicott's innovative theorizing, in other words, can also be understood as tentative attempts to find himself and his own self-cure. His theory speaks to his own condition. As Masud Khan once noted:

> Since one is the laboratory in which all psychological research takes place, it is but inevitable that all new investigations of insight are started off by some subjective experience.
>
> (quoted in Willoughby, 2005, p. 106)

This is not to say that Winnicott's contribution cannot be assessed on its own merits. While theoretical innovations begin in subjective sensibility, they do not end there. Ideas can always be evaluated by weighing evidence, seeking parsimony of explanation, assessing internal consistency, and scrutinizing compatibility with accumulating facts. It is also true that psychoanalytic ideas flourish in a variety of ways: through the elaboration of new metaphors, careful attention to accumulated clinical data over time, observations of child development, open discourse with extra-analytic disciplines, accommodation to shifting cultural trends. But the objective face of theory is not its only face.

To claim Winnicott's theory mirrors his subjectivity need not imply a foray into what is generally called psycho-biography. Psycho-biography tilts toward reducing creative acts and complicated people to the sum of presumed or inferred motivations. There is another way to approach the subjective face of theory making, more akin to how one might enjoy literature or its first cousin gossip, both of which are inspired by the universal impulse to discover other people's secrets. Just as with literature, it is a mistake to seek the heart of the matter *only* in the space between author and text; gossip turns idle unless one allows the material to resonate with the darker recesses of one's own "not me" experience. Wondering if Dostoyevsky really wanted to murder old women or if Nabokov lusted after little girls or if Kafka was really under police suspicion has its place in literary history. But it is a poor way of loving literature.

So the relationship between Winnicott's theory and subjectivity can be approached similarly to how the artist Francis Bacon hung his pictures: he liked to have glass over them so that when people look, what they see is not just a picture; they might, in fact, see a bit of themselves.

"Living just on the dream side of waking"

Within psychoanalysis, Winnicott represents a shift in emphasis from patterns of gratification, frustration, and sublimation to how meaningful and authentic is a person's experience and expression. Whereas Freud fostered a hermeneutic of suspicion—highlighting how people deceive themselves in their refusals to face reality—Winnicott believed in an unconscious search for an environment safe enough to be ourselves without compliance or shame. For Winnicott, the hope to communicate is as powerful as the wish to conceal. It was as if he was perpetually reaching for what was most alive and vital to a personal self. Winnicott's search was for a sort of experiencing that feels real (Goldman, 1993).

The notion of the real is rooted in Winnicott's belief that individuals are in a constant struggle to distinguish fantasy from fact, external from psychic reality, the world from the dream. His problem was how to develop an account of experience not boxed in by either solipsistic subjectivity or claims of objective perception. "I am implying," he once wrote to Victor Smirnoff:

> That actual experiencing does not stem directly either from the individual's psychic reality nor from the individual's external relationships. This sounds rather startling but you can perhaps get my meaning if you think of a Van Gogh experiencing, that is to say, feeling real, when painting one of his pictures, but feeling unreal in his relationships with external reality and in his private withdrawn inner life.
>
> (quoted in Rodman, 1987, p. 124)

The difficulty, Winnicott believed, is tolerating one's essential isolation without fleeing to false relationships or retreating into deleterious insulation.

Perhaps most of all, the notion of the real was Winnicott's visceral reaction to the "Nothing But" quality of certain strands of thinking where human nature is portrayed as *nothing but* the concatenation of conditioned reflexes or *nothing but* the vicissitudes of transformed animal drives or the biochemistry of the brain or the gradients of anxiety in interpersonal situations. He believed there must be more. What interests Winnicott most, what constitutes his great attractor, are nuances of aliveness—something distinct from either sexuality or self preservation—through which meaning is generated.

Because of Winnicott's need to approach things in a way that felt alive, original, and real to him, he often appears poised between the anxiety of influence and the need for company. He avoided reading the works of Ferenczi, lest he discover that he had actually stolen ideas from him. And he was reluctant to employ traditional psychoanalytic terms out of fear that they might substitute for his own thoughts. In a private letter to the American analyst David Rapport, he explains:

> I am one of those people who feel compelled to work in my own way and to express myself in my own language first; by a struggle I sometimes come around to rewording what I am saying to bring it in line with other work, in which case I usually find that my own "original" ideas were not so original as I had to think they were when they were emerging.
>
> (quoted in Rodman, 1987, letter dated October 9, 1953, pp. 53–54)

Theory served a transitional function for Winnicott, offering concepts that he reinvents in accordance with his own sensibilities. Masud Khan (1975) recalls calling one Sunday morning and urging Winnicott to read Lionel Trilling's *Freud and the Crisis of Our Culture*:

> He hid his face in his hand, paused, convulsed himself into visibility and said: "It's no use, Masud, asking me to read anything! If it bores me I shall fall asleep in the middle of the first page, and if it interests me I will start re-writing it by the end of that page."
>
> (p. 16)

Winnicott was a graceful narcissist and a natural performer. He loved people watching him conduct therapeutic consultations and displayed a fierce personalism, pride in his own inventiveness, and a concomitant fear of any inauthentic ventriloquism. Fortunately, Winnicott's "healthy" narcissism was a far cry from the dead end quality of more pathological forms in which empathy is employed to exploit or shame others. If Iris Murdoch (1999) is right that "love is the difficult realization that something other than oneself is real" (p. 203), then Winnicott had a genuine capacity to love.

While obviously blessed with a genius for lovingly entering other people's lives—in the sense of wanting other's to be themselves—Winnicott displayed little concern for how the formal structure and boundaries of analysis might serve as safeguards against potential abuses. By expanding the boundaries of permissible contact with regressed patients through "active management," he incensed more traditionally minded colleagues.

Refusing to define psychoanalysis based on frequency or regularity of sessions, he instead believed in "psychoanalysis on demand" (Winnicott, 1977, p. xv) in which his motto was often: "how little need be done?" (Winnicott, 1962, p. 166). At times, Winnicott went so far as to imply that psychoanalysis was not *what* was done but *who* was doing it (Winnicott, 1958, p. 115).

Winnicott offered tea to patients, sought one out in a public restaurant to change an appointment, had his secretary transport another to his vacation home, and even gently rocked a patient's head. He was late to appointments. He paid the tram fare for distressed families to bring their children to appointments at Paddington Green, which he nicknamed a "psychiatric snack-bar." He brought mentally ill people to live in his house while he paid colleagues for their treatment. A visitor once observed Winnicott shouting advice across a crowded room to a mother whom he had merely overheard having a discussion with another woman (E. Trist, personal communication). Winnicott often agreed to see children on an irregular basis, rather than transfer them to more available therapists. A psychiatric social worker remarked: "It is as if he felt that an ounce of Winnicott was worth a pound of pedestrian psychotherapy." As a result, at least some of the children were sorely "short-changed" (K. Rees, personal communication).

From a contemporary vantage point, Winnicott's approach might seem highly unconventional. But, it should be remembered, he worked for years before social services were introduced through England's National Health Service. His "method" was also a natural outgrowth of his Methodist upbringing, which emphasized *acts* of Christian charity. But it is also true that Winnicott was seen as an "odd" and "self-absorbed," if not downright eccentric, loner who could be quite difficult (Grolnick, 1990, p. 12). One colleague described a session at an International Congress chaired by Winnicott. As someone presented a paper, Winnicott put his head down on the table, his eyes shut. When the speaker finished, Winnicott did not move. An awkward silence filled the room and he remembers thinking that Winnicott was dead. Suddenly, Winnicott sat up as if nothing at all had happened (cited in Clancier and Kalmanovitch, 1987, p. 133).

When Evelyne Kestemberg met him in Stockholm in 1963, he appeared to have an "unconventional side" that, to her, seemed "strange." Watching him cross a street oblivious to oncoming traffic, she recalls a sense of fright he would be run over. "I think the drivers saw that he was not looking," says Kestemberg, "for indeed he gave the impression that he was not looking, as if he were moving in a world of his own" (Clancier and Kalmonovitch, 1987, p. 127).

Shortly before his death, Winnicott confessed "he had been living for many years" in a space that was "*just on the dream side of waking and yet was not dream material*" (Winnicott, 1989, p. 201, emphasis added). And that his struggle in this regard might obviously be difficult for others to bear. "I have this need to talk," he said:

> as though no one had ever examined the subject before, and of course this can make my words ridiculous. But I think you can see in this my own need to make sure I am not buried by my theme . . . Evidently, I must be always fighting to feel creative . . .
>
> (Winnicott, 1986, p. 41)

It was probably inevitable that Winnicott's disposition would alienate some along the way. Charles Rycroft, for example, describes him as a "crypto-prima donna" (Grosskurth, 1986, p. 399). Michael Balint, feeling personally slighted, voices in a private letter what many felt:

> Perhaps I ought to say here that this has happened several times during our friendship. You emphasized on more than one occasion that "though"—(I quote here from memory)—"Ferenczi and Dr. Balint have said all these many years ago, here I am not concerned with what they said," or, "I have not had time to read that but I shall ask the Honorary Librarian to fill this gap," etc. Of course, in this way you always have the audience laughing and on your side—no-one among us likes to read boring scientific literature and if somebody of your stature admits it in public, he can be certain of his success . . . Your way of expressing your ideas forces one into the position of either saying "this is splendid and entirely new" or of remaining silent.
>
> (quoted in Rudnytsky, 1991, p. 86)

Similarly, Elizabeth Spillius, commenting on Winnicott's "self-centeredness," concluded rather unsympathetically that "in spite of his talent, he was more devoted, more in love . . . with himself than with psychoanalysis."

From a different angle of vision, the "narcissistic" qualities that drew the ire of colleagues can be appreciated as touching upon Winnicott's most profound theoretical concerns: how do people manage the difficulties inherent in contact with reality? How do we live with the terror of our essential aloneness, and the part of ourselves that cannot, indeed must not, communicate with the outside world? What is involved in an individual finding and accepting "externality," separating out, putting a psychological distance between oneself and an object? What happens when the archaic need to feel oneself the "creator of the world" is prematurely thwarted? Can one move from the world of "subjective objects" to the world of "objects objectively perceived" without undue loss of personal vitality?

Playing with reality

There was a "great air of freedom" about Winnicott (Clancier and Kalmanovitch, 1987, p. 133). Betty Joseph called him "a bit of a Peter Pan" (Grosskurth, 1986, p. 399) and others use the word "pixie" to describe him. Winnicott said on more than one occasion that if he hadn't turned to psychoanalysis as a profession, he would have liked to have been a comic in a music hall. Late in life, he would ride his bicycle with his feet on the handlebars and drive his car with his head through the roof and a walking stick on the accelerator. When he was 71 years old, his cycling behavior brought a warning from the Metropolitan Police about his infringements of important traffic regulations (Rudnytsky, 1989, p. 347).

In a visit to New York before her death in 1984, Clare Winnicott told Simon Grolnick (1990) how she and her husband often ended up playing on the floor together (p. 15). She recalls him presenting her with a new squiggle drawing every morning at breakfast. If they were separated, she received one in the mail. A visitor staying at their house one weekend said to her:

> "You and Donald play, don't you?" So I said, "Do we? I have not thought of it in that way." He said: "Oh, yes you do. You play with me. You play with all kinds of things. My wife and I, we don't play." And I thought a lot about it, and I could see what he meant. We *did* play with arranging our furniture—chucking this out or—with books, with reading, with—and going out. We had our Saturdays *always* for play. . .
>
> (Winnicott, 1983, p. 5, emphasis in original)

Is it any wonder that Winnicott turned "playing" into a central theoretical concept, a sign of health, maturity, and mental well-being? That he was to assert that the capacity to play was testimony to the individual developing "a personal way of life . . . of becoming a whole human being, wanted as such, and welcomed by the world at large" (Winnicott, 1964b, p. 130)? Or that psychoanalysis could only really begin once a patient was helped to acquire the capacity to play? Play was, after all, Winnicott's personal idiom. An idiom more sensual than sexual, it retained for Winnicott the Old English connotation of taking a risk, exposing oneself to danger from someone or something. "Playing," in Winnicott's hands, is not about jocularity, fun, or amusement, but about creating psychic space to make meaningful use of what the world has to offer. For this to happen, "reality" has simultaneously to be accepted for what it is *and* rearranged in accordance with one's imaginative sensibility. Playing also implies being able to dispose of something when you've got from it what you want.

"Playing" was also shorthand for Winnicott's view of therapy as a proto-symbolic, performative activity rather than one trafficking in information exchange and insight. He was less interested in discursive symbols that *represent* meaning than he was in presentational symbols that *generate* meaning (Langer, 1942). Unconscious life was valuable, in Winnicott's view, not so much as a container of disguised, immature, and hidden meanings, but as a generative organization creating meanings and evoking new experiences. The more authentic experience seems to us, Winnicott suggests, the less deliberate it feels. It comes to us unbidden.

"I am not an intellectual," Winnicott once remarked, "and in fact I personally do my work very much from the body-ego" (Winnicott, 1960a, p. 161). A "body-ego" experience often begins with "muddle." If the inchoate muddle can be *held* in mind, gradually a meaningful and alive experience emerges. At a memorial gathering following Winnicott's death, Marion Milner (1972) commented on his capacity to tolerate and even enjoy both formless quiescence and the restive search for form:

> Over the years, when we had a gap in time and we had arranged to meet and discuss some theoretical problem, he would open the door and then be all over the place, whistling, forgetting something, running upstairs, a general sort of clatter, so that I would be impatient for him to settle down. But, gradually, I came to see this as a necessary preliminary for the fiery flashes of intuition that would follow, when he did finally settle down.

Milner's description mirrors Winnicott's theory of how the Self comes into being. An infant drifts from unintegrated to integrated states and back again, "not minding whether he is many bits or one whole being . . . provided that from time to time he comes together and feels something" (Winnicott, 1945, p. 150). The infant can afford *not to mind* because someone else—mother—*is minding for him.* Winnicott's theory is a virtual cartography of the precarious relationship between the environment and the psychosomatic equipment necessary to sustain alive experience.

Winnicott even articulates a principle of psychoanalytic technique based on his experience of movement from muddle to form: allowing for phases of "non-sense," when no thread of material should be analyzed because what is happening is the preliminary chaos that precedes the creative process. Muddle is not necessarily the expression of conflict, but the necessary formlessness out of which the self, *if held in time*, creates something real.

Home is where he starts from

Born on April 7, 1896, in the provincial area of Plymouth in the West Country, England, Winnicott was the youngest and only boy of three children. The sisters, Violet and Cathleen, were five and six years older. Frederick, his father, was a merchant who, together with a sibling, owned and operated a prosperous business known as Winnicott Brothers. Frederick was chairman of the local chamber of commerce, served as mayor, and eventually knighted. A man of old-fashioned quiet dignity, the few available photographs show him overdressed with a big waxed mustache.

The Winnicott estate was large, lively, and bustling. There was a large garden, an orchard, a croquet lawn, a tennis court, a pond, and high trees enclosing the estate. Young Donald spent much time alone in the branches of one particular tree or else frequenting the kitchen. His mother complained that he spent more time with the cook than with the rest of the family. Even as an adult, whenever Winnicott traveled he would invariably be drawn to seek out the hotel kitchen. Across the road was a second large Winnicott household belonging to his paternal uncle Richard, his wife, and five children. The eight cousins spent many hours together.

The extended Winnicott household—a family apparently blessed with a generally cheerful disposition—were people whose confidence was rooted in relative prosperity and a sense of belonging. Proud of being from Devon, they were so much an integral part of the land and community that a village was named after them. A consistent line can be drawn from these relatively benign social circumstances to Winnicott's belief in natural processes. Unlike many psychoanalysts, Winnicott was never an outsider within his culture. He displays neither the determined struggle for success and acclaim of the self-made man extricating himself from a social class, nor the anxious longings or willful assimilation characteristic of the immigrant.

Peter Rudnytsky (1989) points out that Winnicott's position within the family resembled Freud's description of the son who "has been his mother's undisputed darling" and "retains throughout his life the triumphant feeling, the confidence in success, which not seldom brings actual success along with it" (p. 334). Winnicott's basic sense of security, which he later described theoretically as the "capacity for faith," was born in this early web of loving relationships.

Winnicott (1960b) obviously drew on his own experience when he wrote about how "children find in security a sort of challenge, a challenge to them to prove that they can break out" (p. 30). Elsewhere (Winnicott, 1960c), he claimed that healthy development requires:

> A steady progression, that is to say, a well-graduated series of iconoclastic actions, each in the series being compatible with the retention of an unconscious bond with the central figures or figure, the parents or the mother.
>
> (p. 92)

Winnicott may just as well have been describing his own position within the "family" of the British Society!

At age 13, he was overheard using the curse word "drat." According to his unpublished autobiographical fragments, Winnicott's father "looked pained as only he could look" and then blamed his mother "for not seeing to it that I had decent friends" (C. Winnicott, 1989). On the spot, Sir Frederick decided to send Donald away to boarding school. "So," wrote Winnicott, recalling the incident:

> My father was there to kill and be killed, but it is probably true that in the early years he left me too much to all my mothers. Things never quite righted themselves.
>
> (p. 8)

Winnicott is referring here to the fact that not only was his father a somewhat distant figure preoccupied with public affairs, but that he was the only boy with two older sisters, a nanny to whom he was very attached, a sometime governess, and another aunt living in the house a lot of the time.

A criticism frequently levied at Winnicott is that he underemphasizes sexual fantasy and ignores the role of father in development. This criticism is, at times, somewhat overstated, given the nature of the particular material Winnicott chose to elucidate. After all, Winnicott was invested in making a genuine contribution regarding the importance of earliest infancy. At the time of his writing, the real mother's significance was often denied, either by an exclusive focus on the technique of bodily care, which could be performed by nurses as well as by mothers, or by singular emphasis on intrapsychic libidinal gratifications. Winnicott wished to shift the focus to the emotional development of the infant as it evolved through the facilitating gestures of the caretaker. His emphasis is really more on the maternal function than on the woman as mother.

Still, there is definitely what could be called a felt deficiency on the father side and a maternal bias that permeates Winnicott's writings. Fathers and sexual identity are but small sideshows in development. Father's coming between the child and the mother is of far less interest to Winnicott than the transitional space from which the father is absent, yet, in Winnicott's (1971) words, "initially both joins and separates the baby and the mother" (p. 121).

There is evidence that Winnicott's early upbringing might have promoted some gender confusion, or at least inhibited overt sexuality. Stanley Ede, a childhood friend, suggests that his mother had some difficulty relating to him as a boy. Marion Milner reports that Winnicott told her that he was weaned early because his mother could not stand her own excitement during breastfeeding. When Winnicott gave his broadcast talks on the BBC, many radio listeners mistook his high-pitched voice for that of a woman. Neither of Winnicott's two older sisters ever married. Winnicott's own first marriage remained apparently unconsummated. And the journalist Katherine Whitehorn, in an article in the *London Observer*, even went so far as to describe Winnicott as a "Madonna" (quoted in Grosskurth, 1986, p. 233).

Deeply offended after receiving an advance copy of Whitehorn's article, Winnicott (Winnicott Correspondence, 1949–1970) shot off a letter to her confessing having difficulty reading the material "because the whole thing is highly charged emotionally for me." He was reacting, nevertheless, before having "cooled down." What gave him the "worst shock" was her introducing the word "Madonna." He felt misunderstood and insulted. "I want to say," he continued:

> That while I recognize a maternal identification in myself I think the word female identification is not something I would ever say about myself. At any rate it starts people thinking along the wrong lines; possibly it does not feel like this to you but from my point of view there is an immense difference.
>
> (Winnicott to Whitehorn, September 23, 1966)

Winnicott was always keen to distinguish the maternal from the feminine, as well as homosexual tendencies from a healthy individual's capacity to identify with the opposite sex. When consulted by a male confidant who, after the arrival of a new baby, felt confused about his own sexual identity, Winnicott wrote to him:

> There is a great difference . . . between a unified personality such as that of a man with a capacity for identification with a woman, and a similar but different thing, a male man with a split off woman self . . . I think that the study of man's identification with woman has been very much complicated by a persistent attempt on the part of psycho-analysts to call everything that is not male in a man homosexuality, whereas in fact homosexuality is a secondary matter or less fundamental and rather a nuisance when one is trying to get at man's woman identification.
>
> (Rodman, 1987, p. 155)

Whitehorn, for her part, was "amazed and saddened" by Winnicott's intense reaction to her article. "It's a sad business," she wrote back to him, "that an article in which I meant you so immensely well should have given you only pain . . ." (Whitehorn to Winnicott, undated). She was sorry he objected to the word Madonna, but felt that it was an "image word" she had used "interpretively." Referring back to her original interview notes, she found his exact words had been:

> I'm not a very masculine identified person—not homosexual, it's not the same thing, people don't always understand that . . . I'd be no good as a mother but I've got it in me to know what a mother feels.
>
> (Whitehorn to Winnicott, undated)

Despite feeling he'd be "no good as a mother," the mothering function remained his central preoccupation. Cognizant that this interest had roots that run deep, Winnicott (1957) once noted:

> I suppose that everyone has a paramount interest, a deep, driving propulsion towards something. If one's life lasts long enough, so that looking back becomes allowable, one discerns an urgent tendency that has integrated all the various and varied activities of one's private life and one's professional career. As for me, I can already see what a big part has been played in my work by the urge to find and to appreciate the ordinary good mother. Fathers, I know, are just as important . . . But for me it has been to mothers that I have so deeply needed to speak.
>
> (p. 123)

How might we account for Winnicott's "urgent tendency?" Why was it that he became so preoccupied with the role of the ordinary mother in human development?

A lingering religiosity

There is evidence that Winnicott was bound to his mother by a profound, depressive tie and that in his caring for her and others he carried within a Christlike identification. At the age of 67, Winnicott wrote a poem replete with Christian imagery and sent it to his brother-in-law, James Britton. He attached a note:

> Do you mind seeing this that hurt coming out of me. I think it had some thorns sticking out somehow. It's not happened to me before and I hope it doesn't again.

The poem is entitled "The Tree," which is perhaps a condensation of both the special tree in the Winnicotts' garden to which Donald as a child often retreated and the True Cross of Christ. Part of the poem read as follows:

> Someone touched the hem of my garment
> Someone, someone and someone.
> I had much virtue to give
> I was the source of virtue
>
> The grape of the vine of the wine
> I could have loved a woman

Mary, Mary, Mary
There was not time for loving
I must be about my father's business . . .

There were those sick of the palsy
And the blind and the maimed
And widows bereft and grieving
Women wailing for their children . . .

Mother below is weeping weeping weeping.
Thus I knew her.
Once, stretched out on her lap as now on dead tree
I learned to make her smile, to stem her tears
to undo her guilt, to cure her inward death.
To enliven her was my living . . .

The sins of the whole world weigh less than this
Woman's heaviness

O Glastonbury
Must I bring even those thorns to flower?
Even this dead tree to leaf?
(quoted in Rodman, 2003, pp. 289–291)

One of Winnicott's primary interests as a clinician was in how infants and young children with depressed mothers sacrifice their own development to "look after the mother's mood." They would, as Winnicott wrote in his poem, make a living out of enlivening her.

During a time he was suffering in his first marriage, Winnicott left an assemblage of matches in Marion Milner's office, bent into the shape of Christ on the Cross. And years earlier, after first discovering Freud's writing, he wrote to his sister Violet, "I shall probably be accused of blasphemy if I say that Christ was a leading psychotherapist" (quoted in Rodman, 1987, p. 3). This abiding Christlike identification, filtered through the lens of Wesleyan Methodism, is a little noted aspect of Winnicott's sensibility.

"I did not meet the cultural life (except in the form of an evangelical religion)," Winnicott once said, "until I was at public school" (Winnicott, 1989, p. 508). Raised a Methodist, his home was a 10 minute walk from the church. The family was thought of as "leading lights in the church" (C. Winnicott, 1983), his father acting as treasurer and singing in the choir. Winnicott attended the Methodist church regularly at Cambridge before the war. Later, he joined the Anglican Church, to which his first wife belonged. Sometime around the age of 27, he was even confirmed (C. Winnicott, 1983, p. 3). Although Winnicott's actual church attendance gradually dropped off in his adult years, he retained a "lingering religiosity" (Goldman, 1993) and remained a "believing skeptic" (Rudnytsky, 1989, p. 332). Until the end of his life, Winnicott was often heard humming and singing Methodist hymns.

In his autobiographical notebook, Winnicott gives us a glimpse of his religious upbringing when he writes:

> My father had a simple (religious) faith and once when I asked him a question that could have involved us in a long argument he just said: read the Bible and what you find there will be the true answer for you. So I was left, thank God, to get on with it myself.
>
> (C. Winnicott, 1989, p. 8)

And in a talk given to the Christian Teamwork Institute of Education, he noted:

> Brought up as a Wesleyan Methodist, I suppose I just grew up out of church religious practice, and I am always glad that my religious upbringing was of a kind that allowed for growing up out of.
>
> (Winnicott, 1968, pp. 142–143)

Although Winnicott speaks of growing up out of religious *practice*, he never refers to abandoning everything associated with a religious outlook. Indeed, Wesley's Methodism permeates the Winnicottian sensibility. Unlike Calvin, who sought to *reform* Christianity, John Wesley aimed to *enliven* it. Worship, Wesley believed, should be not only liturgical, but also spontaneous, including extemporaneous prayer. His emphasis was on the experience of God's loving imminence and involvement—His holding presence—not His sovereignty. The heart of religion, according to Wesley, lies in a direct personal relationship with God, not the authority of priests or Pope. Just as Winnicott staked out an "independent" position within the British Society, Wesley argued for tolerance for differences of conviction regarding theological disputes. In the Wesleyan tradition, there is even a notion of spiritual growth that parallels Winnicott's developmental model: the individual is born with an essential inner goodness, rather than original sin. Spiritual maturation is driven by an inclination to mature that culminates in a capacity for concerned "connection." Having grown up within the atmospheric conditions of this church, it is easy to see how Winnicott would be predisposed to a sensibility that emphasized the personal and spontaneous in human nature, a non-dogmatic attitude toward theory, the practical outworking of faith in civic action, and mutuality in the therapeutic alliance.

John Wesley strove to make his work accessible to the common man without trying to forcibly convert him. As he said in one of his sermons:

> I design plain truth for plain people: therefore, of set purpose, I abstain from all nice and philosophical speculations; from all perplexed and intricate reasonings; and, as far as possible, from even the show of learning, unless in sometimes citing the original Scripture. I labour to avoid all words which are not easy to be understood, all which are not used in common life; and, in particular, those kinds of technical terms that so frequently occur in Bodies of Divinity.
>
> (quoted in Phillips, 1988, p. 24)

An echo of Wesley's belief that the fundamentals of doctrine can be communicated in simple language devoid of technical jargon can be found in Winnicott's lectures before lay audiences. As early as 1919, after first reading *The Interpretation of Dreams*, he wrote to his sister Violet:

> May I explain to you a little about this method which Freud has so cleverly devised for the cure of mind disorders? I am putting this all extremely simply. If there is anything which is not completely simple for anyone to understand I want you to tell me because I am now practising so that one day I shall be able to help introduce the subject to English people so that who runs may read.
>
> (Rodman, 1987, p. 2)

A psychoanalyst in the making

Winnicott never felt like a "proper doctor." He "snagged" his License of the Royal Academy of Physicians at a time when one didn't need a medical degree to practice in Britain. But he was also glad to pursue his own course, since it was common practice among doctors to literally not allow their patients to talk. He became a "children's doctor" before pediatrics became an established profession. He was also the first man ever to qualify as a child psychoanalyst.

Straddling disciplines, Winnicott saw himself as a "pediatrician who has swung to psychiatry, and a psychiatrist who has clung to pediatrics" (Winnicott, 1948, p. 157). Pediatrics strengthened Winnicott's conviction that there are natural processes that should not be interrupted. Life's roots (the word "root" appears frequently in his writing) are organic, not calculated or contrived. Children, he concluded, cannot be made to develop; at best, they can be provided with a relatively unobtrusive but supportive setting in which to flourish. "We cannot even teach them to walk," he once wrote to an anthropologist working in Tanzania, "but their innate tendency to walk at a certain age needs us as supporting figures" (Rodman, 1987, p. 186). Winnicott had great faith—perhaps exaggerated—in the "silent integrative forces" of natural growth processes.

Watching what mother and baby did together informed Winnicott's understanding of what went on inside baby's mind. He transformed concrete observations into potent metaphors: *holding*, *handling*, *object presenting*, and *transitional space* are all rooted in concrete phenomena observed in child-parent interactions. Noticing infants instinctively withdraw as impatient midwives shove mother's breast into their mouth led him to see the delicate initiation of breastfeeding as including the infant's need to "create" the breast.

Nevertheless, it was psychoanalysis, not pediatrics, that most deeply informed Winnicott's understanding of children. The year he received his first appointment at the Queen's Hospital and Paddington Green was also the year he undertook a personal analysis with James Strachey. Analysis enabled Winnicott to see children as real people rather than as merely anatomic or somatic beings. As he later recalled:

> It was only through analysis that I became gradually able to see a baby as a human being. This was really the chief result of my first five years of analysis, so that I've been extremely sympathetic with any pediatricians or anybody who can't see babies as human, because I absolutely couldn't however I used to try.
>
> (Winnicott, 1967, p. 574)

Winnicott underwent two extensive personal analyses: the first with James Strachey from 1923 to 1933, and the second with Joan Riviere from 1933 to 1938. At the age of 27, he contacted Ernest Jones, who then put him in contact with Strachey. Psychoanalysis at that time had a terrible reputation as a refuge for witch doctors and tricksters (Kahr, 2016). In recalling his consultation with Jones, Winnicott (Winnicott Correspondence, undated) described himself as a "rather inhibited young man asking whether anything could be done about it"—possible shorthand for sexual difficulties. Winnicott also described a "serious symptom": his larynx would follow sounds that he heard, particularly the voice of someone talking to him."To some extent," he noted late in life, "I always listen with my throat" (Winnicott, 1963a, p. 83). This is a striking symptom given how the illusory boundary between inside and outside became one of his central theoretical preoccupations. It also captures how receptivity to others readily heightens vulnerability to impingements.

Winnicott enters analysis the year he marries his first wife, Alice Taylor, a marriage troubled from the outset. A woman of considerable charm and talent, Alice Taylor was also high-strung and nervous. According to some accounts, she suffered from significant psychiatric disturbance. Masud Khan once made the claim that "taking care of her took all of his [Winnicott's] youth" (quoted in Clancier and Kalmanovitch, 1987, p. xvi).

Although later in life Winnicott expressed admiration for James Strachey, their relationship during the analysis was strained to a greater degree than Winnicott acknowledged publicly. Strachey's private letters to his wife, Alix, offer graphic details from the analyst's point of view. Alix Strachey was in Berlin undergoing her own analysis when her husband took Winnicott as a patient; letters were exchanged on a nearly daily basis. In these correspondences, Winnicott is portrayed as repeatedly derelict in paying for treatment. A typical example, dated, October 9, 1924, reads as follows:

> I'm beginning to doubt whether Dr. W.'ll ever stump up. He finally sent an order to someone to sell something out. And the reply was that the signature didn't stimm with the original signature when the things were bought. He thinks he vaguely remembers or he imagines it's possible, that his father signed his name for him. But I think he's altered his writing on purpose to make further delays. Meanwhile at any moment the Rates may be due and all lost.
>
> (Meisel and Kendrick, 1985, pp. 83–84)

Another letter provides a rather explicit example of how Winnicott's delinquency intrudes upon the analytic space. Referring derogatorily to Winnicott as "Winnie," Strachey writes to Alix:

> The buzzer announcing Winnie was followed by a longer pause than usual today; & I rightly guessed that he was writing the cheque on the stairs. He rushed in & pressed it upon me—die Tinte noch nass ["the ink still wet"]; threw himself upon the sofa & started off feverishly with: "There's someone whose name I keep forgetting." And then long talks about why he should forget names—other people whose names he forgets, etc. It flashed into my mind that he'd made some mistake over my name on the cheque, & I nearly risked walking over to the writing-table where I'd put it down, & looking at it. However, I restrained myself. When he'd gone, I went and looked at it: he hadn't signed it!
>
> (Meisel and Kendrick, 1985, p. 109)

While Strachey's remarks certainly expose both his countertransferential and financial pressures (Winnicott was one of only two patients in his practice at the time), they also reveal something about Winnicott. He was not only derelict in paying Strachey, but failed to pay Ernest Jones for his initial consultation and later created friction with Joan Riviere over the fee as well. There is sufficient evidence to suggest that Winnicott's handling of money in relation to his analysts mirrored a struggle he was having with his own father. When Winnicott was well into his forties, exchanges of letters reveal Sir Frederick's frustration with his son's lack of accountability in financial affairs. Indeed, Winnicott's laxness regarding financial matters may illuminate an aspect of his view of transitional phenomena as an intermediate area between primary unawareness of indebtedness and the acknowledgment of indebtedness. Throughout Winnicott's writings, there is notable privileging—in both how he writes and what he writes about—for self-generated narrative over acknowledgement of what is owed others. Emphasizing authenticity over accountability, Winnicott cared more about the unique than about the good.

Strachey's documented dismissive attitude toward Winnicott was not only because of money. Some of his letters exhibit contempt for Winnicott's preoccupation with "Rankian"-like ideas centering on his mother. Derisively labeling him a "Rankschuler," Strachey writes that

Winnicott was having fantasies of urinating on his mother at the moment of birth (Meisel and Kendrick, 1985, p. 115). In addition, he saw his mother, rather than his father, as a castrating figure. One night, Winnicott had a virulent anxiety dream in which his wife, disguised in a bear-skin, embraced him, took out a penis, and castrated him. The next night he dreamt of a pleasant encounter with his father. Strachey interpreted Winnicott's dreams as defensive—he preferred to think of his mother as castrator because he didn't want to freely express the murderous wishes he had toward his father. Winnicott's normal Oedipus complex, Strachey concluded, was more deeply repressed than the inverted one (p. 330).

Given the mismatch between his concerns and Strachey's Oedipal interpretations, it is understandable that Winnicott might look elsewhere—theoretically and personally—for relief. A theoretical emphasis on feeling real and nuances of aliveness can be understood not only as a retreat from or denial of sexuality, but as an effort to better understand himself.

Winnicott's interest in "aliveness" is also an elaboration of Ernest Jones' notion of Aphanisis. According to Jones (1927), Aphanisis, or the abolition of sexual desire, is a fear more profound than the fear of castration. Having observed men who actually wish to be castrated for erotic reasons, he concluded that "sexuality certainly does not disappear with the surrender of the penis" (pp. 439–440). Jones also described female sexuality in terms other than through the lens of the predominance of the phallus. Winnicott picks up and elaborates this forgotten thread of theory because it resonates with his own experience. Like Jones, his ideas of "aliveness" and experiences that feel real can be seen as part of a search for a common denominator other than the castration complex in the sexuality of both boys and girls. Something before and other than transgression must be in play.

Winnicott's "illness"

Winnicott's analysis with Joan Riviere showed signs of strain not unlike his earlier one with Strachey. On the one hand, Winnicott told a supervisee, Jennifer Johns, that having an analysis with Riviere was like "surfacing and seeing the surrounding territory after having been in a ditch for years" (quoted in Riviere, 1991, p. 32). But a private letter from Riviere to Winnicott three years into the treatment reveals currents of mutual dissatisfaction. The treatment began with Riviere feeling misled into agreeing to accept a reduced fee, whereas Winnicott could well afford her going price. Riviere chides herself for not having made more explicit to Winnicott "what . . . analysis can do and what it cannot, and also what the necessary conditions for it are." She notes they are "working at cross-purposes" and suggests they "put an end to the present tacit assumption on which we have been proceeding" and "have a frank & open understanding about what we both feel able to do" (quoted in Rodman, 2003, pp. 82–83).

Winnicott, for his part, bristled when Riviere remained unreceptive to his theoretical innovations. Once, during his analysis, he told her that he wanted to write a paper on "the classification of the environment" and Riviere "just wouldn't have it" (Winnicott, 1967, p. 576). He privately told John Padel at dinner one evening:

> I said to my analyst, "I'm almost ready to write a book on the environment." She said to me, "You write a book on the environment and I'll turn you into a frog!" Of course she didn't use those words, you understand, but that's how what she did say came across to me.
>
> (Padel, 1991, p. 336)

Winnicott (1967) claimed it took a long time before he "could recover from her reaction" (p.576).

The pattern continued well after treatment ended. Winnicott was particularly hurt by Riviere's insistence he use Klein's language if he wanted a paper of his included in a collection she was editing. From Riviere's point of view, Winnicott's disagreement with Klein and insistence on stating theory in his own language were symptomatic of personal difficulties. She felt he was struggling too hard to be his own real self. She saw this as a "block" in him and did not hesitate to tell him so (Rodman, 1987, p. 94).

Meanwhile, Winnicott cringed at how the "Kleinians," a term he coined, were edging toward a closed system demanding compliance. He was appalled reading the introduction Riviere wrote in which she claimed Klein's theory constituted a fully integrated theory that "takes account of all psychical manifestations, normal and abnormal, from birth to death and leaves no unbridgeable gulfs" (Rodman, 2003, p. 409). Feeling this left no space for him, Winnicott wrote Klein warning that her genuine contribution was being turned into an "'ism' which becomes a nuisance" (Rodman, 1987, p. 37). Psychoanalysis becomes a "dead language," Winnicott told Klein, if people aren't allowed to express what they discover in their own way (p. 34).

Winnicott acknowledged his insistence on his own idiom might very well be "annoying" to others. But he felt let down by Riviere, as he had in his analysis with her:

> I think that I was wanting something which I have no right to expect from your group, and it is really of the nature of a therapeutic act, something which I could not get in either of my two long analyses, although I got so much else. There is no doubt that my criticism of Mrs. Riviere was not only a straightforward criticism based on objective observation but also it was coloured by the fact that *it was just exactly here that her analysis failed with me.*
>
> (p. 34, emphasis added)

Winnicott recognized there was something potentially positive to be gleaned from his subjective struggle. "This matter which I am discussing touches the very root of my own personal difficulty," he tells Klein:

> *So that what you see can always be dismissed as Winnicott's illness, but if you dismiss it in this way you may miss something which is in the end a positive contribution.* My illness is something which I can deal with in my own way and it is not far away from being the inherent difficulty in regard to human contact with external reality.
>
> (Rodman, 1987, p. 37, emphasis added)

It certainly appears Winnicott felt his analyses "failed" him precisely in the realm of what it means to have contact with reality without undue sacrifice of personal vitality. The environment plays a vital role in the delicate and slippery area between subjective and objective objects. "Ideas, like the Word," Winnicott says alluding to his religious upbringing:

> Can fall on stony ground, or they can be received into good soil and so bear fruit. An original idea needs an audience, and the good audience consists of those who have already had the idea; they are glad to find it formulated, and they are angry, too, that a chance for claiming priority has been missed. Thus originality is tricky to assess and to attribute, and *each originator is to some extent a copyist.*
>
> (Winnicott, 1963b, p. 478, emphasis added)

Winnicott's strength as an innovator emerges from his struggle to understand his own propensity toward illusion. He wanted, and perhaps needed, to carry the work of his own analyses further than the point to which his own analysts could get him. Until his death, in 1971, his search continued for self and cure.

References

Clancier, A. and Kalmanovitch, J. (1987). *Winnicott and Paradox: From Birth to Creation*. London: Tavistock.

Goldman, D. (1993). *In Search of the Real: The Origins and Originality of D.W. Winnicott*. Northvale, NJ: Jason Aronson.

Grolnick, S. (1990). *The Work and Play of Winnicott*. Northvale, NJ: Jason Aronson.

Grosskurth, P. (1986). *Melanie Klein: Her World and Her Work*. New York: Alfred. A. Knopf.

Jones, E. (1927). "Early Development of Female Sexuality." In *Papers on Psycho-Analysis*, 5th edition. London: Bailliere, Tindall, & Cox, 1950.

Kahr, B. (2016). *Tea with Winnicott*. London: Karnac Books.

Khan, M. (1975). "Introduction to D.W. Winnicott." In *Through Pediatrics to Psychoanalysis*. New York: Basic Books, pp.11–48.

Langer, S. (1942). *Philosophy in a New Key*. Cambridge, MA: Harvard University Press.

Meisel, P. and Kendrick, W., Eds. (1985). *Bloomsbury/Freud: The Letters of James and Alix Strachey, 1924–1925*. New York: Basic Books.

Milner, M. (1972). "Dr. Winnicott Memorial Meeting." *British Institute of Psycho-Analysis*. January 19, 1972, London.

Murdoch, I. (1999). *Existentialists and Mystics: Writings on Philosophy and Literature*. New York: Penguin Books.

Padel, J. (1991). "The Psychoanalytic Theories of Melanie Klein and D.W. Winnicott and Their Interaction in the British Society of Psychoanalysis." *The Psychoanalytic Review*, 78: 325–345.

Phillips, A. (1988). *Winnicott*. Cambridge, MA: Harvard University Press.

Riviere, J. (1991). *The Inner World and Joan Riviere: Collected Papers, 1920–1958*. Ed. A. Hughes. London: Karnac.

Rodman, F.R., Ed. (1987). *The Spontaneous Gesture: Selected Letters of D.W. Winnicott*. Cambridge, MA: Harvard University Press.

Rodman, F.R. (2003). *Winnicott: Life and Work*. New York: Perseus Books.

Rudnytsky, P.L. (1989). "Winnicott and Freud." *Psychoanalytic Study of the Child*, 44: 331–350.

Rudnytsky, P.L. (1991). *The Psychoanalytic Vocation: Rank, Winnicott, and the Legacy of Freud*. New Haven, CT: Yale University Press.

Winnicott, C. (1983). "Interview with Dr. Michael Neve, June, 1983." D.W. Winnicott Correspondence. Archives of Psychiatry, New York Hospital-Cornell Medical Center.

Winnicott, C. (1989). "D.W.W.: A Reflection." In *Psychoanalytic Explorations*. Cambridge, MA: Harvard University Press, pp.1–18.

Winnicott Correspondence (1949–1970). Courtesy of Archives of Psychiatry, New York Hospital-Cornell Medical Center.

Winnicott, D.W. (1945). "Primitive Emotional Development." In *Collected Papers: Through Paediatrics to Psycho-Analysis*. New York: Basic Books, 1975, pp.145–156.

Winnicott, D.W. (1948). "Paediatrics and Psychiatry." In *Collected Papers: Through Paediatrics to Psycho-Analysis*. New York: Basic Books, 1975.

Winnicott, D.W. (1957). "The Mother's Contribution to Society." In *Home Is Where We Start From: Essays by a Psychoanalyst*. Ed. C. Winnicott, R. Shepherd, and M. Davis. New York: W.W. Norton, 1986, pp. 123–127.

Winnicott, D.W. (1958). "Child Analysis in the Latency Period." In *The Maturational Processes and the Facilitating Environment*. London: Hogarth Press.

Winnicott, D.W. (1960a). "Counter-Transference." In *The Maturational Processes and the Facilitating Environment*. London: Hogarth Press.

Winnicott, D.W. (1960b). "On Security." In *The Family and Individual Development*. London: Routledge, 1989, pp. 30–33.

Winnicott, D.W. (1960c). "The Family and Emotional Maturity." In *The Family and Individual Development*. London: Routledge, 1989, pp. 88–96.

Winnicott, D.W. (1962). "The Aims of Psycho-Analytical Treatment." In *The Maturational Processes and the Facilitating Environment*. London: Hogarth Press.

Winnicott, D.W. (1963a). "Two Notes on the Use of Silence." In *Psychoanalytic Explorations*. Cambridge, MA: Harvard University Press, pp. 81–86.

Winnicott, D.W. (1963b) "Review of the Non-Human Environment by Harold Searles." In *Psychoanalytic Explorations*. London: Karnac, 1989.

Winnicott, D.W. (1964a). "C.G. Jung: Review of *Memories, Dreams, Reflections*." In *Psychoanalytic Explorations*. Cambridge, MA: Harvard University Press, pp. 482–492.

Winnicott, D.W. (1964b). *The Child, the Family, and the Outside World*. Harmondsworth: Penguin.

Winnicott, D.W. (1967). "Postscript: D.W.W. on D.W.W." In *Psychoanalytic Explorations*. Cambridge, MA: Harvard University Press, 1989, pp. 569–582.

Winnicott, D.W. (1968). "Children Learning." In *Home Is Where We Start From: Essays by a Psychoanalyst*. Ed. C. Winnicott, R. Shepherd, and M. Davis. New York: W.W. Norton, 1986, pp. 142–149.

Winnicott, D.W. (1971). "The Location of Cultural Experience." In *Playing and Reality*. New York: Penguin.

Winnicott, D.W. (1977). *The Piggle: An Account of the Psychoanalytic Treatment of a Little Girl*. Madison, CT: IUP.

Winnicott, D.W. (1986). *Home Is Where We Start From: Essays by a Psychoanalyst*. New York and London: W.W. Norton.

Winnicott, D.W. (1989). *Psychoanalytic Explorations*. Cambridge, MA: Harvard University Press.

Willoughby, R. (2005). *Masud Khan: The Myth and the Reality*. London: Free Association Books.

Chapter 7

The outrageous prince

The "uncure" of Masud Khan

Since Masud Khan's forced removal from the British Society in 1988, most psychoanalysts in America have had the luxury of appreciating Khan's writings, without necessarily being burdened with thoughts about who this man was and how he lived his life.

But recent biographical research, as well as published and unpublished accounts, reminds us how seamlessly threads of inspired genius and impaired living are sometimes woven together. These renderings of Khan's personal story—of prolific talent both expressed and squandered; of a brilliant analyst whose personal behavior makes one cringe—naturally lead us to seek some satisfying explanation.

Even in England, the memory of his transgressions—assorted boundary violations, including sexual involvement with patients and candidates, drunken brawls, outright fabrications, an arrest for assault and battery—had nearly faded until suddenly, in February 2001, a four-page expose entitled "Saving Masud Khan," appeared in the *London Review of Books*. Written by Wynne Godley (2001), a well-known economist for the British Treasury, the article was a courageous and chilling firsthand account of the indefensible abuse he suffered in his personal analysis with Khan. It opens with the words, "This is the story of a disastrous encounter with psychoanalysis which severely blemished my middle years." Disastrous indeed: during the initial consultation, Khan expressed disbelief that Godley hadn't read about him in the newspapers since he was about to marry "Svetlana Beriosova, the loveliest of the Royal Ballet's ballerinas." Khan then drove Godley home in his Armstrong Siddeley. Along the way, he asked, "'Did you never think of killing yourself?' but answered the question himself: 'You would not know whom to kill.'"

What ensued is what Godley calls "a long and fruitless battle culminating in a spiral of degradation," during which Khan violated basic rules of decency—assaulting Godley with verbal tirades, gossiping incessantly about other patients, going so far as to arrange a liaison between Godley, who was married, and a female patient who Khan claimed "would be a suitable partner" for him. Khan "induced me to take her out to lunch," writes Godley, after which "we now started meeting a trios," attending lectures, and "spending a whole evening playing poker."

Khan regaled Godley with obscene stories, always demonstrating how he had gotten the better of someone else:

> He had rescued Mike Nichols from a man with a fierce dog in New York. He had fought physically with Peter O'Toole, using a broken bottle. He had got the overflow from his lavatory to pour a jet of water onto the head of a woman who was making her car hoot in the street below . . .

"One evening," recalls Godley:

> I found myself alone with Khan and Beriosova in their flat. Both of them were drunk. They left the room separately so that I was alone for some minutes. I heard a faint moan which was repeated more loudly; the moan turned into my own name—an appeal for assistance from someone helpless and in severe pain. Going into the hall, I saw Khan, lying full length and motionless on the ground. In agony he whispered: "My wife has kicked me in the balls." . . . At the next session I observed to Khan that I might, at some stage, have to say that things had got so far out of hand that I would have to break off the analysis. His reply was that if it got that far, HE would break off the analysis "one day" before I did. So he won that trick too.

This went on for years, until Godley finally "rang up Winnicott and said, 'Khan is mad,'" to which Winnicott replied emphatically:

> "'Yes,' adding 'All this social stuff . . .' He didn't finish the sentence but he came round to our house immediately, saying that he had told Khan not to communicate with me again. As he said this, the telephone rang and it was, indeed, Khan wanting not only to speak to me but to see me, which I refused to do. And that was the end of my 'analysis.'"

I became exquisitely aware of the charged uproar to Godley's article when, in its wake, I was invited to speak at the Squiggle Foundation in London—an institution dedicated to the dissemination of Winnicott's teachings. Devotees of Winnicott were horrified at how Godley implicated Winnicott in his account. Godley claimed, for example, to overhear "a giggly joke about homosexual fellatio . . . accompanied by loud laughter" exchanged between Winnicott and Khan. Godley appeared to place more blame on Winnicott as Khan's analyst than on Khan himself. How could Winnicott have referred patients, Godley among them, to his care? How could he have advanced, supported, and protected this man? And how could Khan's supposed "fifteen years of analysis" with Winnicott done such little good?

Furthermore, colleagues at the Squiggle Foundation were outraged that the British Society responded to Godley's article by holding a "members only" closed-door session, excluding many individuals personally affected by Khan. There was clamor—especially from former patients, supervisees, and therapists organized outside the psychoanalytic establishment—for a more open and public airing of sentiment. Winnicott, they felt, was being unfairly scapegoated by the British Society so as to distract attention from living analysts who were themselves involved in inappropriate relations with students and patients. Some members of the Squiggle Foundation were troubled that Godley's version of events was being accepted without question. Their suspicion was later confirmed when Anne-Marie Sandler (2004) published an official response entitled "Institutional Responses to Boundary Violations: The Case of Masud Khan," accompanied by a commentary by Godley himself.

As a relative "outsider" from North America, I was invited to the Squiggle Foundation to offer some initial thoughts about the Khan-Winnicott relationship that might facilitate an open public discussion. Obviously, I went with a great deal of trepidation, concerned I might be "rushing in where angels fear to tread"—especially with Wynne Godley and other aggrieved patients present. But, I also thought that one way we can express our devotion to analytic work and pay tribute to Winnicott's singular contribution is by candidly and carefully examining both his and our own successes and failures.

Indeed, serious questions have been raised about how, after three prior treatments—Khan had three analysts before Winnicott, two of whom died of heart attacks during the analysis—and work with Winnicott, Khan could self-destruct the way he did. Linda Hopkins (2006), for example, in her biography of Khan, argues that Winnicott's own difficulties with aggression and major deviations from the analytic frame deprived Khan of a true experience of regression to dependence. Much of Khan's deterioration she attributes to his alcoholism, which, she argues, Winnicott failed to adequately address. Roger Willoughby (2005), another Khan biographer, also points to examples of Winnicott's flagrant collusion with Khan and failure to adequately address his destructive envy. R.J. Bacon suggests that Winnicott's notion of the "True Self" contributed to Khan's resistance to change through analysis. It "functioned as an unanalysable persecutory ideal image for Khan" that effectively rationalized his misbehavior (Bacon, personal correspondence, December, 2003). Joyce Slochower (2011) believes the Khan-Winnicott relationship was "characterized by excess and an absence of reflectivity" and that "co-constructed idealization" played a significant role in undermining the treatment (p. 10).

To say I disagree with these criticisms would be oversimplifying, for they have clear merit. It would be more accurate to state that I prefer to approach these matters from a different angle of vision. And that today, more is known about the actual parameters of Winnicott's treatment of Khan than was available to earlier critics. For example, the recent discovery of Winnicott's clinical diary indicates clearly that Khan's claim to have been in treatment with Winnicott for 15 years is simply a lie. The treatment lasted less than three years and ended years before Khan descended into the severe alcoholic stupors described by Godley. But, before I elaborate my own point of view, I have an important personal reservation I think it best to state up front.

Khan's anti-Semitic invective is repugnant to me. When I hear how he referred to Harry Karnac as a "filthy Jewish tradesman," talked about a homosexual patient as having a "dirty Jewish arse," or proudly declared his yearning to "free himself of the rigid Yiddish shackles of the so-called psychoanalysis," I confess to feeling virtually no desire to engage this man. Naturally, I could choose to relate to Khan's anti-Semitism as a symptom of projection, or identification with the racial arrogance of the British ruling class of the Raj. Alternatively, I might think about his hostility as a matter of the narcissism of small differences in which particular pleasure is found in hating immediate neighbors with whom one actually shares much in common. It may also be that Khan was giving voice to the deep strains of anti-Semitism bubbling beneath the surface among British members reacting to the "invasion" of the mostly Jewish émigrés. But for me to think about Khan in any of these ways, I would have to either detach myself or be willing to register his outpourings empathically. In this case, I acknowledge a reluctance to do either.

Having said that, I already find myself in the midst of the fray. Khan has viscerally provoked me. I am repelled, disgusted, angry. Khan has acted outrageously and I am outraged. I am incited and unforgiving for he is intelligent, erudite, insightful, and yet acts hatefully, grossly offends any sense of right or decency, forcing others to bear the brunt of his obnoxiousness. In short: he employs his considerable resources to shock, and in response I want to consign him to oblivion.

Now, what happens if I do allow myself to step outside of this destructive imaginary seesaw relationship? How then might I think about Khan's provocative self-destructiveness? How might I understand a gifted man who, after rising to such prominence, collapsed into a lonely rageful state of sickly impenetrable isolation? And can we usefully generalize from Khan's example to other people who, despite our best efforts, appear to be heading toward a private hell of their own making?

One place to begin is with outrageousness itself. There can be no doubt Masud Khan at times behaved with an intention to shock. Lacanians use the word "jouissance" to capture the rise or kick a person gets from a symptomatic way of being. I think the word fits well for the kind of pleasure Khan appears to have derived from provocative behavior. How can we understand outrageousness? Is it simply an exhibitionist transformation of hostility?

As far as I know, Khan (1986) himself is the only analyst to ever have written explicitly about outrageousness as a distinct affective state. It is not surprising that he would engage this topic. The psychological terrain we know best, after all, is that which we know from the inside out. He was a virtual Geiger counter for the insincerity, phoniness, and half-truths concealed in outrageous behavior. Earlier, Freud pointed out that demands felt to be outrageous were one of the precipitant causes of war neuroses. Shell shock was a dissociative response to an outrageous current demand. Khan looks at outrageousness developmentally, linking maternal overindulgence to a restriction in spontaneity in the child. Obsessional over-care, he argues, inhibits healthy aggression, which can be made up for through outragousness. In discussing such a patient, Khan remarks:

> He did not succeed with me, because I had been a more outrageous person in my private life. I knew all the ruses of that affect, both in private life and professionally. I was a much-cuddled child, who grew up, very precociously . . . . So he could not get the better of me.
>
> (p. 648)

From an intersubjective point of view, a crucial element of provocative outrageousness is the opportunity it affords the individual to see himself making an impression upon another. What is psychologically vital is not so much the making of the impression—the rechanneling of thwarted aggression—as the profound relief in observing the impression that one has made. Observing the impression affords the vulnerable individual a fleeting sense of substance. Like footprints in sand, the impression momentarily reassures the individual that they really do exist. We detect this in the way Khan romped through life with the self-indulgence of a wealthy playboy. He once came to an International Congress with a Habsburg Princess as his guest. They both wore riding habits and brought nearly the whole stable along with them. Glamour—which displays both vitality and decadence—is uniquely designed to generate opportunities to observe reactions. Khan might have been "overindulged" and "much-cuddled," but probably rarely really seen. Perhaps there is something akin to a psychological law: to survive psychologically in the absence of quiet recognition, one's existence needs to be noisily confirmed.

Masud Khan's outrageousness, however, was also the leading edge of a far deeper self-destructiveness. But if what I said about needing to be noisily confirmed is valid, we are, it appears, right in the heart of a paradox. How can it be that self-destructiveness preserves psychological aliveness? There is no easy answer to this question. All I can offer is the following working hypothesis: in the absence of recognition, self-destructiveness becomes a last-ditch effort to preserve a semblance of control as the illusion of the integrity of one's self collapses.

Winnicott (1963) was one of the first people to introduce us to the seemingly odd link between personal agency and the destruction of the self. Even in the infant, he argued, there exists a rather fierce morality, a willingness, sometimes through life threatening refusals to ingest food, to guard the self against threats to the elusive sense that "I AM." In his words:

> The fiercest morality is that of early infancy, and this persists as a streak in human nature that can be discerned throughout an individual's life . . . . For instance, a child of any age may feel that to eat is wrong, even to the extent of dying for the principle . . . . This leads many people who seem to be doing well eventually to end their lives which have become false and unreal; unreal success is morality at its lowest ebb.
>
> (p. 102)

In a similar vein, Eric Erikson (1959) offers the idea that some people would "rather be nobody or somebody bad, and this totally, or indeed, *dead by free choice* than be not-quite-somebody" (p. 143, emphasis in original). For Erikson, such vindictive choices can serve a restitutive function in restoring urgently required feelings of inner stability and control.

Peter Fonagy's (Fonagy et al., 1993) research suggests there is a profound difference between a "pre-reflective or physical self" that is the immediate experiencer of life, and a "reflective or psychological self" that is the internal observer of mental life. Most importantly, these two aspects of experience develop differently and exist in a rather precarious relationship to each other. Mental processes, in another language, are as vulnerable to disruption as are mental representations. This is consistent with a view put forth by Spruiell (1975), who noted that among the strands of narcissism is "the pleasure in efficient mental functioning . . . the regulation of mood . . . and . . . a sense of inner safety and reliability" (p. 590). Well-being means, among other things, experiencing oneself as *simply being*, as opposed to *being at the mercy of* one's mind.

Thus, clinicians of varying orientations appear to be converging on a similar observation: self-soothing and self-preservation do not necessarily go hand in hand. The illusion of the integrity of the self—extending or re-establishing an area of omnipotence—is sometimes guaranteed through self-destructiveness. The problem, of course, is that self-destructiveness as guardian of integrity is analogous to bloodletting; there is a race between cure and bleeding to death.

I would like to turn my attention directly now to the question of Winnicott's treatment of Khan. In doing so, I am reminded of the British historian Philip Guedalla's (2015) quip about writing biography: "Biography, like big game hunting," he said, "is one of the recognized forms of sport; and it is as unfair as only sport can be" (p. 233). That captures what I feel hazarding speculations about what went on in the treatment. There is obviously no way we can ever really know. Perhaps I am a bit of an extremist on this point, but frankly I have serious doubts about what we even know about our own analyses. Often, we make token statements fostering the illusion that we know. The best I can attempt, therefore, is to project Winnicott and Khan's experience onto the screen of my own informed imagination while avoiding the temptation to believe that I possess some privileged vantage point outside the treatment from which I can accurately judge what transpired.

Holding that in mind leads me to propose three distinct, yet overlapping, conjectures: Winnicott helped Khan enormously; Winnicott failed to "cure" him; and Masud Khan could not be helped. I will try to open these up, one at a time. Hopefully, by doing so, we can see our way into discovering how Khan and Winnicott's experience—including their mutually resonating areas of vulnerability—might have some bearing on our own.

Winnicott helped

Masud Khan, despite his tragic end, led an incredibly productive life. He was a prolific contributor to the psychoanalytic literature and a brilliant cartographer of the territory of archaic mental states. We have no way of knowing if Khan could have sustained these achievements without Winnicott's help.

I would like to cite an excerpt from Khan's diary,[1] written four months after Winnicott's death. This entry feels like one of those moments where Khan is being fairly honest with himself. It reads:

> What a difficult thing psycho-analysis is to report about to others. No, even to myself . . . . 25 years of analysis with four analysts is a long odyssey and each of them helped me, without my being able to talk to any of them significantly about myself ever . . . D.W. alone was aware of it and allowed for it . . . . It is for this reason that . . . I did succeed at three occasions to sink into my Self, be silent . . . and related to him. All these three occasions were physical . . . . He was in his chair seated and I had got off the couch and buried my head into the side of his coat. I can still hear his heart and watch beating. All else was still . . . and I was at peace. And D.W. never interpreted those three occasions. He had enabled me to reach to that point . . .
>
> (WB, May 1971)

Now, three occasions may not seem like a lot when viewed from the outside. But it appears to me that moments such as these both tethered Khan as a person and gave him a sense of what it means to care as a clinician. This is not an insignificant gift. Let me cite another excerpt, written, as far as I can tell, about two weeks after Winnicott's death:

> One of the most valuable contributions of D.W.W. has been, that he has changed a catastrophic threat of loss of object into separation anxiety. He is the first significant person in my life who had facilitated me to cope with losing him . . . without it becoming the total loss.
>
> (WB, February 6, 1971)

This, too, is no small achievement. In fact, I believe that it made life relatively bearable and productive for Khan. Winnicott appears to have offered Khan a sufficient sense of recognition so that his worst tendencies were held more or less in check for decades. By saying Winnicott held these tendencies in check, I am suggesting it is unrealistic to expect psychoanalysis to successfully inoculate a person against all future strains. Khan made numerous false claims as to the extent of his treatment with Winnicott. Sometimes, he spoke of 10 years of analysis, and sometimes of 15. Neither are anywhere near the truth. A close examination of Winnicott's appointment diaries from 1949 to 1971 indicate that Khan's five times a week analysis lasted about two and half years between 1951 and 1954. The intensive treatment ended when Khan asked Winnicott if he would be willing to treat his first wife, the dancer Jane Shore, who was severely depressed. Winnicott did not have an available hour, but agreed that Khan could give his hours to his wife. Khan did have ongoing contact with Winnicott, particularly around editorial matters, even after the formal analysis came to an end. While this may appear, from the vantage point of current practice, as "transgressive," it was actually quite common in London at the time. To give a few examples: Joan Riviere, Winnicott's second analyst, had complicated extra-analytic relations, editorial and personal, with her two analysts—Jones and Freud. Rickman, a patient of Klein's, edited some of her papers; Rickman went on to treat Khan and often had tea together with him after sessions. Winnicott's first wife, Alice Taylor, was in treatment with Clifford Scott while Scott was giving feedback to Winnicott on some of his early manuscripts. Alice's brother was in treatment with Klein even as Klein's son was in treatment with Winnicott. Ella Sharpe, Khan's first London-based analyst, showed Khan some of her papers and made social introductions for him.

Indeed, the British Society as a whole was deeply enmeshed in skeins of compromising relationships.

It appears from the available evidence that the notable deterioration in Khan's overall mental stability occurred after the treatment ended. The worst in him came out in full force in the mid-1960s after his personal relationship with Winnicott soured. In the context of Khan's mother's death, his alcoholic wife Svetlana's decision to leave him, the removal of a cancerous lung, and a doctor's mistaken verdict that he had only three to six months to live, Khan engages in a vengeful raging last-ditch effort to regain control over a diminishing sense of continuity through self-destructive drinking and attacks upon the world. If he couldn't conquer death, it seems, he vowed to defeat life.

Winnicott failed

Now Winnicott, of course, had his fair share of blunders. He even told Marion Milner that his analysis of Khan had not been properly completed. Khan wouldn't have been surprised to hear that. In response to a condolence letter following Winnicott's death, he wrote:

> [Winnicott's] genius was in his capacity to fail each of us according to our need to refuse him. If Freud had the Judaic courage to refuse cure, Dr. Winnicott had the Christian humility to take responsibility for the *uncure*. And I, as a Mohammedan, praise them both—since I am the beneficiary of each!
>
> (WB, February 9, 1971)

And in a private entry a few days earlier, Khan elaborated on the link between Winnicott's willingness to go on treating those, like himself, who stubbornly refuse what is offered and aspects of Winnicott's character. "It was most typical of his type of omnipotence," writes Khan:

> That he could never refuse those he knew would compel him to fail . . . . I know all this on my own pulse . . . . Yes, I have known all his failings

> and he never even tried to hide them . . . . He knew and allowed for the margin of weakness and error in every human individual and worked with the 3 per cent that was creative and vital.
>
> (WB, February 4, 1971)

As I imagine Winnicott and Khan together, I would like to offer some thoughts about what might have gone wrong. In his unpublished autobiographical fragments, Winnicott laments never having had a son of his own. Envisioning his own death, he writes about his difficulty dying without a son both to kill imaginatively and to survive him, that is, "to provide the only continuity that men know." It is no coincidence that Winnicott employs nearly identical language in describing, late in his life, his relationship to his own father. In his words:

> My father was there to kill and be killed, but it is probably true that in the early years he left me too much to all my mothers. Things never quite righted themselves.
>
> (quoted in C. Winnicott, 1989, p. 8)

Perhaps the tragedy of Winnicott never having had offspring of his own is that he ended up investing part of his desire for a son in Khan. And, as we know, it is as disastrous to treat our patients as children as it is to treat our children as patients. Although the relationship with Khan might have satisfied some felt need for Winnicott, it probably did little to afford him a genuine opportunity to rework internally and better integrate some of his own dissociated feelings in relation to his father.

Winnicott, of course, was certainly not the only childless analyst to form complicated relationships with patients; he was probably not even exceptional in this regard. I think this is an area we might benefit from studying in some detail. Whatever our conscious intent might be, we sometimes unconsciously use our patients as we struggle to grow or become entangled with them because of mutually resonating vulnerabilities. I am well aware of Freud and Lacan's dictum that we need to somehow "purify" our desire. But, frankly, I find that to be actually a rather odd proposition, more religious than psychoanalytic.

Given Winnicott's complicated investment in Khan, I was struck, in reading Khan's personal diary, by the relative absence of genuine grief in the entries following Winnicott's death. It reminded me of a remark

Iris Murdoch (1999) once made: "Love," she said, "is the extremely difficult realization that something other than oneself is real" (p. 203). But at the same time, Khan was clearly devastated by the loss and furious Winnicott hadn't appointed him literary executor of his estate. To the extent that Khan might not have felt particularly lovable, he needed desperately to make himself extremely valuable. Winnicott, for his part, had cultivated the illusion of Khan as natural heir. For the narcissist, the truth always comes in blows. So, in response to feeling suddenly disinherited, Khan lashed out to destroy Winnicott. If he couldn't do this in the flesh, he would do the next best thing: destroy the father's reputation. He did this both directly—by repeatedly gossiping about Winnicott's impotence, as if to say, "He's not a man, and if I'm not his son let it be known that there could never be a son!" And he also did this indirectly by his outrageous behavior, which would, of course, announce to the world that Winnicott had failed.

But when Winnicott informs us that as a result of "being left too much to all my mothers," things "never quite righted themselves," I think he is referring to more than just a felt deficiency on the father side. Winnicott had a strong inclination to self-absorption that made him, at times, oblivious to his surroundings. "I put myself in the category of people," he once confessed, who, like "optimistic tadpoles":

> Bask in a puddle in the sun, in the shallowest of waters, crowding together and amiably wriggling their tails, totally unaware that the next morning the puddle will have dried up and left them stranded.
>
> (pp. 482–483)

Or, as he acknowledged relatively late in his life:

> It suddenly dawned on me a few years ago that I had been living for many years in a kind of community that was just on the dream side of waking and yet was not dream material.
>
> (Winnicott, 1989, p. 201)

Winnicott's living "on the dream side of waking" might have contributed to his failure to help Khan tolerate being subjected to and being a subject within the regulated community of others. Khan knew Winnicott failed to help him accept disillusionment and thereby find his place among others.

It is no coincidence, therefore, that the clinical exploration of affective states involving rage and anxiety over disillusionment became central themes in Khan's writings. After all, what from the outside appears as theorizing can also be understood as tentative attempts at self-cure. Nietzsche had it right when he noted that every philosophy is "a confession on the part of its author and a kind of involuntary unconscious memoir" (quoted in Pierpont, 2002). Similarly, analysts, I believe, discover and create their theories because they in some way speak to their personal struggles. That is why Freud's staunch determination to be sane and contempt for the "weakness" of illness, Jung's inner torment and fragile sense of self, Ferenczi's wild enthusiasms and symbiotic longings, Sullivan's intense loneliness, shyness, and anxiety in the presence of other people, Winnicott's perpetual strain to keep inner and outer separate but interrelated—to give just a few examples—contributed to how each of these analysts eventually theorized about the human condition. Disturbing personal struggles brought into relief and worked through in relation to patients become symbolized as theory.

Khan, it seems, lived in perpetual dread of the ordinary, as if to say, "If I am like everybody, then I must be nobody." It is precisely around these issues that Khan and Winnicott might simply have had too much in common. Winnicott, like Khan, had a profound, somewhat compulsive, personal need to approach things in a way that felt original and real to him. Elizabeth Spillius gives expression to the annoyance felt by many, particularly among the British Kleinians, who felt put off by Winnicott:

> My response to Winnicott . . . must have been influenced by the fact that I had ten years experience of being taught by him . . . and listening to him give papers . . . . But the ten years of listening were oddly disappointing. At first we found his seminars entrancing. We felt pulled into participating in his ideas . . . . Some of us went on being entranced. I did not. I found it seductive. At times Winnicott seemed to bask in our response; at others he nearly went to sleep and seemed to find us utterly boring. First we were concerned. Is he ill? Should he be doing this? Then we thought, "If he can't be with us he shouldn't try, he should cancel the class." Later I thought that this withdrawal, whether it was illness or boredom and depression, this was really hate in the countertransference . . . . I could never quite take his ideas or his writing with full seriousness because in the background was my feeling

> about his unreliable fluctuating attention, his self-centeredness, his hurt little boy stance. I had come to feel that in spite of his talent he was more devoted, more in love . . . with himself than with psychoanalysis.

I could just as easily provide a very similar description of his behavior told from a much more loving and sympathetic point of view. Winnicott was, after all, what I would call a graceful narcissist. Fortunately, Winnicott's own narcissism remained relatively "healthy" in the sense that it did not preclude imaginatively and lovingly entering into other people's lives. Although he knew what it felt like to be ashamed, he was not crippled by mortifying humiliation. If Simone Weil (2004) is right that "the belief in the existence of other human beings as such is love" (p. 292), Winnicott, I believe, had a genuine capacity to love.

But it is worth considering how Winnicott's narcissism might have caused him to both overestimate what he could do and underestimate the difference between himself and others (Charollete Riley, personal communication, November 5, 1991). He was obviously blessed with a genius for quickly and intuitively grasping other people's core conflicts and communicating in a way the person could take in. He took it for granted that others were equally competent. As a result, he was insufficiently concerned with how the formal structure and boundaries of analysis might serve as a safeguard against potential abuses.

Winnicott's botched treatment of Khan, however, can be understood not only as a matter of ill-provided frame, but also as a failure to more fully take into account overlapping areas of mutual vulnerability. When he entered analysis at the age of 27, Winnicott suffered from what he described as a "serious symptom" in which his larynx would follow the sounds he would hear, and particularly the voice of someone talking to him. He became increasingly preoccupied with the illusory boundary between inside and outside and lived in dread that he might be trapped by either solipsistic subjectivity or the deadened claims of objective perception. As he once acknowledged publicly:

> I have this need to talk as though no one had ever examined the subject before, and of course this can make my words ridiculous. But I think you can see in this my own need to make sure I am not buried . . . . Evidently, I must be always fighting to feel creative.
>
> (Winnicott, 1986, p. 41)

From the point of view of his second analyst, Joan Riviere, the pride Winnicott took in his inventiveness, his "need to talk as though no one had ever examined the subject before," and the concomitant fear that his creativity would be stifled were all symptomatic of his personal illness. She saw this as a "block" in him and did not hesitate to tell him so (Rodman, 1987, p. 94). Winnicott ended up feeling Riviere failed him around this issue. As he wrote privately to Klein:

> This matter which I am discussing touches the very root of my own personal difficulty so that what you see can always be dismissed as Winnicott's illness, but if you dismiss it in this way you may miss something which is in the end a positive contribution. My illness is something which I can deal with in my own way and it is not far away from being the inherent difficulty in regard to human contact with external reality.
>
> (Rodman, 1987, p. 37)

Winnicott's personal "illness"—which was a source of great creative insight—might also have blinded him to more effectively handling certain aspects of Khan's character. Khan fabricated case material. He falsely claimed he was a prince. Charles Rycroft, who nicknamed Khan "the damaged Archangel," notes that those closest to him were never clear about many aspects of his past or whether what he said was true. Pearl King said he "was very skilled at confusing a story" (quoted in Cooper, 1993, p. 4). Khan, for his part, celebrated this very tendency. "All fictions," he wrote, "are true for the person who fabricates them, since they reflect an inner necessity." Indeed, Khan castigated others whose souls are deadened by privileging purported "facts." As he wrote to Zoe Dominic: "Everyone is always jibing at me for never sticking to the facts and so much of modern theater has lost the verve of imaginative truth through escaping into tape-recorder clinical realism." He liked to boast about his "style of flourishes"—exaggerations and distortions that, in departing from facts, invoke the truth.

Khan artfully described the character structure found in perversions as a collage of idolized parts of self and object that are never coherently related to each other. His chosen metaphor was life as a dream. Although a man of immense talent, he was notorious for resorting to ploys. He lost an opportunity to become editor of the *International Journal* because of his lying. In a letter to a friend, he acknowledged suffering from "a delusion of sincerity." The thrust of his theoretical contributions focused on matters of authenticity and the privacy of self. Following Helene Deutsch's (1942) notion of the "as-if" personality, he writes that you don't have to feel much about others as long as you imitate them. The convergence of these aspects of behavior, theoretical interest, and character suggests, in my opinion, an abiding personal struggle to distinguish appearance from reality.

Current developmental research is helping illuminate how the emergence of self-reflexivity coincides with the emergence of pretend play. Prior to age 4 or 5, children have difficulty grasping the distinction between how things look and how they actually are, and in understanding the subtleties of secrecy and lying. A 3-year-old does not yet have the capacity to appreciate the merely representational nature of ideas and feelings. He operates in what Fonagy (Fonagy et al., 2002) has referred to as a mode of "psychic equivalence," behaving as though his own and others' thoughts faithfully mirror the real world. It is only in the fourth and fifth year of life that a child begins to acknowledge that things may not be what they appear to be, that another person may perceive external reality differently, that a person can hold different beliefs at different times. We now understand that the failure to make this developmental leap is related to confusion between the mind of the other and the mind of the self.

There is evidence to suggest that Khan might have been particularly vulnerable in this regard. Khan was the second child of his father's fourth marriage, the offspring of a 76-year-old Pakistani feudal lord and a 17-year-old illiterate singing-and-dancing girl with an illegitimate child. By his own account, he was a "weakly child, always ailing," who was shy, phobic, and, to make things worse, suffered from a minor deformity of his left ear. Judith Cooper (1993), a former patient of Khan's, reports that he told her that "his culture was very cruel about any sort of physical deformity" (p. 10). For three years, between the ages of 4 and 7, Khan was an elective mute. In his diary, Khan makes frequent reference to his intrusive mother's "incessant chatter" and his own response as constituting a "manic expertise to drown her voiceless chatter and muttering in my head." Writing to Sybil Stoller, he claimed to have learned French in an attempt to relieve himself of the "chatter in my mind of my mother's voice."

As late as 1963, Khan sent an unpublished poem to his friend, Zoe Dominic. It reads:

> I cannot hear.
> I cannot hear you,
> Mother.
> Not your wailing or chanting,
> Or the whisperings of maids around you.
> The dead leaves are crumpled
> And stuffed in my ears.
> I heard the shriek,
> knew it was you,
> killed it, mother.
> My mad inconsolable mother.
> I killed your voice insisting in my ears.
>
> I cannot hear.
> What I touch and see is mine,
> Mother,
> And I cannot share.
> I cannot hear.
> Mother.
> Mother.
> Mother.

Khan's profound psychic retreat and detachment—the need to escape from the shrieking, mad, inconsolable mother—contributed to his lifelong tendency toward self-absorption and confabulation. Winnicott—who has taught us more about the positive life-enhancing value of illusion than any other analyst—might have been insufficiently attentive to how Khan was flailing about in its potentially destructive undertow. While exquisitely attuned to vulnerability and the positive value of illusion, Winnicott erred in regard to accountability.

Khan could not be helped

It is not surprising that toward the end of his life, Khan grew increasingly disillusioned with the psychoanalytic enterprise. "One never changes at the root," he wrote privately to a friend:

> But one drastically rearranges oneself, given will, motivation and helpful circumstances from the outside (as analysts we grossly and

> grievously neglect or cussedly disregard that). I would go so far as to say that, to recover from an ailment like mine, reality is destiny.

I imagine Winnicott knew Khan was engaged, as Robert Stoller once put it, in "a prolonged fuck with death," which might be simply another language for describing Khan's hypomanic temperament, or what Keats once described as being "half in love with easeful death." It is fruitless to try to tease apart what part of this was constitutional and what part environmental. Attachment to people and chemical dependency are even mediated by the same neuroendocrine system. Khan obviously suffered enormously from a profound sense of powerlessness vis-à-vis his own mind. And it is this sense of helplessness that constitutes the cumulative psychic trauma that seemed to plague him. Hyper-reactive to the presence of others, he was also easily dislocated by their absence. Put differently: he was vulnerable to shock. To protect himself, he clung ever so tenaciously to the precarious pretense of self-sufficiency. It is not so much that relationships, in this state, are unsatisfying; it is that the dim recognition of the need for any relationship at all engenders reactive rage. One cannot make full use of analysis if one desperately needs not to need. As Khan confessed in one diary entry:

> There are some of us who cannot share our woes with others. This is neither conceit nor arrogance, but a very personal and private stance of stammer . . . . This is why I made such meager use of analysis: Some of us can find our own comfort only from within our own disciplined silences.
>
> (WB, June 28, 1970)

In another language, Khan displayed an insouciant disregard for others. And he even knew that his hateful indifference ripped through the affections of all those who cared the most about him. As he wrote to Robert Stoller, one of the few people who refused to give up on him:

> I am aware of my profound debt to my colleagues who have put up with all the antic and bizarre provocativeness of my temperament and character. I can now see that all these wild antics which antagonized most of my colleagues were almost a magical way of keeping myself reminded that I was not where I was . . . . It is impossible for anybody outside to relate to a person who is hiding himself.
>
> (Letter to R. Stoller, January 30, 1970)

Perhaps the greatest tragedy for Khan was that he could never allow himself the opportunity to benefit more fully from what analysis had to offer. "People like me," he once confessed, "are too private to be analysed." Despite being endowed with a supple imagination and reflective capacities, he apparently could not bear to feel himself a patient. That is why Khan's marvelously astute insights about himself—each of which has the appearance of a turning point—invariably turn out to be cul-de-sacs.

Instead of allowing himself an experience of dependence in analysis, Khan secured preferential patronage through cultivating luminaries. He did this with each of his quite experienced British analysts—Ella Sharpe and John Rickman—before he did it with Winnicott. A mentorship and intellectual lieutenancy masqueraded for a true analytic relationship. What Bion termed "knowing *about* psychoanalysis" substituted for being *in* analysis. There is a cautionary tale here, perhaps an occupational hazard. As Ralph Greenson once noted:

> People who seek psychoanalysis for . . . training . . . should be considered resistant and in need of preparatory psychotherapy. It is my contention that only one who feels himself a patient can be analyzed beyond a certain depth. Only such a person will be willing to try to enter and work in the analytic situation.
>
> (Greenson, 2016, p. 360)

It is tempting to entertain the ironic possibility that Khan's only hope would have been if he had never been interested in becoming an analyst himself. Then, perhaps, he might have been able to have a relationship in which he was a patient and only a patient, rather than a valuable and exploitable apprentice.

Masud Khan had a precocious mind. But a precocious mind is no substitute for the smooth intermingling of the psyche-soma. Insights of the reflective self never adequately compensate for impaired relationships involving the pre-reflective self. Khan knew this about himself. Winnicott had told him as much. As he wrote in a diary entry:

> I have never been able to share my Self with others through language spoken. And yet language has enabled me to know others—and often beyond my own insight into them. D.W.W. often used to say: "You speak wiser than you know." And that is true.
>
> (WB, May 5, 1971)

Although Winnicott might not have been able to alleviate this problem for Khan, he managed to creatively use what he sensed to fashion an important clinical insight: the child deprived of sufficient early experiences of finding his or her own mind in the mind of a devoted Other is left without a personalized, authentic, and vitalized sense of self. If the child is particularly bright, the outcome is often a precocious inauthentic pseudo-vitality that compensates for mother's shortcomings. As adults, such people—and there can be no doubt that Khan was one of them—are inordinately prone to internal collapse.

Despite the tragic dimension to Khan's wasted potential and acute vulnerability, I imagine Winnicott approached the work with a certain acceptance that there was really little he could do. Perhaps, he figured, if he can't cure Khan, he would at least be good to him, particularly as he grew older and weaker himself following his own repeated heart attacks. From the outside, one is tempted to shout "collusion." Khan himself even referred once to Winnicott as "my most generous yet abominable exploiting accomplice" (WB, June 21, 1979). We want to believe that destructiveness, like evil, is eradicable. Blaming Winnicott, of course, keeps hope alive that things could have turned out differently. We are tempted to fault Winnicott for not holding, 40 years ago, current notions of "boundary violations," or possessing contemporary conceptual tools such as "mutual enactments." But it is not even that we want so much to blame as that we prefer events to be rational and people knowable. We can no more abandon the idea that someone must be held accountable than we can resign ourselves to the notion that everything is an accident of fate.

It is precisely the unexpected contingencies of life, however, that psychoanalytic theory is reluctant to take into account. We are experts at searching for childhood determinants, patterned regularities, compulsions to repeat, adhesive object relationships, and unresolved transferences. It is much harder for us to accommodate our theories to what Freud (1927) once referred to as the "great necessities of Fate, against which there is no help" (p. 50). In Khan's case, the loss of his analysis, his analyst, his wife, his sobriety, his mother, and parts of his body combined to overwhelm his basic sense of continuity. As Irwin Hoffman (1998) points out, in psychic life there is a dialectic between a sense of being and an anticipation of nonbeing. For some individuals, there is nothing more shameful than the contingency and finitude of human life, the intractability of our limits. Perhaps, Khan's traumatic encounter with mortality—particularly in the absence of treatment, the presence of pathology, and the vulnerability of his temperament—precluded the possibility of his going-on-being. Enslaved by necessities impervious to his will, Khan suffered unbearable humiliation. Sensing the ever-presentness of death, he wrapped himself in it, corrosively poisoning himself with a reservoir of evil destructiveness.

Freud, following the First World War, had no problem being pessimistic about psychoanalysis as a treatment, particularly given his unwavering conviction in the scientific truth of his theory. We, on the other hand, have become quite shaky—and rightfully so, I might add—about the absolute truth-value of our theories. Unfortunately, however, this is sometimes accompanied by certain zealousness in our beliefs about therapeutic efficacy. There is a very powerful and distinctly optimistic current claiming that almost anything *is* possible clinically. Generally, this takes the narrative form: "If only . . . then." If only Winnicott had forcefully managed Khan's grandiosity and destructive envy, then he wouldn't have behaved so shabbily after terminating treatment. If only Winnicott had maintained the treatment frame, then Khan wouldn't have begun sleeping with his patients. While there may be some truth to this, it is also possible that no prior amount of good enough analysis would necessarily have altered the way Khan, as he aged and fell ill, responded to the accidents of his fate.

Winnicott, too, began his clinical career with no small measure of naiveté. As a young man, he entertained the idea that psychoanalysis could easily mobilize a person's will against unwanted tendencies and that he might even one day join his father's business and practice psychoanalysis on the side as a hobby. But as he matured, Winnicott fashioned a clinical sensibility quite distinct from instrumental notions of cure. He came to believe people differ in their capacity to profit from nurturance and he stopped believing everyone could be helped. He thought it a mistake to explain a person's life solely in terms of analytic results or to reduce a complicated personality to its failings. Winnicott's focus was not on morality, or adaptation to reality, or interpersonal competence. He did not seem to care about the "ego replacing the id" or the "finding of adaptive substitutions." In his quiet non-doctrinaire way, Winnicott saw these as a colossal piece of ideology that instates the analyst as master of reality and knowledge. What was blasphemous about him—and by the way, even as a child his older sisters frequently referred to him as blasphemous—was that he did not see himself as serving any normalizing function. As a result, he was sometimes excessively reticent about telling others what to do. He had an enormous tolerance for patients' symptoms, which is part of both why he was willing to take many cases dismissed by colleagues as hopeless and the reason quite a number of patients committed suicide during the course of treatment with him. A bit of an eccentric himself, he cared, for better *and* for worse, less about the good, and more about the unique.

In 1968, three years before his death, Winnicott spoke before a closed meeting of the 1952 Club on "The Transmission of Technique." According to the notes of one participant, Winnicott remarked, "It is not a very great thing to fail in an analysis. The awful thing is to go on with an analysis after it has failed." Winnicott must have known that awful feeling in his analysis of Khan, perhaps even realizing early on that he could never succeed. I believe he did this because of his wry appreciation of the human predicament, his dedication to the "three percent that was creative and vital," and because he never imagined curing *himself* from taking responsibility for Masud Khan's uncure.

Note

1 The material cited as WB refers to "Khan's diary" or "Workbooks." This material is unpublished and frozen in the archives of the International Psychoanalytic Association until 2039.

References

Cooper, J. (1993). *Speak of Me as I Am: The Life and Work of Masud Khan*. London: Karnac Books.

Deutsch, H. (1942). "Some Forms of Emotional Disturbance and Their Relationship to Schizophrenia." *Psychoanalytic Quarterly*, 11: 301–321.

Erikson, E. (1959). *Identity and the Life Cycle*. Psychological Issues, Monograph 1. New York: IUP.

Fonagy, P., Moran, G., and Target, M. (1993). "Aggression and the Psychological Self." *The International Journal of Psychoanalysis*, 74: 471–485.

Fonagy, P., Gergely, G., Jurist, E.L., and Target, M. (2002). *Affect Regulation, Mentalization, and the Development of the Self.* New York: Other Press.

Freud, S. (1927). "The Future of an Illusion." *The Standard Edition of the Complete Psychological Works of Sigmund Freud*, Vol. XXI.

Godley, W. (2001). "Saving Masud Khan." *London Review of Books*, February 22, pp. 3–7.

Greenson, R. (2016). *The Technique and Practice of Psychoanalysis.* London: Karnac Books.
Guedalla, P. (2015). *Supers & Supermen: Studies in Politics, History and Letters.* Palala Press.
Hopkins, L. (2006). *False Self: The Life of Masud Khan.* New York: Other Press.
Hoffman, I. (1998). *Ritual and Spontaneity in the Psychoanalytic Process.* Hillsdale, NJ: The Analytic Press.
Khan, M. (1986). "Outrageousness, Compliance, and Authenticity." *Contemporary Psychoanalysis*, 22: 629–650.
Murdoch, I. (1999). *Existentialists and Mystics: Writings on Philosophy and Literature.* New York and London: Penguin Books.
Pierpont, C. (2002). "After God." *The New Yorker*, April 8, 2002.
Rodman, F.R., Ed. (1987). *The Spontaneous Gesture: Selected Letters of D.W. Winnicott.* Cambridge, MA: Harvard University Press.
Sandler, A.-M. (2004). "Institutional Responses to Boundary Violations: The Case of Masud Khan." *The International Journal of Psychoanalysis*, 85: 27–44.
Slochower, J. (2011). "Analytic Idealizations and the Disavowed: Winnicott, His Patients, and Us." *Psychoanalytic Dialogues*, 21: 3–21.
Spruiell, V. (1975). "Three Strands of Narcissism." *The Psychoanalytic Quarterly*, 44: 577–595.
Weil, S. (2004). *The Notebooks of Simone Weil.* London and New York: Routledge.
Willoughby, R. (2005). *Masud Khan: The Myth and the Reality.* London: Free Association Books.
Winnicott, C. (1989). "D.W.W.: A Reflection." In *Psychoanalytic Explorations.* Ed. D.W. Winnicott. Cambridge, MA: Harvard University Press.
Winnicott, D.W. (1963). "Morals and Education." In *The Maturational Processes and the Facilitating Environment.* London: Hogarth Press.
Winnicott, D.W. (1986). *Home Is Where We Start From: Essays by a Psychoanalyst.* New York and London: W.W. Norton.
Winnicott, D.W. (1989). *Psychoanalytic Explorations.* Cambridge, MA: Harvard University Press.

Chapter 8

"A queer kind of truth"

Winnicott and the uses of dissociation

A forgotten file marked "DWW's Notes for the Vienna Congress—never given" was recently discovered in the Winnicott archives in London. It contained Winnicott's handwritten preparation for an IPA Congress panel scheduled for the summer of 1971. Although Winnicott had booked a room at a hotel in Vienna, this was a Congress he was destined not to attend. He died on January 25 of that year.

The significance of these notes is that they constitute Winnicott's final word on therapeutic matters close to his heart. They open with the words, "I am asking for a kind of revolution in our work. Let us re-examine what we do" (Abram, 2013, p. 312). "Revolution" is a word uncharacteristic of Winnicott. While he spent his life innovating and extending existing theory, he believed originality is only possible on the basis of tradition. But at the same time, Winnicott recognized "mature adults bring vitality to that which is ancient, old and orthodox by re-creating it after destroying it" (Winnicott, 1960b, p. 94).

At the very end of his life, Winnicott was poised once again to destroy, recreate, and thereby bring psychoanalysis to life by placing his ideas about dissociation front and center. The notes for the Vienna Congress continue:

> It may be that in dealing with the repressed unconscious we are colluding with the patient and the established defences. What is needed of us, because the patient cannot do the work by self-analysis; someone must see and witness the parts that go to make the whole, a whole that does not exist except as viewed from outside. In time we may have to come to the conclusion that the common failure of many excellent analyses has to do with the patient's dissociation hidden in material that is clearly related to repression taking place as a defence in a seemingly whole person.
>
> (quoted in Abram, 2013, pp. 312–313)

One can hear Winnicott's plea as an attempt to more fully integrate into psychoanalytic theory a view of dissociation that had always been important to him. Despite operating within an espoused theory privileging repression as an explanatory construct, in practice Winnicott demonstrates a keen awareness of dissociation—both as a healthy natural capacity and as a defensive response to trauma. For Winnicott, it makes a vast difference how and in what context dissociation is used.

As a natural capacity, dissociation may be employed to allow playful or artistic absorption—a focused tapering of attention that necessarily narrows the phenomenal field. One reason Winnicott valorizes both artistic immersion and playing is the opportunities they provide for healthy "voluntary" use of dissociation. The artist risks entering dissociated states dreading he may either fail in his endeavor and remain "haunted" by presences clamoring for expression, or else succeed and remain stuck in the altered dissociated state. Similarly, in the precariousness of playing, one need not be fully integrated. There is room to be safely surprised by the unexpected so long as there is no premature disruption of the "real"/"not real" double bookkeeping by which playing is contained within its own illusory space. For Winnicott, health includes a relative freedom from needing to prematurely integrate.

As a response to trauma, however, dissociative processes may be triggered fleetingly or harden with deadening effect into a structured disposition as a defense against unmanageable arousal. It remains an open question in a given case whether this use of dissociation is brought about by the overpowering effect of emotions occasioned by a traumatic event or as a defense against those emotions. Whichever the case, unlike repression, dissociation does not simply restrict access to potentially threatening feelings, thoughts, and memories. Instead, it is akin to a "quasi-death," an obliteration of the self to whom trauma might reoccur.

In the course of development, Winnicott suggests, dissociation as a natural capacity precedes repression as a defense. Indeed, unlinked dissociated states are at the root of all self-experience. "Dissociation," he writes, "can usefully be studied in its initial or natural forms." For example:

> There are the quiet and the excited states. I think an infant cannot be said to be aware at the start that while feeling this and that in his cot or enjoying the skin stimulations of bathing, he is the same as himself screaming for immediate satisfaction, possessed by an urge to get at and destroy something unless satisfied by milk.
>
> (Winnicott, 1945, p. 151)

Rather than focusing on the active separation of conflictual repressed mental contents, Winnicott's description of a normal dissociative process places in the foreground how the infant cannot yet be aware of how "he is the same" across disparate states of mind. The excited self is not yet linked to the quiet self. Similarly, in describing a child dreaming, Winnicott contends that:

> There is not necessarily an integration between a child asleep and a child awake. This integration comes in the course of time. Once dreams are remembered and even conveyed somehow to a third person, the dissociation is broken down a little . . . . It is a valuable experience whenever a dream is both dreamed and remembered, precisely because of the breakdown of dissociation that this represents. However complex such a dissociation may be in child or adult, the fact remains that it can start in the natural alternation of the sleeping and awake states, dating from birth.
>
> (Winnicott, 1945, p. 151)

Notice that, according to Winnicott, what holds the potential for bridging the dissociative gap—in both the child and adult—is the telling of the dream to a *third* person. It is the affectively safe relationship with an engaged other that facilitates the linking of naturally unlinked dissociated selves and with it—as dream and awake states enrich each other—the possibility of being more fully alive.

Earlier in the same article, Winnicott notes that:

> There are long stretches of time in a normal infant's life in which a baby does not mind whether he is many bits or one whole being, or whether he lives in his mother's face or in his own body, provided that from time to time he comes together and feels something.
>
> (Winnicott, 1945, p. 150)

At the root of earliest self-experience, Winnicott suggests, is an unintegrated state that periodically gels into dissociated self-states or partial integrations. The infant is free to drift about as there is not yet any built-up version of a self or hardened way of representing "me" and "not-me." What makes the pulses of drifting and gelling life enhancing as opposed to terrorizing is the tether of maternal holding and handling (Winnicott, 1962, p. 59). Mother's love and enjoyment expressed through physical care allows natural dissociative states to be entered into, shifted out of, and gradually integrated such that the infant comes to feel that his body is himself and that his sense of self is centered inside his body. In the absence of adequate care, however, the child's affect states become too discontinuous. An alive drifting and gelling is replaced by arousal, alarm, and abyss. The breakdown of holding and early object relating means the child cannot move seamlessly between dissociated states without a disruptive loss in the continuity of being.

For Winnicott, the self is formed and found through "desultory formless functioning" (Winnicott, 1971, p. 64)—recursive unplanned flow from unintegration through dissociation to relative integrations (and back again). But for this creative coming together (and unwinding) of the self to occur non-traumatically, a particular environment is necessary. "It is only here," writes Winnicott:

> in this unintegrated state of the personality, that that which we describe as creative can appear. This if reflected back, *but only if reflected back*, becomes part of the organized individual personality, and eventually this in summation makes the individual to be, to be found; and eventually enables himself or herself to postulate the existence of the self.
>
> (Winnicott, 1971, p. 64, emphasis in original)

Repeatedly created anew, a Self—the inclusive symbolization of one's own being—follows from the meeting up of the imaginative freedom of the psyche with an environment safe enough to allow the individual to be surprised without being shocked by what comes unbidden from within. Pathology, from this point of view, results from a dissociative disconnect between a person's imaginative and adaptive capacities, a failure to weave oneself with the world (Goldman, 2012).

Winnicott's description of "ego distortion" in terms of "True" and "False" Self is a way of theorizing about the dissociative process in which the "center of gravity of being" transfers from the "kernel" to the "shell" (Winnicott, 1952, p. 99). He is clear that false self-functioning originates in the "infant-to-mother living" and *not* in the "early mechanisms of ego defence organized against id-impulse" (Winnicott, 1960a, p. 144). Indeed, for Winnicott, instinct life itself might be experienced more dissociatively than through the derivatives of repression. As he puts it, "The instincts can be as much external as can a clap of thunder or a hit" (Winnicott, 1960a, p. 141). The question that concerns him is how the True Self, or "sensori-motor aliveness," is at risk for becoming dissociatively split off for adaptational purposes.

A close reading of the text suggests three potentially distinguishable "False Selves": a "shielding false self" whose function is to act as a stimulus barrier, a "defence against that which is unthinkable, the exploitation of the True Self, which would result in its annihilation" (Winnicott, 1960a, p. 147); a "split-off compliant false self" charged with gaining the awards of compliance at the expense of personal expression or growth (Winnicott, 1960a, p. 150); and a "compensatory false self" that takes the form of a "caretaker self" compensating for deficiencies in environmental care (Winnicott, 1960a, p. 142). Whether one prefers to conceptualize these varied constellations as structural entities or as transient processes, what they hold in common is a depleted presence, a shallowness of being, an impaired capacity to allow full-bodied meaning to be created. In short: a dissociative strategy designed to ensure that nothing new, unpredictable, and alive ever happens.

The link between dissociation and pathology is also central to Winnicott's distinction between "mind" and psyche-soma. In health, as mother reliably shields her baby from undue "complications beyond those which the infant can understand and allow for" (Winnicott, 1949, p. 245), the outcome is a smooth "*interrelating* of the psyche with the soma" (Winnicott, 1949, p. 244, emphasis added). In ill health, failures of the environment produce an "over-activity of the mental functioning" (Winnicott, 1949, p. 246). In such a case, there can develop what Winnicott calls "an opposition between the mind and the psyche-soma" such that the "thinking of the individual begins to take over and organize the caring for the psyche-soma" (Winnicott, 1949, p. 246).

To be clear: the "opposition" between mind and psyche-soma is not to be mistaken for "splitting" or internal conflict. Winnicott's focus is not on repressed symbolized content, but rather on a dissociative disconnect whereby the "mind" ends up functioning somewhat autonomously from the center of self to protect from potential traumatization.

Two clinical examples illustrate Winnicott's sensitivity to the evidence of dissociation that often appears as enacted but unsayable in words. With luck and patience, Winnicott hopes the delicate play between therapist and patient might allow a bridging of unhealthy dissociative gaps.

In the paper "Dreaming, Fantasying, and Living," Winnicott describes a middle-aged woman who gradually discovers "the extent to which fantasying or something of the nature of daydreaming has disturbed her whole life" (Winnicott, 1971, pp. 26–37). Dreaming and real living are, he contends, "of the same order," while fantasying is of "another order." Dreams "fit into object-relating in the real world and living in the real world fits into the dream world." By contrast, "fantasying remains an isolated phenomenon, absorbing energy but not contributing-in either to dreaming or to living." That is why dreams and living can contribute to growth while fantasying can "remain static over the whole of [a patient's] life." These two orders of mental life are further distinguished by the fact that whereas "a great deal of dream and of feelings belonging to life are liable to be under repression," the inaccessibility of fantasying is "associated with dissociation rather than with repression."

As the youngest of several siblings, this patient would fit in to other children's games but never really enjoyed or was enriched by them. The games were not personally enriching because "she was simply struggling to play whatever role was assigned to her and the others felt that something was lacking in the sense that she was not actively contributing-in." What the older siblings were unaware of was that their sister was essentially absent. "From the point of view of my patient," he writes, "while she was playing the other people's games she was all the time engaged in fantasying. She really lived in this fantasying on the basis of a dissociated mental activity . . . and over long periods her defence was to live here in this fantasying activity and to watch herself playing the other children's games as if watching someone else in the nursery group." As this patient grew older, she managed to construct a life in which "nothing that was really happening was fully significant to her." Her life, Winnicott concludes, "was dissociated from the main part of her, which was living in what became an organized sequence of fantasying." Her activities "brought no joy. All they did was to fill the gap, and this gap was an essential state of doing nothing while she was doing everything."

Through collaborative work, the patient recognizes that in her choice of wardrobe, she is dressed for a child as well as for her middle-aged self. She also begins to experience "a wave of hate of her mother which had a new quality to it. It was much nearer to murder than to hate . . ." Together they are able to understand how "material that had formerly been locked in the fixity of fantasying was now becoming released for both dreaming and living . . ." Yet even as they explore how the dissociative activity of fantasying makes her ill, the very notion under discussion is enacted between them. As Winnicott speaks, the patient notices distracting herself by fiddling with the zip of her bag: "Why was it this end? How awkward it was to do up!" The patient could feel, Winnicott reports:

> That this dissociated activity was more important to her sitting there than listening to what I was saying . . . . Suddenly she had a little insight and said that the meaning of this fantasying was: "So that's what *you* think." She had taken my interpretation of the dream and she had tried to make it foolish . . . . At this moment she reported that she had already "gone off to her job and to things that happened at work" and so here again while talking to me she had left me, and she felt dissociated as if she could not be in her skin. She remembered how she read the words of a poem but the words meant nothing.
>
> (Winnicott, 1971, p. 32, emphasis in original)

The clinical material captures how as long as dissociation is used to safeguard survival, there is a collapse of the potential space necessary for aliveness. As the dissociative gaps are actually experienced in the new context of Winnicott's holding, the woman gradually becomes aware of how vitally she has relied upon them. She is able to reflect upon how the cocoon of psychic web-spinning to which she retreated early in life eventually entombed her. The relational bridging of the dissociative gap loosens the rigidity of the dissociated structure and allows greater access to self-reflexivity. In the session, she becomes aware of "making Winnicott's interpretation foolish" while simultaneously retaining her connection to him. A new experience of bearing the conflict in mind replaces the old strategy of absenting herself through dissociation.

A second example of Winnicott's work in the dissociative domain involves a middle-aged married man who felt, despite years of beneficial analysis, that "what he came for, he has not reached." He went through life convinced his analysis was doomed to interminability. On one particular occasion, Winnicott found himself saying:

> I am listening to a girl. I know perfectly well that you are a man but I am listening to a girl, and I am talking to a girl. I am telling this girl: "You are talking about penis envy."
>
> (Winnicott, 1971, p. 73)

The remark had "an immediate effect in the form of intellectual acceptance, and relief, and then there were more remote effects." After a pause, the patient remarked, "If I were to tell someone about this girl I would be called mad." Winnicott was quite surprised to hear what he then said in response:

> It was not that *you* told this to anyone; it is *I* who see the girl and hear a girl talking, when actually there is a man on my couch. The mad person is *myself.*
>
> (Winnicott, 1971, pp. 73–74, emphasis in original)

The patient experienced enormous relief because finally feeling sane in a mad environment released him from a dilemma that had plagued him most of his life. As he subsequently said to Winnicott, "I myself could never say (knowing myself to be a man) 'I am a girl.' I am not mad that way. But you said it, and you have spoken to both parts of me." Winnicott writes:

> This madness which was mine enabled him to see himself as a girl from my position. He knows himself to be a man, and never doubts that he is a man. Is it obvious what was happening here? For my part, *I have needed to live through a deep personal experience* in order to arrive at the understanding I feel I now have reached.
>
> (Winnicott, 1971, p. 74, emphasis added)

The understanding Winnicott reached was that "his mother . . . saw a girl baby when she saw him as a baby before she came round to thinking of him as a boy." This man "had to fit into her idea that her baby would be and was a girl." It was the mother's "madness" that was "brought right into the present by my having said 'It is I who am mad.'"

While this constructed meaning appeared to resonate deeply, the patient arrives at the following session and reports that although he had "had a satisfactory sexual intercourse with his wife," now he is ill. What is more, he invites Winnicott to "interpret this illness . . . as if it were psychosomatic." Winnicott says to the patient:

> You feel as if you ought to be pleased that here was an interpretation of mine that had released masculine behavior. *The girl that I was talking to, however, does not want the man released*, and indeed she is not

> interested in him. What she wants is full acknowledgement of herself and of her own rights over your body.
>
> (Winnicott, 1971, p. 75, emphasis in original)

The vignette illustrates how the analytic exchange allows a channel of communication to eventually open between the previously dissociated male and female elements. Winnicott is clear the man's suffering has nothing to do with either repressed homosexuality or a predisposition toward bisexuality. Instead, what plagues is the "complete dissociation" between "split-off male and female elements." An implication of Winnicott's formulation is that the childhood experience of being a boy seen as a girl was an awful one that needed to be avoided. What is avoided is not simply the memory of the trauma, but the entire experience of being that person who went through it. The "complete dissociation" is the means adopted by the patient to guarantee he will never again be the person who suffered what he suffered. At the same time, however, the sequestered experience of being a little girl from the mother's point of view and the little girl's demand for control over the man's body are dissociated elements hollering to be heard. And no less important: both Winnicott and the patient come alive through the shifts in mutual dissociative processes. The unexpected and surprising appearance of the unbidden in the encounter—both Winnicott's and the patient's—indicates relational bridging of mutually dissociated aspects of their experience. By acknowledging he had become the mad person seeing the girl, Winnicott locates the dissociation intersubjectively. He is neither just an interpreter of a patient's unconscious nor an absorber of the patient's projections. Instead, he becomes a subject who deeply identifies with the patient's projection and owns it as his own. By living through together an experience, previously dissociated elements are symbolized in thought and language. What had been unsayable in words is now contained within the self without loss of continuity of being.

Repeatedly, Winnicott notes how some patients' lives become little more than a medium through which dissociated past trauma may be actively sought out in the here and now with the unconscious hope of bringing about some form of integration. Meaningful existence is foreclosed by the repetitive present search for an experience that could not be processed in the past. Why do some people go on compulsively worried by something that belongs to the past? "The answer must be," writes Winnicott:

> That the original experience of primitive agony cannot get into the past tense unless the ego can first gather it into its own present time experience . . . . In other words the patient must go on looking for the past detail which is *not yet experienced*. This search takes the form of a looking for this detail in the future . . . . On the other hand, if the patient is ready for some kind of acceptance of this queer kind of truth, that what is not yet experienced did nevertheless happen in the past, then the way is open for the agony to be experienced in the transference . . .
>
> (Winnicott, 1963, p. 91)

What Winnicott refers to as "*a queer kind of truth*" is the mind's capacity to sequester events that occur without them being felt as something fully real to the traumatized person because "the patient was not there for it to happen to" (Winnicott, 1963, p. 92). At the same time, the patient unconsciously searches for opportunities to engineer the re-emergence in the transference of the original trauma situation. For the "agony to be experienced in the transference," the patient will have to be "ready for some kind of acceptance of this queer truth." Winnicott implies that if a good enough holding environment has been created, the patient will both actively seek out aspects of the analyst that permit experiencing the trauma while temporarily dissociating other aspects of the relationship involving goodness and trust.

The original trauma felt as unreal and the search for an opportunity to relive it are, Winnicott writes, "a fact that is carried round hidden away in the unconscious." But the "unconscious" Winnicott has in mind is:

> Not exactly the repressed unconscious of psycho-neurosis, nor is it the unconscious of Freud's formulation of the part of the psyche that is very close to neuro-physiological functioning . . . . Nor is it the unconscious of Jung . . .
>
> (Winnicott, 1963, p. 90)

Instead:

> In this special context the unconscious means that the ego integration is not able to encompass something.
>
> (Winnicott, 1963, pp. 90–91)

What is required of the analyst, as Winnicott intended to say in his never to be given final presentation, is to:

> Witness the parts that go to make the whole, a whole that does not exist except as viewed from outside.
>
> (quoted in Abram, 2013)

As engaged witness to the "queer truth" of dissociated experience rather than as knowing interpreter of the patient's repressed unconscious, the analyst may open a space for a vital spark of life.

References

Abram, J. (2013). *D.W.W.'s Notes on the Vienna Congress 1971: A Consideration of Winnicott's Theory of Aggression and Its Clinical Implications in Donald Winnicott Today*. New Library of Psychoanalysis, London: Routledge.

Goldman, D. (2012). "Weaving with the World: Winnicott's Re-Imagining of Reality." *The Psychoanalytic Quarterly*, 81(1): 1–24.

Winnicott, D.W. (1945). "Primitive Emotional Development." In *Through Paediatrics to Psycho-Analysis*. New York: Basic Books, 1975, pp. 145–156.

Winnicott, D.W. (1949). "Mind and Its Relation to the Psyche-Soma." In *Through Paediatrics to Psycho-Analysis*. New York: Basic Books, 1975, pp. 243–254.

Winnicott, D.W. (1952). "Anxiety Associated with Insecurity." In *Through Paediatrics to Psycho-Analysis*. New York: Basic Books, 1975, pp. 97–100.

Winnicott, D.W. (1960a). "Ego Distortion in Terms of True and False Self." In *The Maturational Processes and the Facilitating Environment*. London: Hogarth Press, 1979, pp. 140–152.

Winnicott, D.W. (1960b). "The Family and Emotional Maturity." In *The Family and Individual Development*. London: Routledge, 1989, pp. 88–96.

Winnicott, D.W. (1962). "Ego Integration in Child Development." In *The Maturational Processes and the Facilitating Environment*. London: Hogarth Press, 1979, pp. 56–63.

Winnicott, D.W. (1963). "Fear of Breakdown." In *Psychoanalytic Explorations*. Cambridge, MA: Harvard University Press, 1989, pp. 87–95.

Winnicott, D.W. (1971). *Playing and Reality*. London and New York: Routledge.

Chapter 9

Weaving with the world

Winnicott's reimagining of reality

"Did you know," Clare Britton wrote to Donald Winnicott as their relationship was becoming a love affair:

> That Wordsworth for most of his life was preoccupied with the problem of his great good fortune in that his inner world of imagination linked so much with his real experiences? It was a constant marvel & miracle to him—& he was always seeking the clue to it.
>
> (Rodman, 2003, p. 96)

Sent at a time when both Clare and Donald were somewhat awkwardly smitten, the letter hints at their wonder in finding each other. Clare undoubtedly sensed how profoundly Winnicott, like Wordsworth, marveled at the miracle of alignment—he preferred Milner's (1969) word, *interplay*—between inner dreams and outer reality (Winnicott, 1971, p. 98).

Taking particular pride in his inventiveness, Winnicott also, like Wordsworth, sought clues to what it means to have an alive creative relationship to external reality. "I am one of those people," he once confided in a private letter:

> Who feel compelled to work in my own way and to express myself in my own language first; by a struggle I sometimes come around to rewording what I am saying to bring it in line with other work, in which case I usually find that my own "original" ideas were not so original as I had to think they were when they were emerging.
>
> (Rodman, 1987, pp. 53–54)

Feeling "compelled" and having to think ideas "original" might easily be dismissed as symptoms of personal illness. Indeed, those close to

Winnicott, including his own analyst, often did. But Winnicott believed his personal struggle—his being poised between the anxiety of influence and the need for company—reveals an essential driving force in psychic life. As he once wrote to Klein:

> This matter which I am discussing touches the very root of my own personal difficulty so that what you see can always be dismissed as Winnicott's illness, but if you dismiss it in this way you may miss something which is in the end a positive contribution. My illness is something which I can deal with in my own way and it is not far away from being the inherent difficulty in regard to human contact with external reality.
>
> (Rodman, 1987, p. 37)

As Winnicott struggled with the "inherent difficulty in regard to human contact with external reality," he came to conceive psychic life as imbued with a vigor he called *imaginative elaboration* or *primary creativity*. What makes contact with reality "inherently difficult," from Winnicott's point of view, is not that it frustrates. Rather, the difficulty resides in the perpetual strain of keeping inner dream life and outer perceptions *separate yet interrelated*, so that meaningfulness emerges spontaneously from what is created and found. The importance Winnicott places on primary creativity signals a shift in emphasis within psychoanalysis from patterns of frustration, gratification, and sublimation to the way a developing person meaningfully weaves with and is woven into the world.

An unacknowledged root of Winnicott's view of creative meaning making can be found in the writing of the English Romantic poets Coleridge and Wordsworth. Coleridge and Wordsworth are important non-psychoanalytic precursors, part of the broader cultural tradition upon which Winnicott's psychoanalytic originality is based. Winnicott discovered in these poets kindred spirits who deepened his appreciation of the delicate area between what is perceived and what is conceived. Coleridge and Wordsworth were deeply preoccupied with the overlap between *seeing* and *seeing in the mind's eye*, the to-and-fro movement between imagination and environment. Like Winnicott, they were struck by the inherent human difficulty in regard to contact with external reality; they proposed an intermediate area where inner and outer anchor each other; and they recognized a difference between the so-called creativity of everyday life and true artistic productions.

Wordsworth even shared Winnicott's insight that creativity has its origins in the earliest relationship between mother and infant.

At the heart of Winnicott's clinical work lays an abiding concern for what is also a center of gravity for the romantic poets: the vital spark or urge toward creative aliveness. For Winnicott, aliveness refers to a psychological state, not a biological one. Many of Winnicott's seminal formulations—spontaneous gesture, the True Self, potential space, object use—are variations on the theme of how creative aliveness either grows and flourishes, or is hidden or dampened, as the developing child negotiates a personal way of finding a meaningful connection to the environment from which it is also differentiating itself. An experiential sense of aliveness accompanies creative meaning making. Paradoxically, a facilitating environment is required for brute reality to be gradually brought to life in this way.

As an experiment in thinking, I ask: given a sensibility that eschews principles in the sense that Freud employs the term, how does Winnicott think about the notion that a reality principle imposes on a pleasure principle the necessity for delay, detour, inhibition, and compromise? One way to read Winnicott's theory of primary creativity is as a reimagining of what it means for the individual to have contact with external reality. Winnicott reshapes Freud's reality and pleasure principles in accordance with his own sensibility.

To be clear: I do not mean to suggest that Winnicott replaces one set of principles with an alternative one. Indeed, from a theoretical point of view, Freud's principles of mental functioning and Winnicott's primary creativity operate on different levels of abstraction and attempt to answer different types of questions. Freud asks: what energy and constraints drive and regulate the psyche's contact with reality? Winnicott wonders: how does a person acquire a *felt sense* of reality?

In conceptualizing laws regulating a psychic apparatus, Freud proposes non-experiential concepts that niggle Winnicott because of their distance from any felt quality of human experience. For Freud, reality is often conceived of as a hostile force represented by the father and to which the child must adjust. For Winnicott, the mother introduces reality in small doses so that the child retains a secure sense that the environment is also always part of the self. It is not that Winnicott fails to recognize the clash between personal impulses and the compromises that belong to relationships with what is eventually felt as external. He even appreciates the need to flee or fight danger situations. But for Winnicott, the emphasis is less on the *conflict* between "pleasure" and "reality," and more on the *contrast* between *two different kinds of relationship with reality* as it becomes increasingly external.

A "piece of absurd unlogic"

Winnicott proceeds from the premise that the psyche has as its basis the imaginative elaboration of physical functioning. A typical passage from his lectures on human nature reads:

> The basis of psyche is soma and in evolution the soma came first. The psyche begins as an imaginative elaboration of physical functioning having as its most important duty the binding together of past experiences, potentialities, and the present moment awareness and expectancies for the future.
>
> (Winnicott, 1988, p. 19)

And elsewhere, he states:

> The psyche part of the person is concerned with relationships, relationships within, relationships to the body, to the external world. Arising out of what may be called the imaginative elaboration of body functioning of all kinds and the accumulation of memories, the psyche . . . binds the experienced past, the present and the expected future together, makes sense of the person's sense of self and justifies our perception of an individual there in that body.
>
> (Winnicott, 1988, p. 28)

When Winnicott writes of "body functioning of all kinds and the accumulation of memories," he draws out an implication of Freud's neurophysiological presumption that, at the earliest or deepest level of experience, latent memories are somatic ones. Freud (1915), in countering objections to the notion of unconscious mental functioning, notes that:

> When all our latent memories are taken into consideration . . . we encounter the objection that these latent recollections can no longer be described as psychical, but they correspond to residues of somatic processes from which what is psychical can once more arise.
>
> (p. 167)

One meaning of the word "unconscious" for Freud refers to near-physical activity, that which is least available to consciousness. But Freud also aspired to provide a consistently *psychological* account of experience. Building on this aspect of Freudian thought, Winnicott suggests that psychological meaning is generated from the imaginative elaboration of somatic functioning. But for Winnicott, that which is "psychical" does not "*correspond to* residues of somatic processes"; at its root, primary creativity is what the psyche-soma *does*—it generates personal meaning.

Winnicott's "imaginative elaboration" is a temporally binding force concerned with relationships that might be said to "make sense of a person's sense of self." When an infant puts thumb in mouth, for example, it is not solely an instinctive act. The psyche elaborates the function, the thumb eventually coming to stand for other objects gathered together in this way and brought into relationship with the mouth. Function comes to have *meaning* for the individual—at first very simple, but later quite complex. Meaning, Winnicott implies, requires some process that establishes relationships between sensory domains and maps bodily experience onto abstract concepts.[1]

The psyche is the process of radical imagining of relationships at the core of meaning making. Imagination enables the psyche-soma to bootstrap itself from within (Modell, 2003)—what psychologist Frederic Bartlett (1932) described as "the organism's capacity to turn around upon its own schemata and construct them afresh" (p. 213). The psyche, in Winnicott's account, does not perceive and process information; it constructs meaning.

For Winnicott, imaginative elaboration is not another term for "fantasy" or another name for the unconscious. Imagining as carrier of potential meaning making cuts across topographical and structural lines. In unconscious life, we imaginatively create fantasies. In conscious life, imagining plays a role as well. Otherwise, consciousness would be pure repetition, rendering us incapable of arriving at new thoughts or ideas. Idiosyncratic and ungovernable, this radical imaginative force generates a flux of self-experience that cannot be reduced to a series of introjections and projections.

The act of imaginatively elaborating is a process, not a thing or a substance residing in the mind. For Winnicott, the etymological connection between imagination and the earlier Latin verb *imitari*—to imitate, which is also the root of *imago*—has worn thin. The act of imagining is more autonomous, spontaneous, flexible, and inventive than mere imitating.

Imagining does not produce replicas or representations. Rather, it is akin to what Paul Pruyser (1983) calls evocation—a summoning, calling, or conjuring up. "Evocation," writes Pruyser:

> Pertains to such possibilities as eliciting sorrow or languor by the stimulus of a picture of a tree with drooping leaves; of musical tones producing a feeling of relief after a thunderstorm, as in Beethoven's Pastoral Symphony; of producing an apprehensive mood by intoning "Once upon a midnight dreary . . ." Evocation involves images, but does not require imitation.
>
> (pp. 5–6)

Winnicott (1986) acknowledges a certain "absurd unlogic" to the stake he claims regarding the human capacity to creatively conjure:

> I can look at a clock and only see the time; maybe I do not even see that, but only notice the shapes on the dial; or I see nothing. On the other hand, I may be seeing clocks potentially, and then I allow myself to hallucinate a clock, doing so because I have evidence that an actual clock is there to be seen, so when I perceive the actual clock I have already been through a complex process that originated in me . . . . Every moment I have my little experience of omnipotence, before I hand this uncomfortable function over to God. There is some antilogic here. Logic takes the form at one point of unlogic. I can't help this—this is actual . . . . The fact is that what we create is already there, but the creativeness lies in the way we get at perception through conception and apperception. So when I look at the clock . . . I create a clock, but I am careful not to see clocks except just where I already know there is one. Please do not turn down this piece of absurd unlogic—but look at it and use it.
>
> (pp. 49–52)

Reality—which exists independent of the individual—is not passively imprinted but imaginatively elaborated from within. Imagining is an absurdly unlogical force by which we "get *at* perception *through* . . . apperception." Somewhere between the sterility of autistic fancying and the resourcefulness required for survival lies the opportunity for meaningful illusions.

"Both what they half create and what perceive"

The Romantic poets Wordsworth and Coleridge exerted a particular gravitational pull upon Winnicott since their concerns resonated with his own. Winnicott, like them, was "always seeking the clue" (quoted in Rodman, 2003, p. 96) to what enables a person to inhabit, in Wordsworth's (1798a) words:

> The mighty world of eye and ear,—*both what they half create,*
> *And what perceive*; well pleased to recognise
> In nature and the language of the sense,
> The anchor of my purest thoughts, the nurse,
> The guide, the guardian of my heart, and soul
> Of all my moral being.
>
> (p. 134, emphasis added)

Since Winnicott rarely linked his inventive productions with the work of others, it is tricky to trace the direct impact of these poetic precursors. "I could look up creativity in *The Oxford English Dictionary*," he said in a talk before the Progressive League:

> And I could do research on all that has been written on the subject in philosophy and psychology, and then I could serve it all up on a dish . . . . Personally, I am unable to follow this plan. I have this need to talk as though no one had ever examined the subject before, and of course, this can make my words ridiculous . . . . It would kill me to work out the concordance of creativity references.
>
> (Winnicott, 1986, p. 41)

It is also difficult to distinguish actual echoes from accidental resonance. The mere discovery of Winnicott's aesthetic affinity with the poetry of Wordsworth and Coleridge tells us virtually nothing about direct influence. Winnicott, after all, dealt in an area of universal concern. Humans, quite naturally, puzzle over their origins, motives, passions, and creativity. Writers, poets, theologians, and philosophers are as consumed by these matters as are psychoanalysts. Parallels, therefore, may hint at much but confirm little.

Nevertheless, there is sufficient reason to suggest that Wordsworth's and Coleridge's views of imagination enriched Winnicott's own. As a British public school student, he was exposed to their work. Milner claimed that Clare Britton deepened Winnicott's appreciation of the romantic poets;

certain points in his writing are laced with their language (Winnicott, 1952). Winnicott personally communicated to supervisees that he was an avid reader of Coleridge (Issroff, 2005). And Winnicott directly spoke of and quoted Wordsworth to his patients. In one case, he reported mentioning a Wordsworth poem to a patient and being surprised that the patient was not familiar with the text (Winnicott, 1972).

The power of imagination to produce images in the absence of objects, and the "marvel and miracle" of alignment between *seeing* and *seeing in the mind's eye*, is as crucial for Winnicott as for Wordsworth and Coleridge. Indeed, it is foundational to what Winnicott calls "psyche" and what Wordsworth and Coleridge call "mind." While there are notable differences between the two romantic poets—Coleridge's interest as philosopher (and dejected poet) was more in the faculty of imagination, while Wordsworth's was more in the relationships sustained by mental imagery—together they intuited a vision that resonated for Winnicott (Turner, 1988).

"There is creation in the eye," writes Wordsworth:

> Not less in all the other senses; powers
> They are that colour, model, and combine
> The things perceived with such an absolute
> Essential energy that we may say
> That these most godlike faculties of ours
> At one and the same moment are the mind
> And the mind's minister.
>
> (Warnock, 1978, pp. 118–119)

Because of the ambiguity of perception, there is always, for both Wordsworth and Coleridge, a curious meshing between seeing and seeing in the mind's eye. Coleridge describes imagination as a coalescence of subject and object. "Into the simplest seeming 'datum,'" he writes, "a constructing, forming activity from the mind has entered. And the perceiving and the forming are the same. The subject (the self) has gone into what it perceives, and what it perceives is, in this sense, itself" (Richards, 1969, p. 57).

Or, as Coleridge succinctly puts it in his poem "Dejection" (1802): "*We receive but what we give*" (p. 308, emphasis added). Wordsworth (1805) poetically points to the same conclusion when he declares the mind to be "creator and receiver both,/Working but in alliance with the works/Which it beholds" (p. 399).

Coleridge (1817) likens imagination to "master currents" (p. 242) below the surface of consciousness. What we imagine empowers and authenticates perception, allowing it to become personally meaningful (Warnock, 1978, p. 116). The meshing of seeing and seeing in the mind's eye—and this is true for Winnicott as well—allows what is inside to be felt as having substance and what is outside as having significance.

Long before Winnicott proposed potential space as "the intermediate area of experiencing" (Winnicott, 1971, p. 2, emphasis in original), Coleridge referred to imagination as an *intermediate faculty*—that "reconciling and mediatory power, which . . . gives birth to a system of symbols" (Barth, 1977, p. 83). Some special capacity, he assumed, must intermediate the mind's reaching out, even while it surrenders to what is discovered. "Most of my readers," writes Coleridge (1817):

> will have perceived, a small water insect on the surface of the rivulets . . . and will have noticed how the little animal wins its way up against the stream by alternative pulses of active and passive motion, now resisting the current, and now yielding to it in order to gather strength and a momentary fulcrum for a further propulsion. This is no unapt emblem of the mind's self-experience in the act of thinking. There are evidently two powers at work, which relative to each other are active and passive; and this is not possible without an intermediate faculty, which is at once both active and passive (in philosophical language we must denominate this intermediate faculty . . . the imagination).
>
> (pp. 124–125)

Like Winnicott, Coleridge is struck by an inherent human difficulty in regard to contact with external reality: if the mind is full only of a consciousness of itself (an example of energy flowing solely in one direction), it will become solipsistically self-enclosed, lost in an active but isolated tyranny of self-consideration—what Winnicott calls the world of "subjective objects." If, on the other hand, the opposite situation obtains (energy flowing all in the other direction), the mind becomes a passive automaton, responding only to stimuli of nature and circumstance—which Winnicott calls "reacting to impingements."

The dilemma, for both Coleridge and Winnicott, is how to develop an account of experience that is not boxed in either by solipsistic subjectivity or by claims of objective perception. Since we are imaginatively dreaming even while awake, the intermediate area is crucial as a resting place from the perpetual strain of keeping inner and outer separate but interrelated. It is the area where inner and outer anchor each other that allows symbols and culture to emerge and life to feel real.

To take this one step further: both Coleridge and Winnicott link imagination with non-defensive omnipotence associated with God. "Imagination," writes Coleridge (1817), "I hold to be the living Power and Prime Agent of all human Perception, and as a repetition in the finite mind of the eternal act of creation in the infinite I AM" (p. 202).

Thus, for Coleridge, the act of perceiving and of making symbols is essentially a religious act, a participation in the infinite creative act of the supreme symbol maker. At bottom, it is an act of faith in which human beings "partake of the Reality which they render intelligible" (quoted in Barth, 1977, p. 4). As with the supreme symbol, Creation, an act of faith is necessary to perceive the true unity of being within differences.

For Winnicott, too, a creative relation to external reality involves an act of faith. As reality is increasingly experienced as external—gradually differentiated from a primal unity—it becomes "a place from which objects appear and in which they disappear" (Winnicott, 1988, p. 106). In the course of time, with sufficient enough overlap between primary creativity and mother's provision, the infant develops a feeling of confidence that objects of desire can eventually be found, even in their absence. This feeling of confidence is the root of the sustaining power of faith—that good things, even when lost, can eventually be refound.

Winnicott also frequently employs the capitalized "I AM" to denote the earliest experiences of a bounded self—a self that emerges from an actual experience of omnipotence. "From this initial experience of omnipotence," he writes:

> the baby is able to begin to experience frustration and even to arrive one day at the other extreme from omnipotence, that is to say, having a sense of being a mere speck in a universe . . . that was there before the baby was conceived of and conceived by two parents who were enjoying each other. Is it not from *being God* that human beings arrive at the humility proper to human individuality?
>
> (Winnicott, 1987, p. 101, emphasis in original)

Both Coleridge and Winnicott also distinguish between the universal imaginative capacity constituting psychic life and the special talents of the creative artist. In developing this theme, Coleridge proposes the terms *primary imagination* and *secondary imagination*. By primary imagination, Coleridge means that the mind does not mechanically register stimuli and simply arrange them according to the laws of association; instead, mind is active even in the mere act of perception. It knows objects not by passive reception but by its own energy; indeed, it discovers itself through the objects of perception. "If the Mind be not Passive," writes Coleridge (1801):

> If it be indeed made in God's Image and that, too, in the sublimest sense, the Image of the Creator, there is ground for suspicion that any system built on the passiveness of the mind must be false, as a system.
>
> (p. 709)

The "false system" against which Coleridge rails is the tradition of the Associationists, who assumed the mind in perception was nothing but "a lazy looker-on on an external world" (Coleridge, 1801, p. 709).

Primary imagination is like a reliable craftsman, creating our own world even in the commonest everyday acts of perception. But in true poetry—in the making of symbols—a *secondary imagination* is also at work. Not content with the craftsmanship of everyday life and appearances—which can still "leave us cold"—the true poet strives for a vision more intense, more true, than that afforded by daily life. Despite primary imagination, people are too easily reduced to a state of near somnambulism in which they languish amidst what Wordsworth (1814) called "The repetitions wearisome of sense,/Where Soul is dead, and feeling hath no place" (p. 563).

Unlike "Fancy"—which Coleridge says merely recycles or "aggregates fixities and definites" (Coleridge, 1817, I, p. 202)—true poetic imagination fuses disparate things into a new unity. Secondary imagination creates affectively rich symbols that "dissolve, diffuse, and dissipate" the "inanimate cold world" of prosaic consciousness:

> And would we aught behold, of higher worth
> Than that inanimate cold world allowed
> To the poor loveless ever-anxious crowd,

> Ah! From the soul itself must issue forth
> A light, a glory, a fair luminous cloud
> Enveloping the Earth.
>
> (Coleridge, 1802, p. 306)

Winnicott (1986), too, recognized the human vulnerability to lose feelingful connection to life. And while he believed it is in our common humanity to have the capacity for primary creativity, true artists brings to bear a special vision and talent:

> I must make clear the distinction between creative living and being artistically creative. In creative living you or I find that everything we do strengthens the feeling that we are alive, that we are ourselves . . . . If you have ever had a depression phase of the schizoid sort (and most have), you will know this in the negative. How often I have been told:
>
> "There is a laburnum outside my window and the sun is out and I know intellectually that it must be a grand sight . . . . But for me this morning there is no meaning in it. I cannot feel it. It makes me acutely aware of not being myself real."
>
> Although allied to creative living, the active creations of writers, poets, artists, sculptors, architects, musicians, are different. You will agree that if someone is engaged in artistic creation, we hope he or she can call on some special talent. But for creative living we need no special talent.
>
> (pp. 43–44)

For Coleridge, the poetry of secondary imagination redeems human experience from mediocrity and expresses a "higher worth . . . a light, a glory, a fair luminous cloud" (Coleridge, 1802, p. 306). But Winnicott keenly observes that artistic productions, even those of superior value, may actually indicate a *failure* of the artist in terms of creative living. "You can perhaps get my meaning," Winnicott once wrote to a French analyst, "if you think of a Van Gogh experiencing, that is to say, feeling real, when painting one of his pictures, but feeling unreal in his relationships with external reality and in his private withdrawn inner life" (Rodman, 1987, p. 124).

The artist is engaged in a dialogue in which he struggles through his medium to "discover" resonating forms for which he is searching. He reaches out emotionally toward a medium that allows itself to be transformed by the artist's subjective image, so that the artist can then find himself in the significant forms he has created (Wright, 2013). From Winnicott's point of view, this dialogue is a natural extension of the earliest experience in which the mother intuitively resonates and gives form to the infant's own gestures. As such, artistic endeavors often carry the potential of a healing function—but they can also fail to deliver. "The self is not really to be found in what is made out of products of body or mind," writes Winnicott (1971):

> However valuable these constructs may be in terms of beauty, skill, and impact. If the artist (in whatever medium) is searching for the self, then it can be said that in all probability there is already some failure for that artist in the field of general creative living. The finished creation never heals the underlying lack of sense of self.
>
> (pp. 54–55)

What distinguishes creative living for Winnicott is not technical proficiency or originality of production, but the strengthening of the individual's sense of self through experiences that feel real.

When Wordsworth was 28 years old, he penned the first version of an autobiographical poem that was reworked repeatedly over his lifetime but never published. He referred to it as "Poem (title not yet fixed upon) to Coleridge." His widow subsequently published it under the name "The Prelude; or Growth of a Poet's Mind." In it, Wordsworth (1805) intuits the centrality of mother's role in the psychic origins of imagination:

> Blest the Babe,
> Nursed in his mother's arms, who sinks to sleep
> Rocked on his Mother's breast: who with his soul
> Drinks in the feelings of his mother's eye!
> For him, in one dear Presence, there exists
> A virtue which irradiates and exalts
> Objects through widest intercourse of sense.
> No outcast he, bewildered and depressed:
> Along his infant veins are interfused
> The gravitation and the filial bond
> Of nature that connect him with the world.
>
> (p. 398)

Wordsworth can be read as creatively nostalgic. But for him, nostalgia is not a wistful, precarious hold on the inner representation of a lost object. Instead, it is a belief that the living relational warmth of the first relationship becomes an integral and ongoing part of a vital "virtue": the individual's imaginative capacity to encounter and evoke the world rather than merely refer to it. Wordsworth (1807), who also famously declared that the "Child is Father of the Man" (Vol 4, p. 279)—a phrase Winnicott periodically borrowed—pointed to the possibility that the adult need not lose the child's seeing of things afresh.

For Winnicott, too, living creatively—feeling real—is the retention throughout life of the original experience of creatively imagining a world introduced in small doses by mother. In his view, even at the "theoretical first feed" (Winnicott, 1952, p. 223), the infant makes a personal contribution to the productive effort. Mother's adaptation is not simply to provide for the infant as passive recipient of her ministrations, but to afford the infant sufficient opportunity to believe that the nipple and the milk arose out of his gestures, the result of his own creative idea that "rode in on the crest of a wave of instinctual tension" (Winnicott, 1988, p. 110).

Winnicott develops a virtual cartography of how the vestiges of our earliest experiences with mother become the rudiments of our capacity to live creatively. From birth, the human being is concerned with finding elbow room between what is subjectively conceived and what objectively perceived. There is no well-being in this regard for the individual who has not been started off well enough by the mother.

The vital spark

At the heart of Winnicott's work lays an abiding concern for the urge toward creative aliveness and the deadness resulting from failures to create and discover a world that can tolerate one's own aliveness. "In each baby," he once remarked:

> is *a vital spark*, and this urge towards life and growth and development is a part of the baby, something the child is born with and which is carried forward in a way that we do not have to understand.
> (Winnicott, 1964, p. 27, emphasis added)

Primary creativity is the drive that transforms literal happenings into experiences that feel alive and meaningful. What renders this drive *primary* is that it is not an expression or derivative of, nor is it motivated by, anything else. For Winnicott, it is the threat to one's creative aliveness, not one's sexuality, that is bedrock.

What interests Winnicott clinically is the distinction between moments of generative animation and those of empty, lifeless accommodation—how a person imaginatively creates a space between the "thingness" of the world and his own subjectivity, so that brute reality may gradually be brought to life with meaning. The natural urge toward creative aliveness becomes, in illness, a matter of great urgency.

The notion of *aliveness* enters psychoanalysis through the back door (Goldman, 2013). It was only after Freud speculated about a death instinct that aliveness as something distinct from either sexuality or self-preservation became something that needed to be accounted for. What particularly troubled Winnicott was that Freud (1924, p. 160), in speculating about a nirvana principle as expressing "the trend of the death instinct," appeared to violate his own rule of providing a purely psychological description of psychic life. Death, Winnicott argued, is a biological force, not a psychological one.

One useful way of thinking about Winnicott's focus on aliveness is as an extension of Ernest Jones's (1927) idea of aphanisis, or fear of psychic annihilation. Jones suggests the possibility that there is a common denominator in the sexuality of boys and girls more fundamental than castration anxiety:

> In both sexes castration is only a partial threat, however important a one, against sexual capacity and enjoyment as a whole. For the main blow of total extinction we might do well to use a separate term, such as the Greek word "aphanisis."
>
> (p. 460)

With the concept of aphanisis, Jones opens the door for a shift of emphasis from a fear of loss of sexual capacity and pleasure to a dread that all desire or aliveness itself might be extinguished. Winnicott (1958) believed that "the value of [Jones's] term aphanisis has not yet been fully explored" (p. 298). Linking his own ideas about the state of affairs before the ego is able to experience anxiety derived from either instinct tension or object loss to Jones's original contribution, Winnicott (1960) states:

> Anxiety at this early stage is not castration anxiety or separation anxiety; it relates to quite other things, and is, in fact, anxiety about annihilation (cf. the aphanisis of Jones)
>
> (p. 587)

Aliveness—that Winnicott also refers to as "being" so as to distinguish it from physical self-preservation—originates in an undifferentiated field. Rather than a quality located within a distinct individual, aliveness has its roots in a psychic field as mother shields infant from premature awareness of "complications" and "coincidences" beyond its ken. Many of Winnicott's seminal formulations—spontaneous gesture, True Self, potential space, object use—are variations on the theme of how aliveness either grows and flourishes or is hidden or dampened as the developing child negotiates a personal way of finding a meaningful connection to the environment from which it is also differentiating itself. They are all ways of charting the gradual shift in the center of gravity of aliveness from an undifferentiated field to the child as an integrated unit able to keep inner and outer separate but interrelated. Winnicott's preoccupation with the field of play between inner and outer suggests that even as the center of gravity shifts, aliveness itself is never fully localizable.

Development, for Winnicott, proceeds through the negotiation of increasingly more object-related ways of being creatively alive. He speaks little of agencies or structures of mind, focusing instead on movements in relationship that make creative aliveness sustainable. The rhythmic verb "going-on-being" aptly captures what it means to be creatively alive before the infant is anywhere near able to know anything about what time means (Ogden, 2004). A premature awareness of the not-me structure of time preempts the infant's experience of his own rhythms, warping his sense of vitality. Mother's primary maternal preoccupation allows her to live briefly outside of time herself, surrendering to the infant's rhythms of sleep and wakefulness, verve and lassitude, crankiness and agreeableness, hunger and satiation, alertness and distraction, engagement and aloneness. This provides a setting for the infant—through spontaneous impulse, movement, gesture, salivation, and sight—in which to discover the world in his own way and in his own time, strengthening the natural capacity to creatively apperceive (Winnicott, 1956, p. 303). It is creative apperception more than anything else, according to Winnicott, that allows life to feel real and worth living, rather than only something to be fitted in with or as demanding adaptation (Winnicott, 1971, p. 65).

However, if the pattern of relating between child and environment is not good enough—if the child collides with the world rather than creatively finding himself in it—he will be forced to react by "withdrawal from contact for the re-establishment of the sense of being" (quoted in Rodman, 1987, p. 42, emphasis added). To be clear: for Winnicott, the "withdrawal from contact" may even include a preference to die. At some point in life, suicide might be preferable to the agony arising from violation of the integrity of one's *being*, the site of creative aliveness. It is more often than not a desire to be *not-yet alive*—to return to the unaliveness that precedes aliveness, with the unconscious hope that primary creativity can be reinstated—than it is a wish to be dead.

One way of understanding the transitional object is that it contains in condensed form the intensity and aliveness of the baby-mother dyad. By creatively substituting a special object for the mothering person, the infant's continuity of being is maintained. But to serve as a substitute for mother's aliveness, the transitional object—baby's first not-me possession—must be imbued with its own sense of aliveness *by the infant*. Put differently: the infant finds his own way of letting go of the not-yet-fully-differentiated mother while holding on to the mother-who-is-part-of-me.

In health, baby's own devices—his primary creativity—helps mother remain good enough! First, the infant must put himself *into* the object, then realize himself *through* the object. The finding of oneself in and through an objective medium generates a sense of meaningfulness. Thus, Winnicott's theory of development is not simply one of how mother's attunement enables baby to thrive; rather, baby's healthy competence to make use of his own inventiveness and imbue the transitional object with significance enables him to feel alive.

What makes creative aliveness particularly precarious, however, is that so very much hinges upon the quality of response to the inherent destructiveness that is also part of being alive. Calling into question Freud's and Klein's clinical anthropology—whereby the vital helplessness of childhood is thought to be universal, inevitable, non-contingent, and derived from the power of instinctual life—Winnicott (1970) contrasts two dramatically distinct worlds awaiting a newborn, emphasizing that "it makes all the difference which you and I were born into" (p. 287). The first possible world is one in which "a baby kicks the mother's breast. She is pleased that her baby is *alive and kicking* though perhaps it hurt and she does not let herself get hurt for fun" (p. 287, emphasis in original).

In the alternative world, however:

> A baby kicks the mother's breast, but this mother has a fixed idea that a blow on the breast produces cancer. She reacts because she does not approve of the kick. This *overrides whatever the kick may mean for the baby.*
>
> (p. 287, emphasis added)

The infant's psychic health—creative meaning making—is contingent, in other words, upon mother's capacity to survive her own emotional reactions—remaining herself without losing connection to what the infant needs her to be. Only then can the child be enriched rather than shocked by her difference. Whereas Klein assumes that disturbance in the feeling life is the end result of active defense against the destructive force within, Winnicott entertains the possibility that the early individual-environmental setup might thwart the natural urge of the individual to create/discover an external world in which he can be fully alive.

It is mother's capacity to experience and contain the full, alive stream of feelings within herself—love, hate, annoyance, tenderness, joy, jealousy, exhilaration, fatigue—that affords the infant adequate space for the non-defensive omnipotence of primary creativity necessary for vitality.

Reimagining reality

It is often noted that there is little metapsychology in Winnicott's theory. Freud (1911) describes fundamental principles underlying psychic life. Winnicott's predilection is to hold in play clues and facts without building them up into systems. Freud asks: what energy and constraints drive and regulate the psyche? Winnicott wonders: how are people able to "make external reality something of and for themselves?" (Druck, personal communication). While Winnicott shows little concern for energic regulation or the functional "provinces" that structure the mind, he cares deeply about transformations in forms of thought, beginning with primary nonrepresentability and on through unconscious fantasy, conscious subjectivity, and the overlap between what is imagined and what perceived (Widlöcher, 2013).

Still, it is worth considering: given that Winnicott eschews "principles" in the sense Freud employs the term, how does he think about the notion that a reality principle imposes on a pleasure principle the necessity for delay, detour, inhibition, and compromise?

A clue is to be found in the fact that, on the rare occasions Winnicott mentions the reality principle, he often juxtaposes it with primary creativity. In a typical passage, he writes:

> Creativity, then, is the retention throughout life of something that belongs properly to infant experience: the ability to create the world. For the baby this is not difficult, because if the mother is able to adapt to the baby's needs, the baby has no initial appreciation of the fact that the world was there before he or she was conceived or conceived of. The Reality Principle is the fact of the existence of the world whether the baby creates it or not.
>
> The Reality Principle is just too bad, but by the time the little child is called upon to say "ta," big developments have taken place and the child has acquired genetically determined mental mechanisms for coping with this insult. For the Reality Principle is an insult.
>
> (Winnicott, 1986, pp. 39–40)

Winnicott obviously recognizes the clash between personal impulses and the compromises belonging to relationships with what eventually is felt as external. He is well aware of the means—including fight or flight—that aid in circumventing danger situations. But rather than focus on how internal stimulation is regulated to maintain homeostasis or to reduce tension to near zero, Winnicott prods to consider an alternative way of thinking about the bridge between "pleasure" and "reality." He emphasizes that, at increasing levels of complexity, meaning may or may not be spontaneously generated in the to-and-fro movement between inner and outer. To employ an imperfect analogy: Freud's principles of mental functioning depict the physics of the psyche, while Winnicott's primary creativity portrays what Wordsworth (1798b) called the "blood and vital juices of the mind" (p. 103).

More specifically: for Winnicott, reality is not primarily a hostile force, represented by father and to be reckoned with through the compromising of pleasure. Instead, it is the gradually expanding arena in which the psyche generates meaning by imaginatively elaborating bodily functions into increasingly complex relationships. The pleasure obtained is in the richness of an imaginative process meshing with a welcoming world. For Winnicott, pleasure, reality, creating, and meaningfulness overlap as mother and infant communicate. "We have to say," Winnicott notes, that:

> The baby created the breast, but could not have done so had not the mother come along with the breast at the moment. The communication to the baby is: "Come at the world creatively, create the world; *it is only what you create that has meaning for you.*"
>
> (Winnicott, 1987, p. 101, emphasis added)

For Winnicott, the contrast is not between pleasure and reality so much as it is between *two different kinds of relationship with reality* as it becomes increasingly external. One involves creative apperception, whereby the individual is, in Wordsworth's (1805) words, "creator and receiver both, working but in alliance with the works, which it beholds" (p. 399); the other is based on compliance, "the world and its details being recognized but only as something to be fitted in with or demanding adaptation" (Winnicott, 1971, p. 65). What concerns Winnicott is not how a reality principle modifies a pleasure principle, but whether one's sense of reality is experienced as desolate or as spangled by the heart's crayon (Wilbur, 1997).

But there is something else at work in Winnicott's reimagining of how one weaves with and is woven into reality. When all is said and done, he puts little emphasis on the conflictual nature of drives. It is not that Winnicott does not believe in instinctual conflict—he does. But instinctual conflict is not the salient situation of early infancy, nor does it account for all of human experience. "Only comparatively recently," he notes in a review of Fairbairn's contribution:

> Have analysts begun to feel the need for a hypothesis that would allow for areas of infancy experience and ego development that are not basically associated with instinctual conflict and where there is intrinsically a psychic process such as that which we have here termed "primary creativity."
>
> (Winnicott, 1989, p. 420)

Winnicott writes of "difficulties" in regard to contact with reality, which he elsewhere describes as "one of several basic *troubles* that belong to human nature" (Winnicott, 1986, p. 46, emphasis added). Winnicott carefully chooses these words—*difficulties* and *troubles*—so as to signal a shift toward apprehending human experience primarily in terms of paradox rather than conflict. "I find," he once said, that:

> It's almost like trying to count the number of fairies on the end of a pin to see how far you can go back talking about what's happening in an infant leaving out the fact that the environment is, at the beginning, part of the infant. I think that the difficulty is that there's a paradox, and it's the same paradox that turns up in transitional phenomena . . . . The paradox is that the environment is part of the infant and at the same time it isn't. The infant has to accept this eventually in order to become a grown-up at all.
>
> (Winnicott, 1989, p. 580)

Opposites, for Winnicott, are not antagonistic constraints to be overcome, but rather are paradoxical propositions to be lived with—"accepted, not resolved"; reality, paradoxically, "is part of the infant and at the same time it isn't" (Winnicott, 1989, p. 580). A devoted natural scientist of human development, Winnicott relies on paradox as a hedge against what otherwise risks becoming a split-off intellectual scientism.

Turner (1988) beautifully captures this current when he writes:

> Each of [Winnicott's] paradoxes surprises us into new relational thought by shocking the familiar categories of our understanding, and in each case their poetry ensures that the seat of this new thinking is not the intellect but the sympathetic imagination.
>
> (p. 491)

Winnicott thought deeply about paradoxes involved in experiencing limits. For him, reality must be reimagined to be made real.

Note

1 Winnicott's formulation is consistent with the descriptions of contemporary linguists and philosophers such as Lakoff and Johnson (1999), who argue that what makes us uniquely human is the imaginative capacity to generate metaphors. Metaphors arising from bodily sensations are a vital means of understanding the world rather than mere embellishments of speech.

References

Barth, J.R. (1977). *The Symbolic Imagination: Coleridge and the Romantic Tradition*. Princeton, NJ: Princeton University Press.

Bartlett, F.C. (1932). *Remembering*. Cambridge: Cambridge University Press.

Coleridge, S.T. (1801). "Letter to Thomas Poole, 23 March, 1801." In *The Collected Letters of Samuel Taylor Coleridge, Vol. 2*. Ed. E.L. Griggs. New York: Oxford University Press, 1956.

Coleridge, S.T. (1802). "Dejection: An Ode." In *The Complete Poems*. Ed. W. Keach. London: Penguin Group, 1997.

Coleridge, S.T. (1817). *Biographia Literaria*. Ed. J. Engell and W.J. Bate. Princeton, NJ: Princeton University Press, 1983.

Freud, S. (1911). "Formulations on the Two Principles of Mental Functioning." *The Standard Edition of the Complete Psychological Works of Sigmund Freud*, Vol. XII.

Freud, S. (1915). "The Unconscious." *The Standard Edition of the Complete Psychological Works of Sigmund Freud*, Vol. XIV.

Freud, S. (1924). "The Economic Problem of Masochism." *The Standard Edition of the Complete Psychological Works of Sigmund Freud*, Vol. XIX.

Goldman, D. (2013). "Vital Sparks and the Form of Things Unknown." In *Donald Winnicott Today*. Ed. J. Abram. London: Routledge.

Issroff, J. (2005). *Donald Winnicott and John Bowlby: Personal and Professional Perspectives*. London: Karnac.

Jones, E. (1927). "The Early Development of Female Sexuality." *The International Journal of Psychoanalysis*, 8: 459–472.

Lakoff, G. and Johnson, M. (1999). *Philosophy in the Flesh*. New York: Basic Books.

Milner, M. (1969). *The Hands of the Living God*. London: Hogarth Press and the Institute of Psycho-Analysis.

Modell, A. (2003). *Imagination and the Meaningful Brain*. Cambridge, MA: MIT Press.

Ogden, T. (2004). "On Holding and Containing, Being and Dreaming." *The International Journal of Psychoanalysis*, 85: 1349–1364.

Pruyser, P. (1983). *The Play of Imagination: Toward a Psychoanalysis of Culture*. New York: IUP.

Richards, I.A. (1969). *Coleridge on Imagination*. Bloomington, IN: Indiana University Press.

Rodman, F.R., Ed. (1987). *The Spontaneous Gesture: Selected Letters of D.W. Winnicott*. Cambridge, MA: Harvard University Press.

Rodman, F.R. (2003). *Winnicott: Life and Work*. Cambridge: Perseus Publishing.

Turner, J. (1988). "Wordsworth's 'Immortality Ode' and the Play of Paradox." *International Review of Psycho-Analysis*, 15: 481–496.

Warnock, M. (1978). *Imagination*. Berkeley, CA: University of California Press.

Widlöcher, D. (2013). "Winnicott and the Acquisition of a Freedom of Thought." In *Donald Winnicott Today*. Ed. J. Abram. London: Routledge.

Wilbur, R. (1997). "At Moorditch." *The New Yorker*, March 24, 1997, p. 46.

Winnicott, D.W. (1952). "Psychoses and Child Care." In *Through Paediatrics to Psycho-Analysis*. New York: Basic Books, 1975, pp. 219–228.

Winnicott, D.W. (1956). "Primary Maternal Preoccupation." In *Through Paediatrics to Psycho-Analysis*. New York: Basic Books, 1975, pp. 300–305.

Winnicott, D.W. (1958). "Ernest Jones." *The International Journal of Psychoanalysis*, 39: 298–304.

Winnicott, D.W. (1960). "The Theory of the Parent-Infant Relationship." *The International Journal of Psychoanalysis*, 41: 585–595.

Winnicott, D.W. (1964). "The Baby as a Growing Concern." In *The Child, the Family, and the Outside World*. Middlesex, UK: Penguin Books.

Winnicott, D.W. (1970). "Individuation." In *Psychoanalytic Explorations*. Cambridge, MA: Harvard University Press, 1989, pp. 284–288.

Winnicott, D.W. (1971). *Playing and Reality*. London and New York: Routledge.

Winnicott, D.W. (1972). *Holding and Interpretation: Fragment of an Analysis*. New York: Grove Press, 1986.

Winnicott, D.W. (1986). *Home Is Where We Start From*. New York: Norton.

Winnicott, D.W. (1987). *Babies and Their Mothers*. Reading, MA: Addison-Wesley.

Winnicott, D.W. (1988). *Human Nature*. London: Free Association Books.

Winnicott, D.W. (1989). *Psychoanalytic Explorations*. Cambridge, MA: Harvard University Press.

Wordsworth, W. (1798a). "Lines Written a Few Miles Above Tintern Abbey." In *William Wordsworth: The Major Works, Including the Prelude*. Ed. S. Gill. New York: Oxford University Press, 2008, pp. 131–135.

Wordsworth, W. (1798b). "Essay on Morals." In *The Prose Works of William Wordsworth*. Ed. W.J.B. Owen and J.W. Smyser. London: Oxford University Press, 1974.

Wordsworth, W. (1805). "The Prelude." In *William Wordsworth: The Major Works, Including the Prelude*. Ed. S. Gill. New York: Oxford University Press, 2008, pp. 375–590.

Wordsworth, W. (1807). "Ode: Intimations of Immortality from Recollections of Early Childhood." In *The Poetical Works of William Wordsworth (in 5 volumes)*. Ed. E. de Selincourt and H. Darbishire. London: Oxford University Press.

Wordsworth, W. (1814). "The Excursion: Being a Portion of the Recluse: A Poem." In *The Complete Poetical Works of William Wordsworth*. London: Edward Moxon, Dover Street, 1869, pp. 526–602.

Wright, K. (2013). "The Search for Form." In *Donald Winnicott Today*. Ed. J. Abram. London: Routledge.

Index